going after
the beach

a Vietnam veteran looks back
50 years to love, war, and courage

going off the beach

a Vietnam veteran looks back
50 years to love, war, and courage

Robert Garlick

gatekeeper press™
Columbus, OH

going off the beach: a Vietnam veteran looks back 50 years to love, war, and courage

Published by Gatekeeper Press
2167 Stringtown Rd, Suite 109
Columbus, OH 43123-2989
www.GatekeeperPress.com

The editorial work for this book is entirely the product of the author. Gatekeeper Press did not participate in and is not responsible for any aspect of this element.

Library of Congress Control Number: 2021930519

ISBN (paperback): 9781662907685
eISBN: 9781662907692

Prologue

I tell my story as I lived it, or at least as I remember the events, times, and places of the nearly two years spent in the U.S. Army from April 1968 to February 1970, including twelve months in South Vietnam. In some instances, I have been able to go backwards and draw upon history, and use maps, to sharpen my memory or verify what I think I saw. In many cases, I have been spot on. In other cases, it's still a little vague. I admit that in telling my story going forward, fifty years have passed, so it is impossible not also to tell my story looking backward. If nothing else, the experience has given me great perspective, but has come at a high cost indeed.

Some events and places are permanently and forever so deeply burned into my memory banks of my brain and being that they became part of my DNA. They are not like ordinary surface tattoos. The ink used here is beyond permanence, beyond indelible. The ink runs so deep it goes completely through to the opposite side, like a living three-dimensional movie. No erasure is possible. Even if it's cut deeply into, there's no removing it. This is the answer to the question I have been asked countless times over the last fifty years: "What was it like?" It is the story of what happened to me when I was twenty years old. To borrow an old movie line, it's a story of the good, the bad, and the ugly, in which I played a part of each role.

I have written my story using the vulgarities and crudeness of language used by teenage males and twenty-somethings in the 1960's. It was how we spoke during our time in the Army and especially in Vietnam. The use of these words is not an attempt to sensationalize this story. Rather, it's the reality of the way we spoke. I have wrestled with the idea of "cleaning up" the language, but after several discussions with editors (including some veterans), they have encouraged me to tell the story exactly in the language with which we lived it. To be honest, sometimes those curses were actually prayers. As to the depictions of the violence, I have cleansed it a bit, but I cannot take it any further. If one is to provide a truthful and candid answer to the question, "What was Vietnam like?", one cannot play down, hide, or whitewash the answer. The answer brings with it all the baggage, including the ugliness.

Illustrations

The Cardinal Rules

Number I   Never Go Into The Jungle Alone

Number II   Never Forget, It Can Always Be Worse

Number III   Never Get Brave - You Will Always Get Hurt

Number IV   Never Yield To The Lord Of The Flies

Number V   Never Straddle The Boundary - Be On One Side Or The Other

Number VI   Never Do Kids, For There Is No Bottom

Number VII   Never Doubt When Thunderstruck, You Are Always The Right Age

Tracie's Rule   Never Get On The Train

This Is My Story

If one were to review my military records, I am certain one would find them most unremarkable. Drafted on one date and discharged on another date 22 months later. Not a single black mark or smudge of any kind, not one single disciplinary action. But also, not a single medal beyond the very basic standard ones. There is not a single Citation for anything, no certificate of merit, no certificate of achievement, no commendation, no award of any kind. The records would only show an entry date into the Army and a discharge from the Army with almost no history in-between. One would assume a rather bland, characterless, ephemeral stint in the military. It would look as if I were a phantom soldier. And if my brief military career were to be described as a flavor, it would be the flavor of the bargain store brand, the imitation Vanila ice cream found at the bottom of a freezer at the end of an aisle in a supermarket. Just a plain Jane rather ordinary GI Joe.

But that would be a false narrative. I offer a much different chronicle. Every Veteran has a different experience, this is just one of many. Here is my story.

going off the beach

August 1969

"I love the beach." I say this aloud as much to myself as to anyone else. Still, the guy sitting right beside me says, "What?"

I do love the beach; it is my earliest memory. I am about two years old and I am lying on a blanket. To my right is a green house of some unclear shape. The only certainty is its color and the fact that I lie in its shade. I know this because to my left, at some unknown distance, but certainly a short one, there is sunlight brilliantly lighting tan and yellow sand. Beyond that there is blue water. I find this most pleasing and comforting. Surely, I must have been having a good day at such an early age.

"What?" It is the guy next to me again. I heard him the first time, but he has raised his voice this time to make sure I can hear him.

I repeat myself, "I love the beach," but this time I raise my voice, almost shouting, to be heard over the noise of the diesel and "clanking" of the tracked vehicle and the booming surf. Booming, almost like distant thunder, yet it is quite close. This is, unquestionably, the most spectacular beach I have seen or will ever see. I say this with all the conviction and wisdom of a twenty-one-year-old. Still, as I look back on this moment, I know I was probably right. The beach is broadly deep, and the white sand slopes gently toward the surf. And more astonishing, the sand dunes behind the beach tower many stories high. The beach stretches for unknown miles to the south. To the east, the blue Pacific reaches to infinity, and there is absolutely no wind blowing in any direction. It is so flat and calm that the water looks like pale blue glass. There must be something far offshore pushing the huge combers in, and they are huge. They seem to arrive subtly, almost unnoticed, moving through the pale blue glass effortlessly until they near the shore. There, these giant combers climb high and roll forward, falling upon themselves with a crashing thunderous boom.

There is nothing subtle in this continuous collision of monumental wave pounding against immovable beach, an ancient and ongoing battle that has raged for eons. Because there is no wind, there is no distraction to one's senses, there are no white caps to be seen and yet this adds to the mystique. You cannot help being drawn into this scene of a seeming unending flat, dead calm and that of a contradictory, paradoxical Great Pale Blue "presence" that somehow, with extraordinary effort but by no visible means, throws 15-foot combers against this sultry, primeval tropical beach. Pale blue liquid glass, dropping from a height of fifteen feet, shattering itself upon the beach with the sound that can be described by a low frequency "faaaa-wooomp-sss". I feel, even through the aluminum body of the track, the vibration caused by thousands of tons of seawater falling, crashing upon the beach. Do my eyes truly see a perceptible bounce of the beach after every crashing wallop of a wave upon it? The Pale Blue's power is immense and raw, yet equally matched by the steadfastness of this primordial sandy Rock of Gibraltar. The unfathomable purity in this battle is unquestionable.

The mist created by the giants smashing against the beach is gently carried toward the shoreline, and we feel the mist upon our faces and can smell and taste the salty brine. This cool mist is a welcome relief upon my dry face on this mystically still, motionless, early morning in August. The clarity and transparency of the water is extraordinary. As these combers climb high, but just before they fall upon themselves, there is a brief moment where the sun, still relatively low on the eastern horizon, shines through this translucent wall of water turning it to the softest, palest shade of blue. It is mesmerizing to watch. I will carry with me the memory of this brief interlude for the rest of my life, these short-lived few minutes of breathtaking beauty and tranquility. It still brings me such comfort.

This beach is so remarkably, astonishingly pristine; it stuns the senses to think it is possible. It is so unspoiled that it seems ancient and prehistoric, as though I am the first human ever to see it. In a different time, I could feel the way Robinson Crusoe did. One could easily imagine that this beach looked exactly the same way a thousand years earlier. There is not a soul upon it except us. We are most fortunate to find ourselves looking upon an exotic paradise that seems endless. And yet, Hell is so close, so near, and it can show itself in just an instant and seem endless too.

I ride, with more than a dozen others, jammed together on the top of the "command" armored personnel carrier, an APC, a tracked vehicle, but more commonly simply called a "track". APCs resemble small tanks but without gun turrets. More important, they have no steel armor. They are simply diesel-powered aluminum boxes with tread tracks instead of wheels. No one rides inside these "aluminum coffins" except the driver, as they offer poor protection from land mines. We are the last track in a single column of four track vehicles of a mechanized infantry company. The last track is the "command" track, leading from the rear. Each APC follows precisely in the tread tracks left in the ground by the APC in front of it. It's simply safer this way, with much lower odds of running over a land mine as a single column than with all of us spread out. If the lead track doesn't hit a mine, then the following tracks won't either. I don't envy anyone on that lead track, but then again, it's a bit unsettling being last in line too, as last is always a very tempting target and so easily cut off. Any aid or reinforcement is moving away from you. Think of it this way: if you were walking through a jungle trail, would you want to be the last man in line? If I were the enemy, the last in line is the first one I would pick off.

We reach the point on the beach where we had entered in the darkness of the pre-dawn earlier in the morning. We left our encampment at about four in the morning, traveling southwest across dry rice paddies and through green jungle, finally turning east toward the coast. More than once, we are momentarily lost, losing precious time. While riding on top of the track beats walking, it is most uncomfortable. We squat on top with our legs tucked underneath ourselves, holding on with one arm as we hold our M-16's with the other. No one lets his legs dangle over the sides. Far too dangerous.

If the track hits a land mine, the shrapnel will explode into your legs. But with the track bucking and lurching on the uneven terrain, it is difficult to hold on, especially in the darkness while being swatted by brush and branches of the trees. We finally reach the coastline at earliest dawn, but the eastern sky now begins to brighten and turn pink, warning us that we are far behind schedule. We must now push hard. Our driver guns the engine, the diesel growls steadily but happily as the track glides effortlessly over the flat and even terrain of the extreme upper beach.

In retrospect, it doesn't seem possible, but in our rush, we never even notice the beach; we are simply too focused on our mission. Adrenaline pumps through our systems like a dam bursting. We race north up the beach for a couple of miles, vainly attempting to beat the sunrise to reach some hamlet whose name, sadly, I don't think I ever knew. Our unit is supposed to "close the back door", but alas, the dawn now breaks. Though it is barely daylight, we have arrived late nonetheless. Our unintended tardiness will later prove to be immeasurably costly. We have failed to close the "back door". The Viet Cong, aka the VC, or just "Charlie" to us, has slipped away, and there will be hell to pay for our transgression. An unseen phantom hourglass has now been turned. The sand slowly slipping away; it is only a matter of time.

We traveled in an elongated loop to reach this hamlet, but other units coming from different directions reached it well before we did; for us a long, futile, and ultimately sad exercise. All that for nothing. It is not our fault; we have had to travel the greatest distance in darkness, and over the worst terrain, playing out our own personal "bridge too far." Unknowingly, innocently, and despite our best effort, we have so badly fucked up. In a twisted and yet unfathomable *Yin and Yang*, our punishment will soon be meted out. We have not the slightest clue.

This VC controlled hamlet by the sea, our captured prize, seems to be populated by only women and children and two very ancient old men. All the young men have safely fled. Only sullen-faced women and the children they hold in their arms remain. I look carefully at some of the women's faces. They briefly meet my eye and then just coldly stare past me. *They hate us.*

The hamlet has absolutely no strategic value. We find no weapons, no stores of ammunition, no medical supplies, no anything. Having not fired a single shot, we now withdraw. We retrace our steps out of this hamlet to return to our encampment. The trip back down the beach seems like a far longer journey, though a much happier one now. We ride along near the lower portion of the beach, now much closer to the water's edge than earlier this morning, with the water pushed in by the surf and stopping just yards from our APC's. Our pace is steady and unhurried, almost leisurely, as opposed to racing up the beach as we had done but an hour or two earlier. Though no one speaks of it, we all feel relieved that our luck has held and that our company has suffered no casualties. Though we are tired and thirsty, that is trivial compared to the unfortunate fate of others.

Earlier, in the darkness of the night, with all the dust and sand thrown by the tracks and the branches and brush swatting us as we rode through the wood line, almost none of us could really see where we were or where we were going. It is on this return trip, with the sun lifting itself above the blue horizon of the seemingly endless Pacific that we, or at least I, see this piece of Eden.

Our column pauses momentarily at our earlier entry point on the beach, then slowly turns to the west, exiting from the beach, passing through a broad strip of scrubby brush and tall grasses and a few struggling palms to climb the tallest sand dunes I have ever seem. They seem as high as ten-story buildings. We pause again, then the first track begins slowly but steadily to climb up the steep dunes. As it nears the top, the second track begins its ascent. As the first track reaches the top and slowly disappears from sight, the third track begins its ascent. The second track reaches the top, and it too disappears. As the third track nears the top of the dunes, we, now alone on that beach and the last to leave it, pause for one final moment. Almost everyone turns to take one last look. I say quietly, a final time, to the guy next to me, as though we are having an intimate conversation, "I love the beach". He nods his head "yes". I hear the diesel revving, the track lurches slightly, and we turn, *going off the beach* and begin our climb up that sand dune. I sit on the right-hand side of the track with my legs tucked up under myself. I cradle my M-16 with my right hand as I grab hold of the track with my left and as I do, I see my watch at my wrist. I cannot help smiling to myself. It is a self-winding Seiko, my very first "expensive" watch, that I had so proudly bought at the PX in Phu Cat a couple of months earlier for $12.50. I see the second hand as it moves in precise one-second intervals, sweeping evenly around the dial face. It is almost 07:50 AM, a clear, sunny, cloudless morning in early August.

As our track climbs about halfway up the dune, I turn my head to take one final look at that beach, and now from my slightly higher elevation the Pacific seems even a deeper shade of blue. I will never see that beach again.

We leave behind an unnamed, untamed, primordial beach, but one I will remember as an Eden with faultless clarity in such vivid, remarkable detail. I know I can never go back, as it will never be the same. How could it?

One may ask why I have an obsessive need to paint the picture of this faraway place that I spent perhaps 30- or 40-minutes in. I cannot let it go, this place, this beach, this moment in time. So deeply imprinted into me that it is now part and parcel of my DNA. I have to remember this, for to let it go, is to let go of life itself. And one other thing, this surfside Edenic interlude, as brief as it was, will be the first, last, and only good thing to come of this day.

Unbeknownst to us, only moments away and lying just over that sand dune with all the patience of eternity, Hell awaits.

But I am getting ahead of myself. Far, too far, ahead.

Drafted, Conscripted, And Inducted

My military career, such as it was, had started some fifteen-plus months earlier. The "Draft" and my Draft Status had hung over me since shortly after I graduated from high school. I was in and out of college, but the biggest factor was my lack of money. That was exacerbated by the fact that my draft status prevented me from getting a good job. I had hitch-hiked across the country to southern California, vowing to myself that I would lift my position from the near bottom rung of the socio-economic ladder. I had applied to several large companies and had interviews with McDonnell-Douglas and Chevron and had made good first impressions. I came very close to landing a job with Chevron in their chemical division. The manager there was taken by my enthusiasm, clean cut appearance and work ethic, but at the end of the interview, he asked what my draft status was. When I told him I was "1-A," he sympathetically shook his head "Sorry we can't hire you. You will almost certainly be drafted and Federal Law requires us to hire you back when you are finally discharged. We have to give you any raises and promotions you would have received while working here. The company just isn't going to let itself get stuck by that. I'd love to hire you, but not with 'the draft' hanging over your head." He attempts to soothe my more-than-evident disappointment and says "Come back after you get out, I'll have a job for you". I thank him for his time and quietly leave his office thinking to myself, *the climb out of the pit is near impossible.*

Given that reality, and with no money to go back to school, I was truly caught between a rock and a hard spot. I sense that the system is unfairly stacked and that it is about to grab me and chew me to bits. Cheerlessly, I yield to my expected desolate fate. On a Friday morning, I walk into my local Draft Board Office on the second floor above the US Post Office building. I ask the women behind the counter where I stand with my draft status. She checks her files and replies that I am to be drafted very shortly. She tells me there may be still time to enlist voluntarily in any of the various military services, but that the most likely branch for such short notice would be the Army. I have just turned 20 years old, and I try to think logically: be drafted for two years or enlist for three or more? The woman waits for an answer from me. I don't know what to say. After a long moment, I respond "I guess I'll just go with being drafted". Her response takes me by surprise. She asks, "Do you mean this coming Monday or two weeks from Monday?"

It's both a shocking and depressing question. I attempt to process it; I have no job, not even a crappy one. What would I do for two weeks? I search for other options, such as Canada or Federal prison. Neither is viable. I see no other answer. "What's the point of waiting?" I think to myself. So, I reply "I'll go this Monday." The woman then places the form letter into her typewriter and fills in the appropriate spaces and then a minute or two later hands me my draft notice. She tells me I will now be officially listed as a "volunteer" for the draft, but her words bring me no comfort. I walk out of her office and climb down the stairwell to street level and then read my draft notice on the sidewalk: It begins "Greetings. You have been selected by your peers to represent them in the Armed Forces of the United States of America..........." I briefly wonder who my peers are and how I can ever thank them.

The month of April 1968 was one the largest single months for the draft of the Viet Nam war, over 30,000. The Army drafted over

7,500 men each week. How did they ever get away with that? Why didn't I ever meet anyone from Harvard?

On the day of our induction, most of us had showed up earlier that morning at our local draft boards, as directed to do in the draft notices we had received. I had risen early that morning and I dressed in silence so as to awaken no one. My house is as still and quiet as a morgue. I make not a sound as I enter into my youngest sister's bedroom but find her awake on the top bunk that she sleeps on. I do not utter a word, but softly kiss her forehead goodbye, and as I do, she sobs. She is the only one I say goodbye to; I let the others sleep. This is already hard enough. I quickly exit the house. What else is there to say or do here?

I stand in the side yard for a moment. The sun is out and air is mild. The day before was a gorgeous spring day, the temperature nudging 72°, but on the near horizon I see very dark, heavy clouds coming in, and I am sure it will rain soon. I walk from the house to the street where my father awaits me in his bread delivery truck. It resembles a UPS truck but is painted a pleasant yellow with a picture of a loaf of bread on either side. I enter and pull shut the sliding door on the passenger side. There is no passenger seat, so I sit on the top of the engine cowling and face backward. My view is of row upon row of various kinds of bread wrapped in their yellow plastic wrappers. They sit on large movable tan fiberglass / plastic trays which in turn sit in galvanized steel mesh shelves which in turn are secured to the aluminum body of the van. We pull away from the house and begin the ten-minute ride to the Draft Board building. As one would surely anticipate, on even the slightest bump, everything rattles with a metallic sound.

Other than the rattles, we ride in silence with no attempt at conversation between us. I am probably feeling sorry for myself, but I immediately begin to feel sorry for my father despite his habitual cruelty. His is such a dead-end job, but he was one of nine children and went only as far as the ninth grade; given that upbringing, this was the logical and predictable outcome. But I think he actually liked his job; the plant was only a few blocks from where we lived, and he easily walked there. He was out from under his boss each and every day as he drove his van around his route of supermarkets and tiny corner grocery stores. Over time he had come to know every manager or mom and pop store owner, and they always looked forward to his daily delivery. They liked him, and he liked them. Despite that, my father's home persona was most terrible. He had fathered six children and was an abusive alcoholic with a job that did not pay well. We lived at the edge of poverty in my grandmother's triple-decker on US Route 1. He resented that some of his children had already exceeded his level of education. He seemed to be insisting that the cycle of poverty repeat itself. And so, given my own upbringing, my induction into the Army is also the logical and predictable outcome.

I am let off near the Draft Board and I walk across the street to join 30 or 40 other very young men. It is a short wait of perhaps 15 or 20 minutes before we are put aboard chartered school buses to be driven to the induction center. Before we get on the school buses, a member of the Draft Board demands that I show him my draft card. I don't have my draft card any longer -- what's the point of it now? -- and I tell him that. He gives me some crap and then harasses some other kid with the same question. What a prick to harass us in our final few hours of civilian life. I would love to meet him again.

Though it is only a twenty-minute drive, by the time we reach the induction center the sun has already faded behind the clouds. At the induction center we are joined by hundreds of other draftees from all over the state and given a ream of forms to fill out, followed by a mental aptitude exam and a lengthy physical. A very few of the lucky ones fail either one or both, but one can only imagine the poor health or IQs of these guys, as the Army's standard for both categories is abysmally low.

One parent has brought her son to the induction center but not just to see him off. She had been required to sign the waiver to allow her seventeen-year-old to join the Army and had brought him to the induction center to make sure he got there. I actually meet that guy, whose seventeenth birthday is that very miserable Monday. His mother is a struggling single parent, and he seems a decent enough kid, but I am certain he is far more than she can handle on her own. He has already had brush-ups with the police. Besides, they look poor. What are their other options? In some ways, though I was unwilling to admit it then, much of what I saw in him was a younger version of me. I was almost two months past my 20th birthday, but I felt so much older than he and most others.

I think all of us are expecting to be drafted into the Army, but there is a tiny quota of four men for the Navy and two for the Marines. Having been ordered about and bullied by the Army personnel at the induction center, four of the draftees immediately and voluntarily join the Navy, and two immediately join the Marines. I didn't sense that they were more patriotic than the rest of us, but only that the Army had already put a sour taste in everyone's mouth. Those quotas filled, the overwhelming majority of us, well over 400, are pressed into the US Army, which seems to have a voracious and insatiable appetite for young blood. The Army would have happily taken more of us, but there are no more of us left on this day.

At late morning I look out a window and now see a steady drizzle falling with an occasional wet snowflake mixing in. It is a despondent and despairing Monday by any standard, even without this. At this point, having passed our physicals and mental aptitude exams, we are called by name by various clerks to fill out one final form. As it turns out, the very last form is the one used to name the death beneficiary for the Army's life insurance policy. For some reason mine is the last name they call for this final piece of paperwork, but I suspect that this is not coincidental. I take a seat next to the clerk's desk. We have been shouted at, yelled at, and ordered about all morning as if we were all young felons entering prison, but she speaks the first kind words I have heard all day. She smiles. "Are you ready for the biggest day of your life?" Despite the kind tone of her voice, her question scares me, for I think, *what can be worse than this day*? So, I ask "How do you mean?" She replies, "Why you are about to go into the Army." I am somehow relieved, as if in a backwards and upside-down universe. I simply nod my head and answer with an even voice "Yeah, sure". She smiles at me and briefly looks at the form in her typewriter and then benignly asks, "Have you thought about who you would want to receive your life insurance in the event of your death?" The question takes me by surprise, and I almost say "What?" I pause a moment but then think, *given the possible tour of duty, the question is reasonable and logical.* So, I request that my mother be named the exclusive beneficiary, and I insist that my father not be listed in any manner. The clerk taking this information, an ostensibly kind woman, smiles with approval and asks, "What's your Mother's full name and address?" I tell her and she types with a heavy hand, as the form is in triplicate. She pulls the completed form from her typewriter and has me sign my name at the bottom. I hand the form back, and she tells me in a sweet motherly voice that carries pride, "That's what every one of you has done this morning, you have all named your mothers as the sole beneficiary." When I look back on this, I think what kids we really were to have all named our mothers as the sole beneficiary. She goes on to inform me that the Army will pay my mother ten thousand dollars upon my death. It doesn't seem like much, and I am further dismayed when the woman tells me that it will cost two dollars a month for the insurance coverage. Not to worry she tells me; it will automatically be taken out of my monthly paycheck of $90.50. My first thought then was, *how miserly and cheap the Army is*. Much later on, I wondered over the years how many of us she had sent off, but thought she probably felt good that we were all insured and our mothers were the sole beneficiaries.

I am about to stand when the woman says, "Just one last thing." Now my suspicions are confirmed. She hands me the itinerary for our trip to wherever and whatever is coming next. I look and see only one name on it, my own, with the words "in charge" printed next to it. I quickly glance back to her as she says, "You have been chosen to be in charge because of your leadership abilities". I involuntarily look around, as I think she is talking to someone else. She smiles at me, and I am sure that she thinks this news will make me happy. I look blankly at her thinking to myself, *Oh God, doesn't she understand I don't want to be in the Army, never mind in charge?* Still smiling, she points down the hallway and says, "Now go join the others to be sworn in. All the paperwork and signatures of this morning are meaningless until you take the oath." Her voice is reassuring and almost happy, as if she were proudly coaxing me along on my first day of school to walk through the schoolhouse door. I walk in the direction she points, and at the end of a short corridor I step into a very large room which I am the last man to enter. Someone in an Army uniform immediately tells us, "Raise your right arm, state your name, and repeat after me," and we take the oath and are sworn in. It sounds like loud, incoherent mumbling as four hundred thirty of us speak at the same time but who are all slightly out of sync with each other. It's an understatement to say this, but it wasn't much of a ceremony. Joining the Cub Scouts at age nine was a bigger deal, but of course, this time the consequences are incomparable.

A few minutes later we are put on chartered city buses and brought to the train station on that gray, chilly, rainy, depressing Monday afternoon. It is April the fifteenth, 1968. There we wait for our train to begin a 26-hour trip to the reception center at Ft. Jackson in Columbia, South Carolina. There is no brass band. The interior of the train station gives us no cheer, for it is as gray as the day, and not much warmer. To call it dismal does not do it justice. High overhead are a dozen or so pigeons. They roost in corners on the generously wide ceiling molding that juts out from the wall and which their whitish droppings stain. The pigeons look down upon us, and, with what seems to be cold indifference, shake their heads. I look up at them and think, *rats with wings*. What a disheartening sendoff.

There are well over four hundred of us, and I have been placed in charge, I am told, because of my leadership abilities. *Why would they do this to me?* We wait on one side of the cavernous train station, and a short distance away hundreds of relatives, mothers, fathers, and girlfriends have gathered to say a final goodbye. I stand between the two groups holding a bunch of paperwork, and I notice all eyes from both sides are upon me, pleading silently. In my very first act of command, and to the astonishment of the two Army Officers who have escorted us here, I look to both groups and then simply gesture with my arms for both sides to join. It becomes an emotional mob scene. There is no one there for me, and that suits me fine. Earlier that morning, around 7:30 AM, when my old man had brought me down to the local draft board in his delivery truck, our good-bye had been much different. There, on the street in front of the Post Office, we had wordlessly parted company. I had simply shrugged and walked away.

Very shortly our train arrives, and we board it and depart on time at 2:10 PM. My final instructions from the two Army Officers are: "Don't let anyone off the train". I make only a small effort to keep track of everyone; there are simply too many of us. I doubt that this train had a name. It certainly was not an express, judging by the multiple stops we make along the way. People get on, people get off, and occasionally I wonder whether any of us has jumped off at one of these stops. Several hours later after a somewhat lengthy stop at New York's Grand Central Station, we are fed dinner in the crowded dining car. We are served under-cooked hamburger and sloppy mashed potatoes (instant, I'm certain); kind of a prelude and warm-up for Army food. It is a terrible meal. We arrive in Washington, D.C., well after midnight and are taken by a Conductor to another train which has Pullman sleeping cars. I take the bottom bunk, and my bunkmate takes the top one. Sometime during the night hours, the train pulls out of D.C. There is no heat, and it is a chilly night, but my bunkmate tells me the next morning with much gratitude that it had been like sleeping with a bear, as I had kept the cabin warm. We are awakened in the morning by a porter telling us breakfast will be served shortly. I don't remember what we ate.

Our train continues traveling south, and I spend most of my time sitting alone mindlessly staring out the windows. It's not the kind of trip where one plans and dreams of better days. Just before noon the conductor grabs me as we pull into the tiniest of train stations somewhere in South Carolina. We are met on the station platform by a man delivering our lunch. He is dressed in a white suit with long tails, and he wears a white hat. Although it is not actually him, the man looks like a young Col. Sanders, but without glasses or the goatee. Young Sanders hands me some paperwork to sign in triplicate. I do so and hand it back. He in turn hands over several large boxes, which of course turn out to be containers of fried chicken. I will say it was delicious.

So, by some miracle, all four hundred thirty of us (me included) arrive in Columbia in the late afternoon of that day, despite the train making fifty or sixty stops along the way. The train station in Columbia is a derelict of a building that looks as though the Civil War had just ended last week. But in fairness, it wasn't any worse than the one we had departed from in Providence, which looked as if World War I had ended the day before. We are met by a Drill Sergeant (DI) who does not at all seem pleased to see us. He barks some orders, and we board school buses that take us for the short ride to the reception center at Fort Jackson.

The reception center seems to operate around the clock; I guess it would have to in order to handle the thousands of men who enter the Army each week. I don't remember much of that first day other than it was nighttime when we received our uniforms and were fitted with combat boots. We had all been given a small personal hygiene kit from the Salvation Army on our first evening at Ft. Jackson. It consisted of a small but sturdy blue plastic bag, with the red logo of the Salvation Army on the front and secured at the top by a drawstring. The bag contained various toiletries: a can of shaving cream, razor blades, soap, deodorant, and a tiny copy of the New Testament.

The next few days consist of more physicals and shots followed by more aptitude testing. We stay in unheated barracks, which are chilly in the nighttime, and there is no hot water. I shower anyway, but I notice that some do not. Within a few days there is growing hostility between those who shower and those who do not. I don't participate in this as I did not see it coming, and everyone at my end of the barracks has showered, so I have no cause. But further down the barracks floor, those few who have not showered have a surprise one night. Some persons (I assume more than one) take those cans of Barbasol shaving cream given to us by the Salvation Army and put generous amounts of "mentholated" shaving cream between the sheets of the offenders. All awaken at some point in the night and amid much cursing finally take showers. After that everyone took a shower every evening. Better this way, as later on in "basic training" the penalty for poor hygiene becomes much more severe.

Fort Gordon

After about a week or so at Ft. Jackson, we are broken into two groups, and half of us are to be bused further south to Ft. Gordon in Augusta, Georgia, for "basic training". We are joined by a large group of draftees from New York City and Pennsylvania. We are all put aboard chartered Greyhound buses for the two-hour trip; it is a brief respite from the bullying. Our buses enter the base, and within minutes we are near our training company headquarters. From the bus windows, we can see several Drill Sergeants pacing back and forth, with urgency, like caged animals hungrily awaiting fresh meat. We slow to a stop and, in a scene reminiscent of old movies, the bus door opens, a Drill Sergeant steps aboard and screams, "Get off of my bus". Art imitates life, life imitates art, but either way the abuse starts, and both life and art suck. We hurry from the buses and are greeted by several more Drill Sergeants who scream at us to grab our duffle bags from the cargo bays of the buses and to fall into formation at a very nearby field. Once in formation, we are ordered to dump the entire contents of our duffle bags onto the ground. We do as we are ordered, and out fall socks, underwear, the shirts and pants of our uniforms, and the Salvation Army blue bag of toiletries. I am grateful it is not raining. The Drill Instructors / Drill Sergeants then go through everything looking for contraband, but there is none to be found. We are now ordered to put everything back into our duffle bags and marched to a nearby grandstand where we take seats. The Company Commander introduces himself and explains a few things, but then very quickly turns things over to the Senior DI, Sergeant Tittle, who tells us the rules and the penalties for breaking them. He is the antithesis of a Dale Carnegie course; he is not here to make friends. Our names are then called, and we are broken into four very large platoons of over a hundred men each and each of those platoons has its own personal DI. Our DI is Sergeant Penn.

It is now late afternoon, so we are taken to our sleeping barracks and assigned a bunk by Sergeant Penn. At around 5:30 PM we are "whistled" into formation outside the barracks and marched a very short distance to the mess hall to eat supper. We form a line of about 450 men which moves very slowly as the dining hall is very small and will only hold about 60 people. We must wait until someone finishes eating before we can enter.

After eating, we return to our barracks and line up for showers; it is so overcrowded. As to our sleeping barracks, they are left over relics from World War II, if not World War I. There is nothing modern about this Army. It is as though things and time have stood still for nearly a quarter century, and now this crappy old base is forced back into life. The barracks are nearly decrepit and built with white asbestos siding. An ancient coal furnace provides heat and hot water for the showers. Both floors of the barracks building are filled with double rows of bunk beds. It has the look and feel of the prison barracks of *Cool Hand Luke*. No one is allowed to smoke inside the barracks, as the second floor has only one exit, but later on, some of my barrack mates do smoke. They fall asleep at night with a lit cigarette and set their mattresses on fire. A couple of them are burned. Oh god....

We finally get to bed around 9:00 PM, and at 9:30 PM it is officially "lights out." Our training begins in earnest the very next morning when we are awakened at 6:00 AM by the lights coming on and DI Sgt. Penn screaming at us to get up. We dress and are whistled into formation in the dark and then marched to a nearby field where we run a mile before breakfast. It's not that much fun. The first week of basic training is such a blur that I lose track of the days. It is when I awake on the first Sunday at 8:00 AM to the sound of singing that I realize that it is finally a day off. I dress and walk around our barracks and seeing how cloudy it is outside, I relize it is about to rain. But the singing comes from several small groups of the brothers that find each other and begin to harmonize and sing. They are actually very good and it hits me to realize that through song a way can be found to get through this ordeal.

My comrades-in-arms are of a mixed assortment. Some, I will come to realize later, can barely read or write. Others have a lengthy criminal history despite their youth or maybe because of it. I inquire of my young bunkmate why did he ever enlist for six years when he could have simply been drafted for two years? He replies very somberly, "I killed another kid". The judge had, at my bunkmate's sentencing, informed him he would be serving six years somewhere and was given the option of six years in prison or six years in the military. After a moment or two, I asked him why he had not joined the Air Force or the Coast Guard. His reply said it all. "None of the other branches would take me, not even the Marines. I had to bring a letter from the Judge just to get the Army to take me." It has been said by many that the Army was the big catch basin at the bottom of the street of life; it would take in just about anybody and anything. In wartime, the Army will take 'm sixteen to sixty-six, blind, crippled or crazy, or criminal for that matter. So went the joke, but of course, there was more than just an element of truth in that.

Our Basic Training is a most unpleasant experience. It's not supposed to be a Boy Scout Camp, but every aspect of it is exacerbated by the severe overcrowding of our training company that is three or four times larger than normal. Our barracks and mess hall are bursting at the seams. So how are four hundred and fifty men to be fed in the allotted time of just thirty minutes in a mess hall that will only seat about 60? The Army's solution is to allow us three or four minutes to eat our meals, and then we are forced out of the mess hall. Any conversation is strictly forbidden; the Senior DI, Sergeant Tittle, paces among the crowded tables and reprimands any man who even says "Pass the salt". He barks "You don't have time to talk, so shut up and eat. Your three minutes is up, get out."

Our actual training is rather mediocre. Don't get me wrong; this was no fun, and it was a most miserable experience. But there were just too many of us and therefore everything was rushed and inefficient. There were only so many hours per day that the rifle range could be allocated to each training company. With each training company at least triple its normal size, there was not enough time for any one individual to be properly and thoroughly trained in the use of his weapon. If you're going to do it, then do it right. McNamara, Johnson and Nixon, all wanted to wage war; they just didn't want to have to pay much for it. It is as if someone had turned the conveyor belt up to its highest speed in an attempt to stamp out as many Government Issue soldiers (GI's) in the shortest possible time. The Army didn't seem to have much of a plan, or perhaps the plan no longer worked because of the huge numbers of draftees. So, for us, from beginning to end, this seems to be a barely organized process that is filled with much yelling, screaming, bullying, and more than an ample amount of stupidity. The months of May and June in Georgia are hot and humid. The training days start early and finish late; they are long and grueling, one following after the other with no end in sight. I try to see the method to the madness, but I can see no leaders, only screaming bullies.

Everyone copes in a different way. The fat guys who cannot meet the physical requirements near the end of training get recycled. They are sent to a special training company, nicknamed "F Troop," for a month of nothing but exercise. From "F Troop" they are then sent back to start basic training all over again; surely a most hellish cycle. I meet one of these guys as I am going through basic training. He tells me he has been recycled through "F Troop" twice. But he is starting to shape up and has lost much weight, and I am certain he can make it through this time around. I sympathetically ask how he ever puts up with it, and it is then that he tells me his plan. Somehow, he has found out that the Army Rules and Regulations state that if a recruit is recycled three times through "F Troop" and still cannot pass the physical requirements of basic training, the recruit is then discharged. He is just about to be sent back to "F Troop" for the third time. One more failure and he will reach his goal. I am, momentarily, envious.

Others use a much more drastic plan that will yield the same desired result but in a vastly shorter time. The Army is so over-strained and so ill prepared, there are no M-16's available for the training companies. Instead, we are being trained with M-14's, an older rifle. Compared to a M-16, it is a "blunderbuss". Why not just train us with muskets and be done with it? But the M-14 is big, heavy, and powerful, and it shoots a very large round. It's almost a cannon, and we have nicknamed it the "Elephant Gun." Every afternoon, as we are about to leave the rifle range, we must individually state to the Range Officer that we are not carrying any live rounds back to the barracks. The Army's fear is that one or more of us will shoot the Drill Sergeants some evening. Their fear is not irrational, as this has happened before.

After every evening meal, as part of our nightly entertainment ritual, we are required to clean our rifles, lest we have any free time. But on one rather unpleasant hot and humid evening in late May, we hear the roar of an M-14 going off at close range. The noise comes through our open windows from the barracks next door only thirty feet away. We rush outside and look in to find that one of our comrades in arms has executed his plan to escape from the Army. He has placed the barrel of his M-14 against the outside of his shoulder and has pulled the trigger. The round, does in fact, wound his shoulder just enough that he will be given a Medical Discharge. But the plan has its flaws, and there are some serious examples of the Law of Unintended Consequences in this scheme. Principal among them is that the muzzle velocity of the round is astonishing; it leaves the barrel at an almost inconceivable 2800 feet per second. Given such velocity, the round's momentum is not slowed or deflected by a small amount of flesh. Only the briefest time is required for the round to travel the remaining 11 inches from his shoulder to the side of his head and shatter the latter all over the ceiling. He falls, from his top bunk to the floor, already dead. This scene is not for the faint of heart. An accidental suicide; how gut wrenching the news of this must have been to his parents. He is another unintended casualty of Vietnam.

One thing the Army did attempt to get its arms around is health and hygiene. Our barracks are very crowded, and if someone picks up a cold it is easily passed around. I know this, as I spent four days in the base hospital fighting some awful bug. So, every effort, including group punishment, is made to keep those pitiful old derelict barracks and ourselves clean. Some of my peers, especially in the first few weeks, find the adjustment to barracks life difficult. Many of them are the self-professed "tough guys," but their mothers always made their beds for them. They would be weepy-eyed the first few times they had to make their own beds to the satisfaction of some DI. A few of them even cry when they are finally allowed, after many weeks, to call home. I never ever call home, but I never want to. But for one poor kid, who doesn't keep clean enough, it is public humiliation. One afternoon, immediately after our "five minute" noon meal, we are all assembled in a large open area behind the barracks. The offender is called out in front of all 450 of us, whereupon the Senior DI explains that private John Doe will now give a demonstration of "field hygiene". The poor bastard places his steel helmet open side up on the ground and then kneels in front of us as water is poured into it. He then takes his toothbrush and then uses the water in his helmet to brush his teeth. That completed, he next washes his hands and face. The final step is to use this water for shaving. This is not pleasant to watch and we all stand in silence. There is no whistling or shouting or jeering; we all just want this to be over. I give the guy credit; he doesn't crack and without any emotion, he quietly completes his demonstration of "field hygiene," much to our collective relief.

One of the most degrading and hateful things about basic training is the whistle. The Drill Sergeants blow on a shrill whistle as if calling in the dogs. When we hear this whistle, we have to stop whatever we are doing and then come running, screaming at the top of our lungs, and fall into formation. The Army's rationale is that it was good exercise for us to run and scream as we rush to the formation, but I hated that whistle. You start to react to it as Pavlov's dogs did. You would hear or think you heard the whistle and would tense up to respond to it. One afternoon upon hearing it, I realized I was responding to it as a dog would. I was no dog, so I stopped myself and purposefully waited a bit as many of my barracks mates ran out the door in a mad dash. After a few seconds I did run to join the formation. I wasn't looking to be late and then punished, but after that I never responded like a dog. It was a psychological game that I would not allow myself to be defeated in.

One of the more vivid memories of "basic training" was the day we went into the gas chamber to experience tear gas. This is "military grade," powerful stuff, especially in a small room, which has no ventilation, as opposed to out in the open where the wind might disperse it. We are all given gas masks and are instructed in how to put them on and wear them. I am among the first group of about 30 of us who are led into a small windowless building in which a rather long narrow table occupies the center. The instructor has us walk slowly around this table, and as we do, he describes the effects of the gas. He then places a single small canister of the stuff on the table and pulls the pin. It does not explode but merely releases a very thin whitish wisp of smoke. I am unimpressed and think "that's it", but to be on the safe side I have taken a deep breath and I hold it. We continue to walk slowly counterclockwise around the long table and no one seems affected by the gas, so I begin to breathe and I am fine. But after another minute or two, the instructor tells us to remove our gas masks, and we do so. At first, I feel nothing, but soon my eyes begin to sting and then I take my first breath. Big mistake. It is most wretched, and we cannot escape this small room. We continue walking in a circle around the long table, all of us coughing and wheezing, and our eyes are burning. Just after I pass the instructor, he tells us to state our service number as we pass him, and then we can leave the building. It will be some time before I can do this, as I am now next-to-last in line, but about halfway through this process, the gas becomes so overwhelming that the instructor lets us evacuate the building. Two or three guys actually need medical attention, but they shortly recover and rejoin us. Now I know what military grade tear gas is all about. The next group of guys is called. They look terrified, but in the end, every one of us has had the gas.

As basic training grinds on, we are allowed a few perks, one being that we are allowed to visit a nearby but tiny PX on a Saturday. I probably buy a Coke or Pepsi that day but have misunderstood this is only a one-time privilege. The following Monday evening I walk the one block to the PX to buy that Pepsi and run into our Senior Drill Instructor. He makes me put the soda back and tells me I will be punished later. A few days later, immediately following our four-minute lunch, we are whistled to our formation. We are informed that there will not be any training that afternoon because we will be attending a special outdoor show put on by some TV network to entertain the troops. It's not Bob Hope, but something like that. Of course, the Senior DI tells me because of my earlier infraction of the rules I cannot go. He tells me that one of the remaining Sergeants will find some work detail for me later. I nod and say "Yes sir" and then drop out of the formation. But I am glad I am not going. It has been cloudy all morning and now it is beginning to drizzle, and everyone going is ordered to put their rain poncho on. Sitting in a field in the rain isn't going to be fun. I return to my barracks but go to the second floor and find a bunk in the very back that cannot be seen from the stairwell. I hear my training company marching off to wherever the event is being held and I soon fall asleep. I am awakened only once when I hear some Sergeant downstairs shouting, "Is there anyone in here?" I lie perfectly still and, in a moment, I hear him depart, and I sleep like a baby.

In the late afternoon I awaken to hear my training company marching back in. I go outside and fall into the formation. They are all wearing wet ponchos and they look miserable as hell. My DI looks at me very suspiciously as I still have the sleep in my eyes. He is about to say something, but we have mail call and he doesn't bother. I do get a few pieces of mail, including a large manila envelope, which I roll and stick everything inside my shirt to keep it dry. But the mail makes my shirt stick out. The DI happens to walk back by me and now slaps my stomach saying with great disgust, "You've got a hell of a gut." I pull the mail from my shirt and my shirt falls flatter than even his trim waistline. I give the DI my best version of the disgusted look of "You're an idiot." He is embarrassed but says nothing. But in the end, this incident pays dividends, as he eases off me for the rest of basic training.

I ask a newly-made friend from Pennsylvania how the show was. He replies, "It sucked; it rained the whole time. There were no seats; we had to sit on the ground. So, we all took our helmets off and sat on them trying to keep our butts dry. It really sucked and so did the show." I nod sympathetically, and he asks, "How was your punishment?" "Oh, I slept like a baby." He curses and then laughs out loud.

Other than that, I simply try to blend in; I don't get into much trouble, I don't cause any, and I don't volunteer for anything, other than to give blood. I pull my own weight and without fanfare try to offer decency and encouragement to others; I attempt to quietly go unnoticed. Somehow this plan fails me. At the end of basic training, my four hundred and fifty peers vote me as the number one in leadership. I do not see this coming, and neither do my Drill

Sergeants, who at the very least have mildly disliked me; now they hate me. A couple of Officers, shocked by this turn of events, encourage me to sign up for another year and go to Officer Candidate School, but I decline. I loathe being in the Army.

In early June, as we near the end of basic training, we are told we may go off the base on a one- or two-day pass into downtown Augusta (also known as Disgusta by the soldiers stationed there). But just a couple of days later, during the morning formation, we are informed that Robert Kennedy had been assassinated in California. Only 11 days before my induction into the Army, Martin Luther King had been assassinated as well. We are told there had been riots in Augusta back then and therefore there would be no weekend passes because there were fears this would happen again. It was a turbulent time.

After basic training, every soldier is sent to some sort of school for further training. A few have voluntarily enlisted, in order to be guaranteed a particular school. Others, upon receiving their draft notice, enlist before their draft date, also to be guaranteed a place in a school. But there are also about three dozen others, mostly but not all draftees, who are sent to a special Reading and Writing School before any attempt is made at further training. It amazed me that so many of my comrades could not read and write. I personally knew a few, their penmanship so poor that we had to address their letters home to their families and read to them any letters they received. These guys were from Providence, Pittsburgh, and New York City, all over. Of course, the Drill Sergeants found this exasperating and were furious when training or testing was held up so that instructions or questions for some simple test had to be read to them. But for most of the guys in this group, if they survived it, the Army was probably the best thing that ever happened to them.

On Saturday morning, the final day of "basic training," we are dressed in our khakis and marched to an open field that has some stands at one end. We are here for our graduation ceremony. There are a couple of short (thank God) speeches; then a group picture is taken in grainy black and white. We are then dismissed, and several of my comrades run toward the grandstand to be hugged and greeted by their parents, who have driven down from New York City, Providence or Pittsburg. I think, *These guys are proud to have graduated from Army Basic Training???* Then it hits me. This may be the first time in their lives that they have graduated from anything.

In the meantime, the Senior DI spots me and bawls me out for not keeping the brass on my uniform untarnished. He is the same one who had earlier caught me with the can of Pepsi. "If you think you can slack off, you've got another thing coming. I'll personally take care of you next week." But of course, this never happens. By the very next morning, Sunday, I am placed with many others on a chartered DC-6. It's an older four-engine prop plane; no jet service in this Army. Before I get on a bus to take me to the airfield, my new friend from Pennsylvania shakes my hand and wishes me well. He had enlisted and is heading to cartographers' school. He asks where I am headed; I shrug and say, "Artillery." His final words to me are: "Don't let the assholes get you down." I am unsure whether he means my comrades or the lifers? By 10:00AM, we lift off the runway of the Army airfield of Fort Gordon and fly west to Fort Leonard Wood (Fort Lost-in-the-Woods) in Missouri. There, about half of us get off the plane to start Advanced Infantry training. We shortly lift off again and fly to the final destination.

Fort Sill, Oklahoma

As a draftee you are most likely to end up at the bottom of the Army barrel; armor, artillery, or infantry. These are the places that not many enlist for. Hell, even my killer bunkmate is going to clerk school. But of course, he has enlisted (well, sort of) for six years in order to be guaranteed a place in a school. The rest of us draftees are, well, cannon fodder. I end up in Lawton, Oklahoma, assigned to the Fort Sill Artillery Surveying School. But at least I do not end up on a howitzer as a gun bunny. I can think of no greater agony than that of the cannoneer, spending hour upon hour, days on end, hand-loading thirty-pound rounds into a 105 Howitzer and going deaf doing it.

Someone meets our plane when we land at the Fort Sill Army airfield. We are loaded onto a bus and then dropped off, a few at a time, around the post at our designated barracks and the place where I finally report in. I must have gotten something to eat and then fallen deeply asleep. I awaken to find everyone dressing in a hurry and scrambling to report to a formation outside the barracks, to which I am late. But I notice, as I approach the doorway exit, the lifers taking the names of those who are late. I just hold back inside the doorway as the lifer Sergeants scream and lecture. After a few minutes, they dismiss the formation, and I simply blend in as we go to breakfast. After breakfast we are marched off to start our classes in Artillery Surveying. Our class is large, maybe a couple of hundred guys, but it goes well enough, and it seems as if it will be a decent school. There are also half a dozen Marines taking the course. In the late afternoon, when we are marched back to the barracks, the Marines, all of whom are Sergeants, hold us for a meeting before our dismissal. They look us over. Then they approach me and then unanimously appoint me to be in charge of the Army guys. They tell me they like what they see. I cannot say no, so I force a smile and say, "Great." It's not like this is a promotion; there's no increase in rank or pay. But it's probably slightly better than not being in charge. Besides, I'd rather be on the right side of six Marine Sergeants than on their shit list. My aspiration has always been to go un-noticed, but my supposed leadership abilities keep screwing up that plan. And so it goes.

Most of my comrades-in-arms accept me as their leader. After all, I am not a bully about it; I don't see myself as better than they are, and to the best of my ability, I am very fair about directing various work details. Nevertheless, two or three are very resentful about it; they object less to me personally than to the fact that they were not chosen. They seem obsessively to hate the situation. One guy in particular gives me a lot a crap and is as belligerent as he can be. He is a white guy from New York City and tells me that when he gets out of the Army, he is going to be a New York City cop. I see no leadership abilities in him; all I see is a desperate guy who is angry at the world because he is not in charge. He also strikes me as a bit of a racist. Just what the world needs more of. May God help New York City. The Marine Sergeants didn't like him much either; they knew an asshole bully when they saw one. But he didn't dare give them any crap; they would have delighted in cleaning his clock, and he knew it.

I got along with the Marine Sergeants very well. Sometimes after hours, especially on the weekends, we might do a few things together. But mostly it was a blind date kind of deal. One of the Sergeants would get a date, and his date would have a girlfriend who needed a date; that was when I was called in. I met a lot of tall women from Lawton and Chickasha. Nothing romantic, but it was a lot more fun than hanging around the barracks. But all of that ended with the completion of our school, and I never saw those Marine Sergeants again.

In the very beginning of my time at Fort Sill, I would watch some TV in the recreation room. On July 4th, I saw a story on CBS evening news about a parade back home. I thought I saw some friends; they looked as if they were having a good time. But it depressed me, so I never watched TV again.

With the Marine Sergeants gone, I would on occasion leave the post to venture into downtown Lawton, Oklahoma. It was not a very big city by any standard, really no more than a big town on the desolate, barren, windy plains of Oklahoma near the bottom of the Texas pan-handle. No one had used much imagination in naming the streets of the town; it was just a big grid with consecutively named streets: First, Second, Third, Fourth, Fifth, and so on, with the cross streets named Avenue A, B, C, D, E, and on and on. The downtown section, which was only a few blocks long, consisted mostly of bars, pawn shops, and dry cleaners. The surrounding blocks had more bars, pawn shops, and dry cleaners.

Fort Sill was an artillery training base. The big guns, which the cannoneers trained and practiced on, were capable of sending heavy high explosive rounds at least 20 miles. This meant-- it absolutely demanded--that the base be both physically large and situated somewhere very remote. Therefore, Lawton's sole purpose seemed to be to provide some kind of diversion and entertainment or dry cleaning to tens of thousands of Army GI's who had no other place to go. It would have been perfect for a movie set, except that most people would have found that the movie set was embellished and exaggerated. But Lawton, Oklahoma, was the real deal, the epitome of an Army town, clinging to life just outside an Army base, located in the middle of nowhere.

Most of us did not like the town; it was only a distraction from life on the Army post, and not a particularly good one. There were bars full of hookers, strip joints, with the occasional pawn shop that would always see a lot of action towards the end of the month when everyone was broke. The Salvation Army had a store front over on Avenue E, and I think the USO had a small storefront a few blocks away, but I never saw much activity at either one. But on one particular street on which there was one bar after another, squeezed in among them was the tiniest of storefronts with a white Cross in the front window. The Cross was illuminated by small white Christmas lights which seemed to be lit around the clock. The door was almost always open, and inside was a man of the cloth, eternally dressed in black, holding the Good Book. I guess he was available for Christian counseling around the clock as well, but he wasn't getting a lot of walk-in traffic. Later that Fall, I noticed he had changed his tactics a bit. He would put a couple of plates of cookies on display with a huge glass pitcher that looked as if it was filled with lemonade, next to them. He would get two or three guys in there on a Saturday night, but I never went in. Oh, occasionally I might be tempted by something sweet, but there is no such thing as a free lunch, and I was unwilling to pay the entry fee of being preached to.

Decades later, I heard a song on the radio, "Walking in Memphis" sung by Mark Cohn. Near the end of the song there are the following few lines:

"They got gospel in the air,
Reverend Green be glad to see you,
When you haven't got a prayer,
Boy, you've got a prayer in Memphis"

Whenever I hear that song, I always think of that tiny storefront with its white Cross in the front window on that decadent street of downtown Lawton, Oklahoma. I still see that man of the cloth, dressed in black, holding the Bible and that plate of cookies... I wonder whether it's still there. The bottom line is that Lawton was not much fun. Evenings usually ended up being a bunch of GIs in a bunch of bars staring across at each other, with every one of us bored as hell.

The artillery surveying school itself wasn't too bad; more than a few guys had enlisted to be in this school. I guess I got lucky. Upon completing the school, I am temporarily assigned with a few others to an Artillery Battalion on Fort Sill. But as we report into our new unit that day, we are in for a shock. The unit has been put on alert to travel to Chicago. It is 1968, and the U.S. government is sending Federal troops to quell the riots at the Democratic National

Convention being held in Chicago. Our new unit isn't sure what to do with us, but overnight "they" decide we should take some leave time and go home. This is just as well, as some of my unit actually went to Chicago and ended up spending a week in a National Guard Armory. Fortunately, they were never called out onto the streets. I was quite pleased to have missed that trip.

I take the leave and return home. It starts well enough. I fly military stand-by, and because there is no space left in coach, I am put in First Class. What a treat. But the rest of my leave becomes bittersweet. I visit my grandfather, who is in his late eighties and who is suffering from what was un-diagnosed Alzheimer's. It shocks me to see that he has so rapidly declined from the last time I saw him five months before. It doesn't look as if he has shaved in several days, so I shave his face with my electric shaver. He seems appreciative and possibly a little embarrassed, but I say nothing. Looking back on that day, I am glad to have done that for him, as I owed him far more. I finish my leave and return to my new unit at Fort Sill. My mother calls me at Fort Sill six weeks later telling me that my grandfather has died of pneumonia. He was my best friend from day one onward. I had barely 20 years with him. Not nearly enough. To this day I still grieve his passing and my loss.

I don't like the Army at all, but I can do nothing about that. I just try to go un-noticed. The survey section that I am in doesn't even have an NCO (non-commissioned officer) running it; consequently, we do no artillery surveying. Instead, we do generic work details like cleaning the latrines (bathrooms), washing and waxing the barracks floors, as well as guard duty, KP, and other mind-numbing crap. But I have made friends with a guy from Idaho who happens to work in Personnel. He mentions that they are short one clerk. I beg him to let me talk with the NCO he works for. The Sergeant, an E-6, is actually a decent man and I am able to convince him that I would make a good clerk. I am a marginal typist but good enough to be a clerk. He gives his blessing, and I start working for him. This keeps me off the "KP and guard roster" list, and I no longer wash and wax floors. For a short time, my life in the Army is endurable. But my luck turns sour after just two months. There is a change of Sergeants in personnel. The new guy is nasty and insufferable. He's another lifer asshole who is going to show everyone who is in charge. He alienates all of us. What was once not a bad job quickly become unbearable.

The Sergeant has an obsession about answering the phone on its first ring, lest some other lifer, who may be calling personnel, complain that the phone wasn't answered fast enough. When the office phone rings, he tries to beat us to picking it up and then reprimands us for not picking up sooner. To a man, we greatly dislike him and talk about how we would love to screw with him somehow, but no one comes up with a viable plan. Or do we? The friend who originally got me this job, unbeknownst to all of us, arrives at work very early, well before any of us show up. He lifts the hand set from the cradle of our Sergeant's desk phone and then places clear Scotch tape over the cradle, holding it permanently down. Now when the phone rings and the Sergeant lifts the phone hand set, it will just keep on ringing.

Shortly after the personnel office opens, the phones begin to ring. Of course, our NCO picks his phone up before us, but my friend picks his up and takes the call as the NCO keeps shouting Hello? Hello? A few minutes later the phones ring again and our NCO is champing at the bit to answer the phone. He is first on the draw, but of course on the second ring one of us takes the call. He can't figure it out. In a few minutes the phone rings again, with the same result. On the fourth time with the same result, the Sergeant is steaming and slams his phone down. He gives us the dirtiest look and storms out of the office. My friend quickly pulls the Scotch tape from the phone cradle. Our Sergeant returns in a few minutes; his phone rings, he picks up instantly and screams into it. We now hear the voice of the Sergeant Major's voice, who doesn't take anybody's crap, screaming back at him. We all bury our faces in paper work trying desperately not to laugh out loud. But he doesn't learn and he only becomes more harassing and belligerent. Things only worsen, and I finally ask my First Sergeant for another assignment; he agrees and tells me that another co-worker has requested the same thing. By the end of the week, I return to the artillery surveying section, and by Monday I am back on crappy work details and KP again.

Our typical day in the Army, though stupid and miserable, becomes very predictable. We rise around seven or so, shave, dress and then go to get some breakfast in the mess hall. I usually have only toast, juice, and coffee. There are other choices, but nothing I want. These include burnt scrambled eggs and the universally despised "creamed chipped beef on toast." This concoction is aptly known as "shit on a shingle," and I have never seen anyone ever eat it; yet it is served every day. It is food and effort wasted seven days a week. The Army seems incapable of change.

After breakfast we report to the morning formation. There is always an announcement, usually about something that matters little; it is generally some kind of complaint. We are never praised. After that, the formation is dismissed, and unless you have a particular assignment or job (such as my former clerk job) we begin our "work details," which we call "shit details." These are usually mundane work projects whose sole purpose is to keep us busy. We are often marched to the motor pool where we perform preventive maintenance on our trucks and jeeps. We check the oil level in the engines, but the biggest task is to check the battery terminals for "snow," as the lifers put it. Sometimes there is some corrosion where the battery cables attach to the battery posts that appears as a white fuzz. If you find any, you clean it off. Of course, you do this again the next morning, so it is pretty rare to find any "snow." It is a way to waste a morning.

At noon, lunch is served in the mess hall, usually potatoes and beef or chicken. I cannot remember what we did in the afternoon. Something mind-numbing enough to be forgettable. Around 5:00 or 6:00 PM, dinner is served, which is often a repeat of lunch. In the evening, you can change out of your uniform and take a 15-minute bus ride into downtown Lawton or stay on the post and go to a movie. I probably go to the movies four or five nights a week. Sweet Jesus, the Army sucks.

KP or "Kitchen Police" duty makes for an intolerably long day. You are awakened well before anyone else to report to the mess area. There you assist the cooks with whatever help they need, but mostly you wash dishes, pots, and pans, cleared tables, and washed floors. The cooks change shifts after the noon meal, but we have to stay on for the entire day and well into the evening, probably a 16-hour shift. It is hellish drudgery, and we all hate it. On one particular day when I am on KP, the head cook, a height-challenged Sergeant (E-5) lifer bully, marches me down to our Battery commander's office and tells our Second Louie that I haven't been working hard enough. The Lieutenant, who played football in college and is not much older than me, thanks the Sergeant and says "I'll handle this." After the lifer leaves, the Lieutenant smiles and asks what happened. I ask, "Is this supposed to be punishment?" He replies, "No, of course not." "Well sir, I'm doing the best I can." He nods and says, "I know, okay, better get back there then." I return to the mess hall. The lifer smirks, thinking he has really gotten me in trouble. What a jerk! Though I do not know it at the time, he is the kind of guy who would have a live fragmentation grenade tossed at him in Vietnam. He is the kind of guy who gets "fragged."

I cannot stand much more KP or other "shit details," so I ask for a re-assignment to South Vietnam. I put the paperwork through personnel, and a few days later our battery commander calls me into his office. The Lieutenant, being the decent enough guy that he is, asks if I know what I am requesting. I tell him I do. He tells me that, in the end, I will just end up with the ground pounders and gravel crunchers. Little do I know how right he will turn out to be. He tells me he will not approve the request, but not to worry; it will be overridden further up the chain of command, once the paperwork hits the Pentagon, as every volunteer for Viet Nam is immediately taken. It may seem counterintuitive, but going to South Vietnam is part of my plan. I have learned that after your one-year tour of duty, if you have less than five months remaining on your induction, the Army discharges you. I would get out several months early. It is easily worth the risk, or so it seems. Therefore, I rationally and intentionally volunteer to go.

I then return to the daily grind of shit details of looking for "snow" on battery terminals, checking engine oil levels, and washing and waxing floors. I hope my transfer will come quickly. But before much time goes by, one of the duty drivers goes AWOL (absent without official leave) again. He has already gone AWOL once before, which is why he has become a duty driver. That job is for the screw-ups. He had gone to the stockade for a short time before being made a duty driver. Now he is back in the stockade. There are two duty drivers. They work a 24-hour shift, and then have 24 hours off. Basically, they hang out at the Battalion Headquarters (HQ) with a small truck and drive anyone who needs a ride around the base. But the best part is that they are exempt from "work details," KP, and guard duty. Hell, sign me up.

My First Sergeant calls me into his office; he is not at all happy that I want to become the "duty driver." This job, he tells me, is for the "screw ups," for the guys who can't do anything but drive a jeep. It does not require "leadership" to drive a jeep. He seems genuinely concerned and disappointed with me for choosing this job. He is Puerto Rican, a bright and educated man, reasonable and fair, a capable leader. I don't know why he is in the Army, but he has done well nevertheless. He is relatively young to be a First Sergeant (E-8), and no doubt he will make Sergeant Major, E-9. His retirement will be comfortable. He is the rare exception; most lifers are promoted ever-so-slowly by staying in the Army for life.

My Puerto Rican comrades tell me they have also asked the First Sergeant why is he in the Army, as they hate it as much as I do. The First Sergeant cannot understand why we do not want to be here, and we cannot understand why he is here. I tell my First Sergeant, that duty driving is only a temporary assignment; I will be leaving in one or two months, as I have requested a duty assignment for South Vietnam. He gives his reluctant okay, and now I am off KP, guard duty, and shit work details. I am staying one step ahead of the curve. This sets the course for the rest of my military career: go as long as you can, and if it turns really shitty, find something else.

Of course, it takes some time for the Army-Pentagon machinery to roll over and actually work and issue orders. It is not until mid-January that I receive my orders to Vietnam.

At this point I am not so certain about my grand plan to beat the system. By the time I get to View Nam and complete the twelve-month tour of duty, I will have less than two months remaining, not the early discharge of five months I had planned on. My "duty driver" job is no career maker. But I'm not a "lifer," and it is usually an easy enough job with the benefit of no KP or other shit details. Besides, I have a girlfriend now, a local girl from Faxon, a tiny farming town outside of Lawton. I met her during the fall when an Army friend had been kind enough to invite me along to a small party off-base. She is blond, a sweet kid, and can sing like an opera star. But with orders in hand there is no way to undo this; you cannot simply un-volunteer, especially for South Vietnam. The die is cast; I must live with this decision.

Before shipping off to Vietnam, I take my obligatory one-month leave and return home. To save some money, I get one of the guys to drive me to Tinker Air Force base to see if I can hitch a ride east. I am in great luck; as soon as I get there, I step on to a six-passenger Air Force jet that is heading to Washington, DC. Other than the two pilots I am the only person on this flight. I spend the night at a Naval Air Station barracks, and the next morning I almost immediately catch a ride to Boston. The only other passenger is a Three-Star General who sits in a private cabin in the rear. Per military protocol, the highest rank leaves the plane first. As he strides down the aisle, he slaps me on the back and says very cheerfully, "Well son, we made it." I call a cousin who picks me up at the airport.

Being home is not that much fun or interesting, but my parents are divorced now, so the household is at least a more pleasant place. But the weather is as cold as hell compared to Oklahoma, and I really don't have much to do here in the middle of the winter. It's not like it's July and one can head for a day at the beach.

In the end, I cut my leave short and head for Ft. Lewis, Washington, near Seattle; it is the jumping off point to South Vietnam. I have one last Saturday night fling before going, much to my regret. My cousin picks me up, and we go out for a final send off, which it nearly became. We drink too much, and on our way home, he loses control of his car as we travel across the steel mesh of a very old bridge. We hit a massive steel girder—luckily-- which prevents us from falling into the river far below us. He hits the steering wheel, and I put the top of my forehead into the windshield and break it, leaving a large perfectly circular spider web in the glass on the passenger's side.

I momentarily black out but seem to come around quickly, though I haven't the slightest sense of time. My cousin is muttering to himself, half out of it. I realize I am holding something in my right hand. It is the arm rest that I had ripped out of the door upon impact. I attempt to get out of the car, but I have difficulty opening my door. I finally force it open, make a quick assessment of the damage, and then walk behind the car to the driver's side. I pull my cousin from the driver's seat, and he says, "You probably should drive." I agree but I doubt the car will start. I haven't yet told my cousin that the front passenger side is wrapped around a steel girder and that the front tire is folded up under the car. I attempt to start the car but it won't even crank at all. I tell my cousin I think we should get rid of the beer, and he agrees, and I begin throwing unopened cans of Pabst Blue Ribbon off of the bridge into the river below. (I never had much luck with Pabst.) It is 1:00AM and there is absolutely no traffic, which is a good thing, because my cousin keeps staggering out into the middle lane. But as luck would have it, a cop pulling into a nearby diner spots us and begins backing down the bridge towards us. My cousin asks me for a big favor, "I just got out of the high-risk pool. Tell the cops you were driving. You're going to Vietnam anyway, so what does it matter?" I agree. "Yeah, what does it matter?"

The cops ask the obvious question, "What happened?" I make up some story how there must have been some ice on the bridge, but he looks around and isn't buying it. He looks at my driver's license on which I have doctored my birth date in order to show that I am 21 so I can drink. He shakes his head; this isn't going well. But before he says another word, I show him my military ID and tell him I am going to Vietnam next week. He looks at his partner, and they both shrug. He hands me back the ID and says "I'll call you a wrecker and you can take yourself home."

I decide the next day that I should leave the following morning, before anything else goes wrong. On my last night home, I say good bye to my Grandmother. She wishes me well, and I am certain that she thinks I will return in a year, especially given the stern advice she insist I hear. I am convinced that she fears that I may become lonely so far away and is worried that at age 20, I will be too young and foolish and will bring home a war bride. She shakes a finger at me and says, "Don't you bring home a little Chinese girl." I think, "right continent, wrong country," but I know she means well, and I promise my Grandma I will not bring home a war bride.

The following morning, I take an Eastern non-stop flight to Seattle. To the astonishment of the personnel clerks at Fort Lewis, Washington, I have reported in several days early. Not a problem they tell me, as many guys report in late. Only 36 hours later, they squeeze me on to the flight to Cam Ranh Bay.

Before the flight, we are put on buses and driven to McCord Air Force Base, which abuts Fort Lewis. We board a stretch Boeing 707; a chartered Flying Tigers Airliner. The flight is absolutely jammed, every seat taken by military personnel. We fly nonstop from near Seattle to Tokyo, where we lay over for about an hour and a half as the jet is re-fueled. We sit in a special area of the terminal for the U.S. military. After a short time, we see members of the US Army entering from another side. These are the guys who just left Vietnam and are returning to the States; they are waiting for their jet to be refueled as well. I look at them closely and then stare past them; they seem older than we do, and I think, "this will be a long year." After some time, we are called to our waiting plane; we depart Tokyo and then fly the final leg of our journey.

February 13th Cam Ranh Bay

After an exhausting flight we land in Cam Ranh Bay, South Vietnam. It is a massive base used by every branch of the service: Army, Navy, Coast Guard, Air Force, and Marines. The Air force has a huge air base here, the Navy has a huge port, and the Army has a huge staging area. Almost everything and everybody that moves in and out of South Vietnam goes through Cam Ranh Bay.

We exit the plane. Having come from the continental winter of the U.S., we walk into a wall of heat, and I find it staggering. We are herded onto buses and driven a short distance to a reception camp. We will spend a couple of days here as "they" sort out who is going where, when and how. We are given the usual make-work details to keep us busy, but this only embitters everyone. Most of us find it difficult, if not impossible, to sleep, given the heat. A year later though, I will find the evenings cool and will sleep with a light blanket on me.

After a couple of days at Cam Ranh Bay, about forty of us are put aboard a noisy prop-driven freighter, and we fly north, making a couple of briefs stops along the way. We stop at small bases, where a few guys get off and a few get on, and eventually we arrive at Phu Cat Airbase. There, a small truck meets me at the terminal, and I am driven a couple of miles to Service Battery, where I am processed into my new unit. I spend a couple days and nights there doing the usual Army paperwork in triplicate. Having completed that process and being assigned to Headquarters Battery, on the following morning I and a few others head about 20 miles north up Highway 1 to my new home at LZ (landing zone) Uplift.

Welcome To Uplift

The trip is not without mishap, as our truck dies halfway there. We are a bit nervous being stuck on the side of the road, but we have radioed to Uplift to send a truck, which actually arrives without too long a wait. We climb aboard, and after another 30 minutes of driving, we finally arrive at LZ Uplift. But what a disorganized dump of a place it is. It's a moderately sized camp, with four or five different Infantry or Artillery HQs based there. There are several helipads at different places within the camp, but it's too small to have a runway for planes to land. There clearly was no plan in organizing the place. As each new unit moved into the LZ, they pushed the perimeter back a bit and then built more small sandbag-covered buildings that we commonly called hooches. It has become a hodgepodge, and the place is as ugly as sin. As our truck enters my Battery's section of Uplift, I see several short steel burn barrels. They are emitting heavy black smoke that is sickeningly sweet; its stench is nauseating. Later I will learn what they are burning. Uplift has the look, feel, and smell of a third world POW camp. It is almost completely filled with lowly built hooches that at first glance look as if they are partially built into the ground. But it's their dirty green rotting sandbags that begin at ground level and that are stacked against and over the hooches that causes them to appear so cave-like. The sandbags are in various stages of decay caused by the blistering tropical sun. There is reddish-brown clay everywhere, which comes in two forms: dust and mud. Both suck. I guess you can get used to anything, but at first glance LZ Uplift is depressingly butt ugly. And I haven't even seen it in the mud season..............

The driver points me in the direction of the battery's office, which is just a dozen steps away. It's a building of just two very small rooms, and I enter the outer one to find the battery clerk sitting at his desk. He's probably a little younger than I am; he looks thin and wears wire-framed glasses, but his persona seems decent enough. The glasses give him a slight sense of style. He takes my paperwork, looks briefly at it and says rather flatly, "Well, better go report in," and points to the tiny office behind him where the battery commander sits at his desk. The clerk silently rolls his eyes, wordlessly warning me that Capt. Fruit is an asshole.

I stroll through the doorway and stand in front of Fruit, salute and then say, "Reporting for duty, sir". I doubt that Fruit is much older than I am, but does he ever look like a dork. He wears RPG's (Army Regulation Prescription Glasses) -- better known as Rape Prevention Glasses or Birth Control Glasses as they are so repulsively homely that any woman would run from them. Poor dumb Fruit. I realize as I come to know him that he thinks that if he does everything by the book, the Army will reward him. But he is only a punk bully, desperate to be far more important than he will ever become. He has no leadership abilities; he is as paper thin as the sheets that the Army Regulations are written on. As I quickly learn, he is universally despised by every man here, be it Officer, NCO, or enlisted.

Fruit doesn't waste a moment before starting his pointless shit, by asking me, demanding to know, how long have I been in country? It is obvious that I have just arrived in Vietnam. I immediately know where this is going, so I refuse to co-operate and work on frustrating him. I start with, "Gee, I don't know exactly." He responds, "Come on, you must know how many days." To which I respond "I'm not sure" … "I just got here."

Fruit grows desperate. He needs to know exactly how many days I have been in country, so he can boast how many more days he has been here. He tries again. "You must know how many days you've been here." But I play dumb; I pretend that I am counting the days on my fingers. "Let's see, I left, but we stopped in Japan." "So, one, two, no, no…one, two, three, then four, then, no, no, no." Fruit is now pacing behind his desk. I continue, asking myself a rhetorical question, "Was I in Cam Ranh Bay three days or four? No, no that's not right. I was in base camp for three days I think." Fruit can't stand it any longer. "Well, it doesn't matter how many days you have been here, because I have been here longer. And you need to remember that I have been here longer." I simply give him a blank look and then say, "Sir, I'm not sure how many days I have been here." He mumbles something then says "Dismissed." I salute and then walk out the door. The clerk briefly catches my eye and gives me the thumbs up.

Outside, I immediately run into the First Sergeant. He introduces himself to me in a most decent and friendly manor. "Top" as we respectfully and lovingly called him is from Florida and has the most pleasant of southern drawls. He turns out to be a rather decent man, capable of great leadership. He offers to show me to my section as well as the mess hall, showers, and latrines. I tell him about Fruit, to which he unhesitatingly responds, "Oh Fruit is an asshole. Everyone hates him." This speaks volumes of how things are in this unit, and I have only been in LZ Uplift for fifteen minutes.

"Top" walks me down to my new quarters, which look like a dusty sandbag-covered cave. He introduces me to my new platoon, "Artillery Surveying," and its NCO, Sergeant Patterson. Top pats me on the shoulder, saying "Okay, you're all set now," and then leaves. But it barely registers, as I do a double take and then look once more at Sergeant Patterson. The man is so immensely fat that he has trouble going through a doorway. He is the fattest Sergeant I have ever seen. There is no equal; in fact, there is not even a distant second.

Sergeant Patterson begins by telling me he has been in the Army for nearly 27 years. He joined the Army during WWII, and tells me in a comforting way that he has yet to lose a man in combat. But I look at his girth and wonder; forget combat, how many have been lost to starvation? He tells me he plans on staying in for as long as he can, but fears in three more years the Army will force him out. I think that if he doesn't drop dead before then, he will surely be dead shortly after from boredom. The Army is the only thing he has; talk about a lifer! He asks if I will be staying in. I try not to disappoint him, so I tell him I'm not sure yet and hope that my nose doesn't grow like Pinocchio's. But in fairness, my first impression was that I could be working for someone far worse than he.

Over time I got to know him slightly better. Sergeant Patterson wasn't too bad a guy, and though he could be disagreeable at times, the guy wasn't a prick. He just wanted you to kiss his ass a little, and everything was fine. But most of us in the survey section refer to him as Sergeant Dufus behind his back. He's not dumb, but he's not especially bright either. Throw in his gross weight and the fact that he always smells a little, and it's a little hard for any of us to kiss up. Months later a new guy from the Massachusetts National

Guard shows up and, hoping to get a promotion, sucks up big-time to Patterson. That causes the rest of us to quickly despise the newbie.

The other thing I learn rather quickly about Sergeant Patterson is that the man is rather predisposed to farting; I suppose it was no surprise given his appetite. He would later tell us-- repeatedly I might add-- his favorite fart joke. "See, now there's these two guys who are in England, you see, and they are watching the Queen go by in her carriage. See, so one of them farts as she rides by. So, the other guy says, 'How dare you fart in front of the Queen?' 'See, so the first guy replies,' 'Oh sorry, I didn't know it was her turn.'" Then Ol' Pat would rip a loud one that really stunk; I guess you had to be there. Welcome to stinking Uplift.

We almost never do any actual artillery surveying, in which an artillery position and a few prominent landmarks or targets are precisely surveyed as to provide reference positions for a bombardment. It's a leftover from WW II and WW I, but it doesn't seem to be used much in Vietnam. So instead, our section catches all the shit details. That includes plenty of guard duty on the perimeter wire. Life at Uplift begins to suck.

I make friends with everyone in my section, some better friends than others, but I have no enemies. There is a guy from someplace in Vermont with a very quiet personality. The guy from California is alive. Another guy from I forget where, is a little dull. And a dude from Texas is our buck Sergeant and is a decent enough guy. It is what you would expect, a real mixed bag. I just want to survive my time and then get the hell out of the Army.

But unless you have a specific job or duty for every day, you are at the mercy of whatever shit work details come up, be they necessary or simply invented. That is the situation the survey section is in. Every day is some brain deadening work detail like filling sandbags. It seems that we never have enough sandbags, mostly because the cloth bag rots pretty quickly in tropical sun and humidity. At some point we get "new plastic-fiberglass bags," but to our great disappointment, they do not hold up very well at all with the ultraviolet rays of the sun beating down on them. But Sweet Jesus, the sandbags are everywhere. They are stacked around, against, and over our low buildings to prevent or at least slow down exploding shrapnel from rockets and mortars coming through the side walls or roofs. But the bags rot so quickly that we continuously replace them; it is endless.

We do have some help from the local population, though. Top, our First Sergeant, has hired a small group of refugees from a Vietnamese camp for IDP's (Internally Displaced Persons). They are not paid very much, but we give them a free lunch at which they may eat as much as they want. Top also hires several women to work in the kitchen as well. This relieves us from having dreaded KP. Of course, the funds to pay for these workers come from money collected each month at payday from the enlisted men. It's not a lot of money-- maybe a few dollars each-- but the NCO's and the Officers don't pay, despite their much greater salaries. The theory is that they would not have to do KP or shit details anyway, so why should they have to pay? The elitism and incredible cheapness of these men are hard to fathom. A real display of leadership… And they wondered why some of them were hated so much or that so many were fragged.

But our Top makes every attempt to look after our welfare, far more than most Officers or NCOs ever would. He is the right man in the right position at the right time and is greatly respected and liked (almost loved) by all the enlisted men, many of whom are really just 18 and 19-year-old kids. There was supposedly a prohibition against placing 17-year-olds in combat positions, but that prohibition "leaked" occasionally. I turn 21 years old a few days after arriving in Viet Nam and am in fact one of the old men among the kids.

There are some small generators at the camp that keep the radios and other electronics powered up, but that is about all. Very shortly after my arrival, the First Sergeant has one of the senior supply Sergeants work his magic with his counterpart at the Phu Cat Airbase. I am sent along to help out, which is better than filling sandbags, though I do have to suffer through several hours of hearing how great a supply Sergeant he is. The supply Sergeant takes a brand-new jeep and trades it for a brand-new diesel-powered generator. Of course, the "jeep" is written off as a "combat loss," destroyed by enemy fire, on the same day and time that an Air Force diesel generator was destroyed by an enemy rocket. I honestly think we got the better part of this deal, because now with a diesel generator we could make power around the clock. Our electrician ran wiring into every hooch, so that each of us can now run a tiny fan, a radio and a couple of light bulbs. Somehow, we also got a bunch of sheets thrown in with the deal, so we now sleep on a single cotton sheet on our wooden bunks in our tiny hooches. The home-made bunks, as well as our hooches, were built from wooden ammo boxes that once each contained 105 artillery rounds. Life got a little easier at Uplift.

The Air Force was always eager to trade anything for a new jeep. The air base at Phu Cat was fairly substantial, and their maintenance shop took only a few hours to change that olive drab green of the Army over to the pale blue of the Air Force. We could always write almost anything off as a combat loss, often legitimately, as there were frequent rocket attacks at Uplift as well as our other batterys. And the Air Force never tired of getting new jeeps.

Top always is as fair as he can be with guard duty. But there are a substantial number of guys who are ED (Exempt from Duty). They need to be at their posted position, so they never catch any time on "the line," aka, "the perimeter," aka "the wire." This still strikes me as inherently unfair. Every one of us should pull guard duty, no exceptions. It would not be too bad that way; guard duty would not come up that often if everyone shared in this duty. But it is the other "lifers" who make a mess of things. They insist that they need their guy or guys fresh every day, so it always falls upon the same small group of us to pull guard duty. So, Top would try to his best to spread guard duty around. But with such a small group to choose from, it is often every other night, with an occasional extra night off, then back to every other night.

Our unit covers three of the many bunkers that run around the perimeter of LZ Uplift, which is our unit's contribution to the security of the LZ. But it is always the same bunch of us who catch this, and guard duty generally sucks big time. We report for duty at 6:00 PM. Then we are read some instructions or other bullshit by some lifer Sergeant, or occasionally even by screwball Capt. Fruit with his god-awful RPG's. The lecturing completed, we then load up an open 1-ton truck with dozens of claymore antipersonnel mines, three heavy M-60 machine guns, three grenade launchers, and many boxes of ammo for each as well as a big bunch of hand flares. The Sergeant of the Guard drives us out to "the line," and three of us are dropped off at each one of our bunkers. Then the truck heads back inside the perimeter and we are on our own for the next twelve hours.

We set up the Claymore mines out in front of the bunker, always taking great care to point them outward, away from our position. We then run the wire leads back to the bunker and tie them into their hand-held detonators. The final step is to put an ammo belt into the machine gun and then pass the night away.

The bunkers themselves are two stories high, either consisting of a ground floor at grade or even slightly dug into the earth with a rear entrance. Each side is almost completely covered with sandbags except for some small openings in the front and sides. But it is up top where we pull guard duty. We would climb up the stacked sandbags from the rear side of the bunker onto the second story. The second story is about seven feet tall and has sandbags stacked about three feet high on all four sides and at each corner, a post supported a slightly pitched shed roof; it too, is covered with sandbags.

There the three of us while away the night in each bunker. We usually all stay up together until about midnight, and then begin two-hour shifts. Two guys go downstairs to sleep, while one stands guard up top. After two hours, the shift rotates until about 6:00AM, when the Sergeant of the guard drives out to the perimeter to pick us up. It is usually boring as hell and is often difficult to stay awake during our shifts, so we almost always bring a radio along. We find the nearest Armed Forces Vietnam Network station, playing the top forty, which gives us something to listen to and helps keep us awake.

There are rainy nights from time to time, and of course this makes things suck even more. Sleeping on a cot in the bottom of some sandbag bunker is not exactly the Ritz-Carlton to begin with, but the absolutely worse thing is the rats. The more it rains, the more the rats take shelter in the bottom of the bunker. They are big, and you awaken to find them crawling over you; the ultimate injury and insult is to realize they have just bitten your hand. *I hate the rats.* So, on many a rainy night I take a folding cot from inside the bunker and place it outside in the open behind the bunker. Then lie on it and pull my water-proof poncho over me. Yeah, it is more dangerous this way as I have no protection from any shrapnel that might explode nearby, and maybe I get a little wet, but the rats never bite me after that.

Top's Morale Booster

Top, being the very good leader he is, attempts to the best of his ability to provide some kind of recreation or entertainment outlet to keep our morale from slipping too far. One of those items that probably falls under both categories was the "Skin Flicks".

I suppose back in those days, long before "video stores," "Netflix," or the internet, "skin flicks" as we called them were an Army staple. I suspect that these "art cinema" films were obtained probably from the same air force Sergeant that had handled the jeeps for generators deals.

Normally, the nightly movies we see are picked up daily from a supply depot at LZ English. English is about 20 miles or so to our north and is just big enough for a short runway that allows a prop-driven cargo plane to land and take off. The regular nightly movies are the usual Hollywood crap, though as it turned out, I have already seen most of them back at Fort Sill, Oklahoma. These movies are played outside, projected upon a white sheet hung from the side of the mess hall, for all to see.

But the "art cinemas" are handled much differently. These are a very rare treat indeed! Because they are on loan from the Air Force and there is such a high demand for them, we have them for a special "one night only" showing which takes place inside the mess hall. Of course, the main reason that these "art cinemas" are shown inside is the fact that our Colonel, the battalion commander, is a proper Southern Baptist from Alabama. Oh, I have heard the man curse before, as well as any trooper, but I guess hard core porn crossed the line, hence, at the First Sergeant's insistence, we see these movies indoor. As it turns out, this makes it even more fun.

We are notified by word of mouth at dinnertime that there is to be no Hollywood movie this evening, but instead, Top has a special treat for the enlisted men only, which is to be held inside the mess hall at 8:00 PM that night. We are clueless, but we have complete faith in Top and therefore know it will be good, whatever it is. We all return to the mess hall at the appointed hour well after dark. There are three movies this evening and I have the great fortune not to have guard duty that night.

We all seem to enter into the mess hall at the same moment; our high anticipation guarantees that no one is late. We are greeted by Top, who tells us all to take seats. The first thing I notice is that every plywood shutter has been lowered. They are usually wide open, to allow whatever breeze that may come along to enter and provide a little relief from the heat. The second thing I notice is a movie projector at the back of the room. Top begins by telling us that Supply Sergeant So-and-so has been able to secure some training films and that we need to look carefully and pay close attention. He tells our projectionist, "Okay, start them," then leaves, and the training films begin.

While we are not 100% certain, we are all pretty sure of what is coming. Judging by the small size of the film reels sitting in the projector, we know that they are not the usual feature length B-grade Hollywood crap. And we are correct.

None of the movies have sound, and the first two are in black and white; the color one is shown last. Always save the best for last.

The first movie starts, a rather grainy black and white, which seems a bit dated, judging by the clothing worn and the backdrop of the apartment setting. There's not much of a plot; a couple are in bed when there is knock on the apartment door. The husband opens the door to find it's the landlord demanding the past-due rent. Of course, the husband is broke, so after some brief negotiation, all parties agree that the landlord will settle the debt by fucking the wife. With no sound, we see the "actors" speaking their parts, as well as their dramatic hand gestures, but the lack of a soundtrack is neither an obstacle nor a detriment; it becomes an opportunity. There sits among us a black dude from Cleveland or Detroit, who is the Eddie Murphy of this time and place. He fills in the voices of the characters that we cannot hear but only see. And he does this as only a street-wise black dude from Cleveland or Detroit could. His "sound track" is spontaneously funny, and we roar with laughter till our guts hurt. That movie ends; the lights come on momentarily as our projectionist changes to another small reel. He shouts, "Kill the lights," and our second training film begins.

This one is another grainy black and white, also with no sound. At this point in the evening, we would have turned the sound off anyway and had "Eddie Murphy" do the play-by-play. The opening scene starts with a couple screwing on the couch; he doesn't seem to be much of a lover and she is becoming quite annoyed by his lackluster performance. Finally exasperated, she jumps from the couch and yells, shaking her finger at him. She momentarily leaves the room, returning in just a few seconds wearing only leather chaps and accompanied by a German Shepherd, a rather large German Shepherd! I guess you might call the next scene "bestiality". Even "Eddie" is taken aback and pauses for a moment but then quickly recovers and resumes his play-by-play of this event. We are all screaming, laughing out loud crazy, when the lights suddenly come on, the projector stops, and we hear the unmistakable voice of Top. "Now men . . . now men, you have got to keep it down. I don't want the Colonel waking up and coming on down here. The Colonel doesn't like this sort of thing. Now men, you just have to keep it down." We all promise Top we will keep it down, and we say this as sincerely as we can, despite the enormous grins on our faces. Now we know why the plywood shutters were closed.

Top leaves, and our projectionist, who has already loaded film number three, shouts to have us kill the lights. Somebody hits the light switch, and we sit back to watch round 3. This time the movie is in color and the higher quality of the film is immediately apparent. Again, there is no sound, but it is not needed or wanted, as "Eddie Murphy" begins his play-by-play. The scene opens with a young, pretty blonde sitting on a couch. She rises to answer the door and greets her boyfriend. They return to the couch and begin to fool around. The next scene abruptly opens in the bath tub which is full of water and into which the blonde enters wearing a short but form fitting blue cotton dress with some printed Daisy flowers on it. I remember that short wet dress with its printed flowers. We all do. They have sex three or four different ways.

We play all three movies over again and then again, a third time, but by the fourth replay we become more than a little too boisterous, and Top comes by to tells us that it is getting late and tells us to go get some sleep before the Colonel finds out. We cheerfully comply with Top's wishes. He is the kind of leader who genuinely cares for the men under him, and we know it. If he asked for ten volunteers on a suicide mission he was leading, then one hundred and ten of us would have stepped forward. We loved him and would have followed him to the far side of hell and back, knowing without a doubt that he would bring back every one of us. He was a career man where most of the rest were "lifers". All in all, this is the funniest night of the nearly two years I spend in the Army.

The Daily Grind

Time marches on and to a certain extent there is some routine in my daily life at Uplift. There is always guard duty, often three nights a week, and in between are the usual work details around our section of LZ Uplift. The work details almost invariably involve filling and stacking and/or replacing sandbags on, around, and over the various buildings (hooches as we called them) that make up the buildings in our camp. The hooches are usually constructed of narrow wooden boxes that once contained artillery rounds. These boxes are laid out to form the rectangular shape of the hooch, with each wooden box filled with a sandbag. Then they are stacked, overlapping the boxes underneath, nailed together, and each in turn filled with sandbags, and so on, and so on. When the walls reach about seven or eight feet high, some wooden beams are placed overhead. They in turn have the wooden boards from the ammo boxes nailed to them to form the roof. Then a large tarp is stretched over the whole roof to keep us dry underneath, and a layer or two of sandbags is placed on the roof and against all four outer walls in an attempt to slow down the shrapnel from an incoming round.

But we have help. As noted earlier, "Top" has arranged for the hiring of about eight laborers from an IDP camp about three or four miles down Highway 1 from Uplift. This is in addition to the four women hired to help out in the kitchen. We pick them up every morning, six days a week. It is mostly women of various ages, one older man we called Papa-san, and one young man who for unknown reasons has not been drafted into the South Vietnamese Army. I think Troy is his name; he is a good and decent guy. He wears a "pork pie" hat instead of the common broad-rimmed, woven leaf type. It makes him look a bit more Western and slightly more sophisticated, though a bit silly. He speaks fairly good English and was chosen as their foreman, but not just because of translation skills; he is a capable leader.

Troy is a happy guy and always maintains his good humor despite the grim reality of the war. Later on, when he brings his girlfriend along to work at our camp, we can see why. She is an extraordinarily pretty girl, an amazingly beautiful and sweet kid. They are engaged to be married. She looks to be 17 at the most. She is such a pleasant kid who seems happy to have such a good job with a free lunch thrown in at mid-day. We learn very little of her family life, but if she lives in an IDP camp, she may not have much of one. Her name is Hoar, which is pronounced as "whore," which she most definitely is not. Our Battalion Doctor was struck by her beauty but is taken aback when he asks me what her name is and is told "Hoar." But the poor girl has a terrible cough that sounds like TB to him. She only comes to work for five or six weeks, and then stops because she is sick. Life is hard in the camps.

I work with this group almost every day, and at some point, I am put in charge of the "gooks." This is a derogatory term, which I never use when I speak to them. I treat them fairly and kindly and with respect, and we shortly become friends, in an odd "daytime only" and "while in our camp" kind of way. Of course, at 6-4, I tower over them. As time goes on, since I spend almost every day with them, a few of my comrades give me the nick name Super Gook, but I bristle whenever this is said and eventfully it is dropped.

Our Artillery Survey section probably only performs one or two surveys the entire time I am there, which is why we are always selected for some crappy work detail, a.k.a., "shit detail." But not for the "true" shit detail, which falls upon the medics to perform; they get to burn the actual shit.

To handle the sanitation issues of our unit, three "latrines" or "outhouses" have been built; a two-holer for the Officers, a four-holer for the NCOs' and a 12-holer for the enlisted men. They look about the same, differing only in their length, and they are all placed in the same area. They are built of plywood, each basically a long narrow box about six feet wide with a shed pitched roof of corrugated steel. There is a door at one end, and where you enter, there is a long, raised platform placed against the side wall that runs the length of the building. This long enclosed "bench" is about a foot and a half high and maybe two feet wide, with a series of "holes" in the center located about three feet apart. It is kind of nice, as every hole has a toilet seat. The seats look out toward a screen, starting about three feet off the floor, which goes to the roof line and runs the length of the building, providing plenty of ventilation as well as a good view.

The medics' only duty, other than treating us or anyone else who is brought in, is to literally burn the shit. As one sits in the latrine, his deposit drops from that raised bench into an open steel drum about sixteen inches tall that contains a few gallons of diesel fuel. Every morning, the medics come to the back of the outhouses, drag the "pot" out to one side and then set the diesel afire. The smoke that this emits is thick and black, like grease burning, and the odor is sickeningly sweet, the same as bodies burning. To your brain it is chemically unforgettable. But the actual medical reason that the medics burn the shit is to check for worms, which are spotted on occasion. And, unknowingly, we are treated.

Unfortunately, I spend a fair amount of time at the latrine, especially the first few months, as I am constantly sick with dysentery. Just outside the mess hall there are two large containers of either purple or orange colored Kool-Aid. They are kept full 24 hours a day, so that anyone can get a cold drink, day or night. I remember on a few occasions when I was very sick, taking a glassful of the purple stuff. But before I had finished drinking it all, I would run to the latrine as the Kool-Aid rushed through my intestinal track that fast. My diarrhea was so severe that I would often bleed while in the latrine. I would then visit with the medics and be given huge doses of Milk of Magnesia. I would pass that quickly too, but eventually it would stop me up.

After about three months, and after acquiring every possible bug, I finally stop being sick. But everyone suffers from dysentery at one point or another. The only really good thing about the outhouse was that it is sanctuary of sorts. If you are in there, the "lifers" leave you alone, as they don't want to be hanging around the latrines. Of course, old Sergeant Patterson has quite the outhouse reputation. He was and is, to this day, the fattest Army Sergeant I have ever seen. On occasion we would see him rumbling down to the NCO latrine. If there were any lifers in there they would leave in a hurry, before he entered if at all possible. And once he was in there, any other NCO heading in that direction would stop and turn around when they saw that he was in the latrine. Ol' Pat must have easily weighed on the very far side of three hundred and fifty pounds. When he went to the latrine, it was serious business, and every man gave him a wide berth. He would sometimes be in there for thirty or forty minutes. Every once in a while, one of the young buck Sergeants, a non-lifer, would come into our latrine. We would tease, "Hey, this is enlisted only." His response would be "Oh come on, big old Pat is in the other one."

Of course, it is very easy to remember the funny moments or pranks that we played out, but generally our time at Uplift is not fun. In fact, it is most often a miserable grind, especially in our section. We are stuck on a small LZ where there is little to do besides gruelingly boring shit details and guard duty, which is often every other night. My time here is scarcely bearable, but what else is there to do but bear it? I would not have chosen to spend my life in an institution that by and large seems to reward stupidity and ignorance; why else would the Army be so chockablock full of both?

Many of the lifers-- I dare say most of the lifers-- are poorly educated, and they seem uninterested in changing that. Most of the senior officers are educated men, though I don't know why they would choose this profession. Some of the junior officers are college grads. A few have some college behind them and probably have gone the route I was offered, Officer Candidate School (OCS), but which I turned down. But on the whole, the enlisted men are much better educated than most of the lifer NCO's. Several of the enlisted men in my battery were already college graduates and are here only because they had been drafted. No wonder the Army functioned so poorly, who wants to be led by a moron? Generally, the Army was in poor shape, neglected by its country, which wanted to fight wars on the cheap. I suppose the Army worked well enough in peacetime. But now being forced to ramp up quickly and putting over a half million troops in Vietnam just wasn't going to work very well. I often felt in my own unit that we were close to mutiny, which in fact, many months later, did happen.

The only person keeping the place from exploding was our First Sergeant. "Top" as we usually called him, was also known among us as "Top Dog" and "First Shirt" though we never addressed him that way. He was tall and lean, and kept himself quite fit, unlike so many of the other out of shape and fat lifer NCO's. I suspect they disgusted him. Top seemed to handle any situation with quiet aplomb. I don't think I ever heard him raise his voice. He was no pushover; that was immediately evident, as he was not a man one would dare fuck with. Yet when he gave an order, it seemed as if he were your favorite uncle who had just requested a favor that you would of course fulfill; you could not possibly be so rude as to refuse to do it. He seemed to lead effortlessly. He was the antidote to Fruit.

One might begin to feel badly for Fruit as he had not a single friend. Over a short time, one would see which Officers paired off or hung out with each other, but Fruit was always alone. But given only a short time, you would soon see why he was not to be pitied, as he was such a complete and total prick. Most of the functions and sections within Headquarters battery are directed by equal or higher-ranking Officers than Fruit; so, he would dare not screw around with any of those sections or people. But where he could, he would find any excuse--or create one--to increase the misery factor by interfering with anything, anyone, or any group, when he felt he could get away with it. As I think back, he was a coward. His actions or conduct did nothing to improve things or morale, but he did things only to make himself feel better by exerting some false sense of control.

One sweltering day, as I am supervising our "native" help as they replace sand bags around some hooch, Fruit approaches me and tells me to make sure that we take away the old rotted sand bags. Of course, we always clean up the area we have worked in. Fruit is only doing this out of boredom, but I respond, "Oh yes sir, I'll try to have this cleaned up before lunch." He reprimands me, "Don't 'try,' mister. *Can* do, *can* do," and then walks away. What a desperate asshole.

There is a reason Fruit is in charge of Head Quarters battery: he is not trusted to be placed in charge of a firing battery that takes guts and brains to run. The Colonel hates him and is often heard shouting at the Executive Officer, "Major Shaky," the words "and don't let Fruit fuck it up." The Colonel says it so often that it seems to be his favorite expression. Imagine how poorly Fruit is regarded if the Battalion Commander has to order his Executive Officer, a Major, to watch Fruit so that he doesn't screw things up. Being made CO of HQ's battery is like being appointed "Laundry and Morale Officer." The Colonel would have appointed Fruit to that if the position actually existed.

Of course, Major "Shaky" has his own problems. "Shaky" is not his real name, but rather the nickname we give him because he has "the shakes" every morning. He is actually a rather decent man, but he has a serious drinking problem. He and the Colonel are the only two to have individual sleeping quarters; the rest of the officers are housed together in one big hooch. This privacy probably works against Shaky's well-being as he might not drink so much if he were housed with a group of fellow officers. But off by himself, he drinks like a fish every evening. When we see him in the morning, he has the "shakes" that last half the day; poor bastard.

He is not a bully or full of himself and seems to conduct himself well. He is a capable leader, but the drinking is taking him down. He is a career man, a lifer for sure, but he is getting a little past his prime as a Major. He probably should have made light Colonel by now, but I suspect "they" have passed him over once or twice already. He wanted to make Lt. Colonel on this tour of duty in Vietnam, but they are never going to let him join that club, not the way he drinks.

Any fool can be promoted from 2nd Lieutenant to 1st Lieutenant to Captain; look at Fruit. To make Major isn't as easy for sure, but to make Lt. Colonel is a high hurdle, and Major Shaky wasn't ever going to get over that bar. His driver later recounted to me that the Major had told him that if they were ever shot at while on the road, which happens with some frequency, they were to turn around and charge the shooter(s). Major Shaky was hell bent on getting a medal and therefore a promotion. But I'm certain the only thing Shaky would get with a stunt like that was a posthumously awarded Purple Heart. Yeah, and his driver's mother would get her son's insurance money. On this point, Shaky was a little selfish.

Cardinal Rule Number III

Late one hot and sunny afternoon, as I walk towards my hooch at the end of the work day, I cut through behind the mess hall as the cooks are about to prepare our evening meal. The cooks use gasoline as a fuel for some of the stoves and are filling them when something goes horribly wrong. One of the cooks screams in terrible tortured pain as one of the stoves bursts into flames. He must have been re-filling a stove, but has spilled gasoline doing so, which ignites in a flash; his hand and his arm are on fire. A couple of other cooks pull him away from the stove and rush him to the nearby medical hooch. But in the meantime, a full can of gasoline lies in the middle of a circle of flames. Though it still has its cap on, I fear it may explode. I rush forward and grab its handle with my left hand and pull the can away from the flames. But what a fool I am. The handle is nearly red hot, and I severely burn my palm and fingers as I grab it. I rush to the medics, who treat me and I visit them daily for nearly a week as they change the bandages. The wound heals. But I have broken **Cardinal Rule Number III: Never Get Brave – You Will Always Get Hurt.**

I get no thank you from anyone, no placement on light duty, but just more of the same crappy work details and more nights in a bunker on the line. Bravery most often results in injury or death. But being the slow learner that I am, I will break Cardinal Rule III several more times.

The Fools On The Hill

There is one somewhat peculiar "detail" that falls upon the Survey section to perform almost daily. Just barely outside Uplift to the southeast is a rather steep and tall hill. Duster Hill, as it is known, could almost be called a low mountain because of the way it rose rather abruptly from the low and level plains that surround it. This hill is so steeply pitched that the only drivable access is a road that twists its way up its south face, and even then, four-wheel-drive is required. The hill is about 650 feet high, but there is a reasonably level, if narrow, plateau on its top. There are perhaps a half dozen different HQ Companies or Batteries located within Uplift, and each has its radio relay station set up on the narrow plateau of Duster Hill. The survey section's job is to bring our radio operator his lunch and any mail that has arrived from the afternoon before. The reason our group is assigned this task is that on a rather irregular basis we perform some artillery targeting. Targeting is an exercise in which a nearby battery fires off a few rounds that do an airburst and we confirm the location and angle from the top of Duster Hill. We have only done this a few times, but we still keep bringing lunch and mail up to the radio operator anyway. The "visiting hours" are strictly limited to the daylight hours, as the Hill is just outside the perimeter wire of Uplift. Once the main gate of Uplift closes off Highway 1 at 5:00 PM each evening, that's it; the residents of Duster Hill are isolated from us until the next morning. There are maybe a half a dozen radio operators up there and perhaps 20 infantry grunts to guard the place.

Duster Hill, whose northwest face is close by, is just outside our wire and towers hundreds of feet above us. Its only entry point is reached by traveling in an elongated U. One does not walk to or from it, but travels there only as an armed group in a jeep or truck. We leave the gate of Uplift and drive south on Highway 1 for a half mile and then turn left to the east for a short distance and then turn left again, now driving north to begin a long tough climb up the south face. With such limited access during the daylight only, this tiny place always feels a little spooky, but add the nights, and it crosses the line. It is this long nightly isolation that sets up an unbalanced dynamic that propels most of the Hill's residents to spiral downward and inward. There just isn't enough to do during the day or night. If idleness is the devil's workshop, the Hill is the main factory floor.

Our radio operators seem not to last too long up there. It probably looks like easy duty at first glance, but then the monotony of each boring day, followed by a long dark night, drives almost all of these guys crazy. There seems not to be anyone in charge up there; in fact, there cannot possibly be anyone in charge there, as the Hill is so crazy. When we go to the Hill, we usually don't stay too long, maybe an hour or two if we do some "targeting," but usually much less. As time goes on, there are a few times I am taken up there and dropped off alone to do the targeting. Going there might seem like a good way to stay out of sight and be away from those sandbag details, but it is not fun up there. The place is an insane asylum, but without any guards. The only time I ever see an NCO up there is when a lifer Staff Sergeant is supervising a fistfight between two enlisted men. They are about the same size weight and height and seem evenly matched, but after a few rough minutes one begins to win. The guy losing then grabs his M-16 to equalize the situation, but the Staff Sergeant then puts a 45 to the guy's head; he drops his M-16 and the fight continues on. After a few more minutes the fight ends, and the Staff Sergeant and his guys leave the asylum to return to the relative normalness below at Uplift. I am not impressed by his display of leadership.

On another afternoon, I briefly see a Major from the 173rd, which shares a big section of Uplift with us. He is a "greenie," his newness in the country indicated by his still very green uniform that has not yet been faded by the tropical sun. I think he has come up just to check the Hill out, but I can tell he is very uneasy about being here. He gives me a nervous smile, somehow instantly and intuitively knowing that I am not a resident of the Hill and therefore that he can safely communicate with me. I nod and smile gently back; I look to either side of me and then shrug my shoulders, saying wordlessly, "Yeah, the place is insane." I then go into the "targeting bunker," and he leaves shortly afterward, never to return.

The truth of the matter was that the Hill is out of control and living here was bizarre and drives people dangerously insane. There are two or three young Vietnamese boys perhaps ten years old living there who have become "boy soldiers." They have been kind of adopted by the GIs on the Hill and wear little-boy green Army uniforms. They have been trained with the M-16 and are good marksmen. They might earn their keep as house boys, cleaning the hooches for the GI's. They cook Vietnamese dishes. I once watch them boiling the chopped-off claws of roosters and hens to make some kind of soup. It does not look appetizing. A few GI's even keep stray dogs as pets. Hardly any of this is considered Army "normal," but this is only the start.

With so much time on their hands and with no one in charge, many of the residents begin to play with the guns. And there are many games that goes dangerously out of control. There is an M-50 machine gun that sits up on the highest part of the Hill. This is a very large machine gun; the thing weighs nearly a hundred pounds; one does not John Wayne it. It has a ravenous appetite and is "fed" via a lengthy cartridge belt. Each cartridge that makes up that belt is itself nearly six inches long, and the round that it fires can travel and kill at more than a mile distance. At close range, the round can penetrate nearly an inch of steel. Designed to shoot down aircraft, it is used here on Charlie. It is horrifically damaging; if a round "only" hits your arm, it not only wounds you, but more likely removes the whole arm. Though it is mounted on a turret and can be pivoted in any direction, the fifty generally faces away from Uplift and down the southeast side of the Hill. This side of the Hill is thickly wooded and is the most likely direction Charlie would attack from.

One afternoon after being dropped off for "targeting," I watch from our nearby hooch as one of the full-time residents of the Hill finishes loading a new belt into the fifty. He invites me to shoot a few rounds down the hill, and I do. I hold the fifty with hands on either side of the grip, and with both thumbs I press down on the "butterfly." It roars and I send three brief bursts down the hill into the thick woods. It is fun. But my compadre tells me, "Here's how you do it." He raises the gun sight upwards and aims at an open field about a mile away upon which a herd of cows peacefully graze. He sends a very long burst towards the cows and a few seconds later, we see a couple young boys running, frantically shooing the herd to the far end of the field. Gratefully neither the young boys nor the cows are hit. The gunner stops his firing and laughs, saying, "Now that's how you do it." I say, "Great," and then go back to the targeting hooch to pretend I am busy.

About a week goes by and about five of us are sent back up on the Hill to do some targeting that never actually takes place, as targeting is almost always cancelled shortly after we arrive. Our section decides to stay a while. There's no sense in going back down to Uplift for another shit detail. But in the meantime, the boys on the hill begin to play with their toys once more. This time, however, several of them are playing with the M-79 grenade launcher. They compete to see which one of them can shoot a grenade farthest. The grenade launcher resembles a short, yet very fat, single-barrel shotgun; in fact, one might describe it as obese. It pivots open like a shotgun and a fist-sized cartridge is placed inside the barrel and then closed. Just aim and squeeze the trigger. It has a pretty good kick and makes a loud "thump" when fired, but the boys brace themselves and shoot the grenades off the backside of the Hill away from Uplift. One of them is finally declared the winner, but now a much more dangerous game begins; who can shoot it the highest?

They begin by aiming upwards, but not quite perpendicular to the earth. But each in turn begins to aim a little closer to perpendicular, and it quickly becomes clear where this is going. The boys with their toys aim high, and the actual round, the grenade, is large enough that one can see its flight. Each grenade shot is now just barely clearing the plateau of the Hill. This becomes a lethal, deadly game of brinksmanship. There are about twenty of us watching as the last and final shot is taken. The shooter aims directly and precisely straight overheard and lets it go. The grenade soars straight upward and for the briefest moment disappears from our sight, but only a moment later it reappears and we immediately realize its projection has no arc in it at all. It will not drift over the hillside; it is coming straight back at us. Each of us dives for cover; I slide under our truck as the grenade explodes. No one is hurt, and the fools on the hill have finally scared themselves straight for at least the short term. We take this opportunity to leave and drive back down and around to Uplift.

We can escape the madness there, but our radio operators cannot. On one trip up to the Hill, our radio operator simply gets into our truck as we arrived and says pleadingly, "Take me back to Uplift." We take him back down, and the next day bring his replacement back up to the hill. He seems fine for about six weeks. But one afternoon we find him shirtless; he looks haggard and seems to twitch involuntarily. He tells us that he doesn't sleep well because of the mosquitoes. We look into his small hooch and can see many holes in the back wall and roof; we look back at him, but he won't meet our eyes. We ask about the holes, and in a quiet voice he tells us that he threw a hand grenade into the hooch to kill the mosquitoes, but that it didn't work. We grab his stuff, what little remained, and bring him back down with us. We drop him off with the medics; better to let the Docs handle this one. We got to hate going to the Hill.

Operations

Three months drag by and they are not three months of fun. There are probably 50 nights of sitting in a sandbag bunker on the perimeter wire pulling guard duty, with day after day of shit details, highlighted by asshole Fruit and Sergeant Dufus. One morning I finally catch a break from my near slave like existence of unending work details. As we are about to start another day of filling and replacing sandbags, the First Sergeant calls me off the detail. Top introduces me to Captain T from the Operations Section. He tells me to grab their jeep from the motor pool and drive the Captain around to wherever he needs to go.

Capt. T is black, tall and lean--my height at least-- and at first glance seems decent enough. I grab the jeep, and we drive out of Uplift and head south on Highway 1 toward Qui Nhon some forty plus miles away. He seems approachable, so I engage him in conversation, and we end up talking the entire trip down and back. I can't remember what the reason for the trip was, but he and I hit it off. When we return to Uplift, the Captain asks if I want to be the permanent duty driver for Operations; I tell him yes, just square it with Top. He tells me he'll take care of that and that I am to be at his beck and call 24 hours a day but that I will be ED (exempted from duty). Now I am off the guard roster, and no more sandbag filling. Capt. T also tells me I must move over to the hooch that is directly next to "Operations," which is the nerve center of the battalion, as he may on occasion need to find me in a hurry. I happily do so, as it is bigger, cleaner and a somewhat nicer hooch than the survey section hooches, which are right next to one of the helipads and are always having sand and dust blown inside them from the Hueys that land

and take off. Besides, my former hooch mate is getting a little too squirrely, as he has been here a long time to begin with, and his time here has done nothing to improve his psyche.

I don't waste any time, but move over to my new home immediately. The sandbag-covered barracks is considerably more spacious than the small four-man hooch I have been living in. There is one large area which houses about sixteen guys, most of whom worked in FDC (Fire Direction Control). But at one end is a smaller room that only two or three of us live in, which has just a bit more privacy.

The FDC guys actually do something. When a battery is called upon for a live fire mission, the FDC section figures the firing direction, the charge used to propel the round, and the angle of elevation. They have to be quick and accurate and they always are. FDC works around the clock, as a firing mission might be needed at any time day or night. They generally work a screwy shift of 6 or 8 or 12 hours, which I can never figure out as I see these guys at different times on different days. Most are pretty bright, almost all had some college, and several were college grads. Except for one or two guys, most of this group living in the FDC hooch was exempt from guard duty.

A guy nick-named "Grandpa" is the FDC leader. He has been promoted to Spec. 5, which is very good for a draftee, as most of us never get past Spec 4. He is a college grad, and at age 23 or 24, is one of the oldest draftees I know. He is mostly bald on top, wears glasses, and given his ancient age and his leadership position, he has been given the honorable title of Grandpa. Of course, a big factor in the nick-naming is that this group is bright and educated and has a honed-knife edge sense of humor. Looking back, I would call it "pre-Letterman," though it is much more jaded. But I make friends with all of them, especially a guy from Illinois. I begin to call him Big D, as he is as tall as I am. He was drafted from his small hometown from somewhere in central Illinois. Big D hates being in the Army as much as I do, which actually is most comforting to me. He repeatedly tells me, far, far more than any other person, over the next nine months, "If you're stupid enough to get into the Army, then you deserve everything that happens to you." I must admit, his logic and cynicism were impeccable and flawless.

Big D would on occasion say this to "Bitter John." Big D first mentions him after some incident in which Capt. Fruit has made life slightly worse for somebody who then bitterly complains to us. Big D and I both listen to the complainant; but as he walks away Big D says "That's nothing, wait till you meet Bitter John."

I meet him the next evening. Big D is right, but bitter is an understatement. He is off the chart. I can't remember if Big D or "the group" tagged him, but it has stuck and fits him perfectly. I truly like "Bitter John," who is a bright guy, a good decent, honest man with a good sense of humor, but his bitterness is larger than life. Someone who doesn't know him well enough might not like him; the self-made huge black cloud around him covers up most of the good things about him. He is from Pennsylvania or New Jersey somewhere and completed college with an accounting degree from a good school. He even had a rather decent job working for a large firm, but the good life ended for him just a few months later when he was conscripted into the Army. Oh, he is bitter! He will, at the drop of a hat, rant on how unjust this was. "Why me? I had an education, I had a great job, I was making great money, and I paid taxes, so why me?" It never ends. "Why me, why not some of those stupid guys? There's plenty of them. Why not some of those bums who don't work, why, why, why…"

Occasionally he stops in mid-sentence and pauses, as some lifer Sergeant can be seen entering or exiting the Operations hooch, and then says with quiet, yet great, sarcasm, "What a moron he is." And we all laugh. I guess we laugh because he is having as hard a time as any of us coping with our Army life. Being in the Army is much like doing time in prison. You are stuck in a place you sure as hell do not want to be, wearing ugly green prison uniforms, often surrounded by people you would not associate with on the outside. The lifers, our tormenters, are the guards. The only other alternative to doing your time inside the wire at Uplift is to do your time outside the wire, out in the boonies, where you'd only meet different tormenters. Which flavor of hell do you prefer? My only complaint about Bitter John, which I never share with him, was that he sees himself as the only guy that the Army and the country has ever screwed over, never anyone else. He just doesn't get it; this Army, this stinking place called Uplift; this stinking war is a real shitty deal for all of us. However, I am not too hard on Bitter John, as I have some sympathy for him. But my gripe, my complaint, my bitterness asks a much bigger question. Almost all of my boyhood friends remain untouched by any of this. "So why just some of us; why isn't everyone going through this?"

Some months later, Bitter John finally gets it, finally understands it, and I am glad for him, as I think it eases some of his pain.

The Pluses Of The Duty Driver

My military life, relatively speaking, is greatly improved as the misery factor has easily been cut in half. I just drive a jeep, taking a Captain around to wherever he needs to go. No long miserable nights on the perimeter wire, no more sandbag details, just drive the jeep. I think of my First Sergeant back in Oklahoma who told me that "driving a jeep does not require leadership." Maybe not, but I also fail to see where sandbag details require much leadership. I am glad to be away from such drudgery. The job has a few quirks but far, far more benefits than just being ED. The trips can on occasion be a little long, sometimes running a hundred miles round trip, which in an open Army jeep is not necessarily all that pleasant. But these trips often go to places like Phu Cat or Qui Nhon which have PX's, thus allowing for a little shopping.

One mid-morning I am in the Phu Cat PX killing a little time as Capt. T attends to some business. I look at watches and spotted a self-winding Seiko; it gave the date and day of the week as well, and its luminous hands glow in the dark. It is only $12.50, and I buy it as it is such an incredible value. I am on a roll now. Nearby is the perfume counter. It seems odd to me that perfume is being sold in Vietnam, but there are some nurses stationed here. I notice that one particular brand is $32 per ounce, which seems astonishingly high. I ask the young Vietnamese woman behind the counter to let me smell it. She is most amenable; she tells me it is "Joy," a French perfume, and then removes the cap from a sample bottle and holds it under my nose. Little do I know it, but "Joy" is considered one of the greatest fragrances ever created. It smells most wonderful, a floral fragrance to be sure, but not one I can place. Still, it seems terribly expensive to me and I move on to look at other items in the PX.

Capt. T finishes his business, and I then proceed to drive him to several locations that day. From time to time as we drive on the roadways, I smell flowers, even if I am driving next to a rice paddy. But I can never see or find the flowers I smelled. Finally, that evening after I take a shower, the smell of flowers finally disappears. It's then that I understand and appreciate the lasting quality of Joy; I guess it is worth the $32 it costs.

Where there were no PX's, one can find supply depots along the major highways, some of which only provide fuel and pallets of Pabst Blue Ribbon. Of course, the fuel is free and a case of beer costs just $2.40, cheap enough, but served at the ambient temperature of +95°F, it isn't a favorite beverage.

One place we visit almost every day was LZ English. English is about 20 miles to our north, where it too sits alongside Highway 1. It is a much larger LZ than Uplift, and it even has a runway that can land prop-driven freighters. The runway seems a bit short and primitive, especially compared to the runway at the Phu Cat Air Base. The runway isn't level, as it appears to a have a noticeable hump in it about three quarters of the way down. There are steel barrels that were cut in half and placed every so often along each side of the runway. They have a few gallons of diesel in them so that they could act as landing lights at night if needed.

There is also a small "business strip" that runs along either side of Highway 1 just before you enter English. It is the usual collection of tiny shops, restaurants, barbershops, massage parlors, and whorehouses that can be found outside of any of the larger military bases in Vietnam. Of course, Uplift is too small and too oddly located for anything like this. The closest thing we have to any kind of business is a dinky little car wash at a stream about a mile to our south; just a guy with a tiny gas-powered water pump and a couple kids with rags. They don't seem to get much business.

On the other hand, the town of Bong Son just south of English sizzles. I doubt any GI is legally allowed to go there in the evening, though I am sure more than a few find a way. But during the daytime the strip is always busy. Especially the combination bar-massage-parlor-whorehouses that probably make up half of the establishments along the main drag of Highway 1 as it bisects Bong Son. Even if you aren't there to get laid, you can always buy a beer or a soda (Coke or Pepsi) for fifty cents and talk a little with the "ladies". Of course, we feel a bit ripped off by this price, as we can buy the beer or Coke for a dime at the PX. But then again, one does expect to pay something for the ambiance and other overhead expenses. As to the price of the "boom-boom," that is five bucks. It seems the entire economy of the country is based on fifty cents and five bucks. From time to time, I see a pair of Army medics walking along the strip from one whore house to the next, making house calls, checking on the health of the girls and giving them a "shot" as needed. The whore houses are "de facto" Army-certified, in a non-official way. The brass figures it's better to keep things clean and healthy, as opposed to trying to close them up. Free enterprise at work, I suppose. The whores, the boom-boom girls, are not necessarily held in high esteem by the local population, and any woman who works the oldest profession in South Vietnam is known as Madame K. For any GI to even tease a woman, even a boom-boom girl, by calling her a Madam K sets off an immediate angry reaction as it is such a grievous insult.

I never understood with any certainty the origins of the Madame K designation, but wondered whether it had something to do with another Madame: Madame Nhu was perhaps the most detested woman to have ever lived in Vietnam. She was the "First Lady" of South Vietnam in the early sixties when her brother in-law Diem was President of South Vietnam. Her ideology was extremely pro-Catholic and strongly anti-Buddhist. The small Catholic minority was 5% of the population, yet held 95% of the wealth. She had publicly mocked a Buddhist Priest, Thich Quang Duc, who had soaked himself in gasoline and then committed a self-immolation on a crowded city street in Saigon, protesting the shooting of Buddhists by Diem's government. So here we are, backing a bunch of crooked thugs because they are anti-communist? Hell, this war is already lost. Though by this time there is a different government, it's corrupted too. We're never going to win this.

But be it Madame K or boom-boom girl, most of the locals, if not the entire country, find this occupation to be number 10, aka, very bad. But what are the employment opportunities when the whole country is literally just one big war zone? What was once a pleasant small town now has a fair-sized military base plopped down next to it. LZ English is the new Ft. Sill, and Bong Son has become the new Lawton.

From time to time as I get ready to drive from Uplift to English, someone, usually from FDC, asks a favor. The FDC guys might have just finished the night shift, and with the day off to rest, they ask if I could drop them off at a whore house along the main drag of Bong Son and pick them up on the way back. I always said, "Yes; just don't keep me waiting in front of the whore house."

There is always some kind of paperwork to be dropped off and picked up at English, but probably the most important thing I do at English is to drop off the semi-nightly movie and pick up a new one. If I don't, there will be hell to pay, as almost everyone has become dependent on a movie in the evening. There is nothing to do at Uplift in the evening, it's just too small to have enough critical mass for anything to happen. We once try playing volleyball with some ARVN's who are part of an artillery battery at their section within Uplift, but after just two or three games, the lifers make us return to our compound; no mixing is allowed.

And on the nights when we have no movie, the lifers drink to get on to a pleasant buzz if not on to oblivion. And the rest of us discover the very strong Vietnamese "pot." Talk about getting a pleasant buzz on: it is like taking a magic carpet ride.

It didn't start out that way. We can buy beer very cheaply; it is only ten cents per can, and somebody will have a tiny Japanese refrigerator which will cool it down enough to drink, and we are quite happy. Whisky and scotch are very, very cheap as well, only two dollars a bottle at the PX, and these are the first choice for the hard-core lifers. The only down side to drinking a little too much beer might be a dry mouth in the morning or a headache. But marijuana doesn't have those annoying side effects. Big D is the one who turns me on to the weed. I've tried it a few times back home but it never did anything for me. And now in Vietnam, the first couple of nights I puff on a joint it doesn't do much either, but by the third night…ba-boom. From then on, we often get stoned. Big D is driving a Major around who demands that his jeep be kept spotless; consequently, Big D heads down to the tiny car wash just to the south of Uplift. Which, as it turns out, is selling pre-rolled joints.

Not wishing to be smoking all of his stash, I begin to buy my own, very discretely, at various stops I make as I drive my jeep around. Big D is greatly impressed, and when he asks where I bought the pre-rolled joints, I simply name the city, town, or hamlet I stopped at. Hence, we give the joints names like Bong Son Bombers, which are long and fat, Qui Nhon 100's, which are much like the cigarettes, and Phu Cat Mini's. The Phu Cat Mini's being somewhat thin and short, are deceptively potent. But it's not just us, the whole Army is smoking. Several months later, a new battalion commander asks the enlisted men to fill out an anonymous survey about our drug use; no strings attached. He keeps his word, but he must have been bowled over. The findings are never released, but I ask my Captain friend a couple of days later what were the results; he tells me over 90%. Of course, if there were an anonymous, no-strings-attached survey of the NCO's and Officers asking about their alcohol use, I am certain it would be over 90% as well.

There is, in general, a huge generational gap between us and the NCO lifers and the senior Officers. The average age for a draftee in Vietnam is about 20 or so; most of the lifers are at least 15 years older, and some are 20 years older. We don't get them and they don't get us, and that is never going to change. How can it?

The Minuses

Over time the Captain and I become good friends, at least while we are on the road. While inside Uplift, we maintain the usual military protocol, but once we drive out the gate onto Highway 1, we both relax. We spend many hours together each day sitting only three feet apart in an open jeep; we have to be friends. We can generally talk about almost anything, though our viewpoints on a few things are radically different, and I am smart enough to know when to keep quiet. He is probably a dozen years older than I, and so far, he has spent most of his adult life in the Army. Those two factors are probably the bases of our divergent views. It isn't quite generational, as he is still a young man, but we see some things very differently.

One of the things most certain to be seen during our travels, as it never fails to happen, is to see the peace sign flashed. Whenever any U.S. Military vehicles pass by each other on any highway, almost all of the GIs on the vehicles flash each other the peace sign. This has happened tens of thousands of times as it is the universal greeting of the enlisted men. One morning as we are traveling south somewhere, we pass by a convoy of about six trucks headed north. As we approach, I naturally flash the peace sign, and it is returned by several guys in all six trucks as we pass. The Captain says pleasantly, "Great to see the Victory sign." I'm shocked, so I respond, "No sir, that's the Peace sign. It means peace and get high." He is not at all pleased, and tells me a little sharply, "No, that's the Victory sign, see the V for Victory." I don't bother to respond. He actually thinks we are going to win this thing; he just doesn't get it. He is a very decent and good man, but he is in lockstep with the company line. What's the use?

There are speed limits in South Vietnam, but they have not been imposed on us by the local jurisdictions, but by the U.S. Military, and they are strictly enforced. There are no seat belts in jeeps or trucks, or even tanks. Besides, if you need to get out of vehicle quickly, you don't want to waste time unbuckling. There aren't even doors on jeeps, and I've rarely seen one with even a canvas top, so there is little protection offered in the event of a crash. Therefore, we have been directed, ordered, to drive at no more than 25 miles per hour, unless of course we are fired upon.

The Captain tells me that if he dies in Vietnam, he does not want it to be because of a traffic accident. I don't have a problem with that at all. Whenever we drive south, I always drive at a steady 25 mph. It is when we go north from Uplift that he has me drive a little faster. We have been shot at many times as we drove toward or from English. Of course, you never see the sniper or his muzzle flash, or even hear the sound of his rifle fire. But you occasionally see a little puff of dust on the road in front of the jeep, or even at its side, or even hear something go by your head. The first time that a round goes between our heads, I just look over at Capt. T to see him gesturing with his left hand and yelling, "Go, Go, Go." The sniper pretty much works the same couple of miles of road, so the Captain always has me drive at 30 or 35 mph whenever we travel by there. On that same occasion, he starts holding my M-16 on his lap as I drive. He wears a side arm 45 in a holster, which is useless at a range of more than six feet. The first time he does this I complain, telling him he should use the M-60 machine gun mounted on a turret behind us. But he says not to worry, he'll protect me and I should just drive. He is right; only a-hole John Wayne could drive a jeep at 50 mph with one arm while holding an M-16 in his other shooting at Charlies.

Getting shot at by Charlie in his back yard is an expected and predictable consequence of traveling in an unescorted open jeep; the jeep is an easy target. But the worse thing is "friendly fire," when one of your own comes after you. One bright and sunny midafternoon while we are driving south on Highway 1 from LZ English, back towards Uplift, a US Air Force jet buzzes us. He comes in behind us at an elevation of perhaps hundred feet and traveling at 400 mph. We are a clearly marked US Army jeep, and yet just for fun, this Air Force bully blasts by us. The suddenness of his uncalled-for action takes us by complete surprise; I nearly lose control of the jeep. The sound level of the jet blast at this speed and close elevation is off the charts. I am certain that both of us have suffered significant hearing loss, all because this Air Force a-hole coward wanted to have a little fun.

Meet The Colonel

From time-to-time Charlie shoots a few rockets in at us at Uplift. The frequency varies a bit, from two or three nights in a row to nothing for 15 nights. Same deal with the number of rockets: sometimes five or six, sometimes a dozen or more. But it is always at night when Charie has the cover of darkness, as he is no fool. The rockets are always fired from the south or southwest, as Uplift is surrounded by hills in the other three directions. The heavy forest growth in that southerly area also offers great cover.

One evening, about a half dozen rockets hit the LZ as we are watching our forgettable Hollywood Movie Matinee projected against the outside wall of the mess hall. The movie cuts out and we take cover in the nearby sandbag-covered bunkers. The rockets do no damage, as they fall short, most of them hitting just short of the perimeter wire. A few guard bunkers in that area spray the wood line with machine gun fire, but they have no real target. It's all over in five or ten minutes, and we come back to the outside of our bunkers and the movie starts up again.

Only a few minutes go by and I hear my name being shouted. I respond, "Here," and the voice tells me to report to operations. I immediately do so and I find Captain T standing in front of the Colonel and wonder what kind of deep shit trouble I am in. I report to the Colonel, but he says not a word. The Colonel silently stares at me with great intensity, as if mentally recording every feature and detail of my face. I don't know what I might have done to have warranted this. But then still staring only at me, he speaks to both of us in an almost angry tone: "Take your jeep out the front gate. The MPs are waiting for you. Then drive along outside the perimeter wire with your lights off until you reach the impact area of those rockets." He now shifts his stare directly at Capt. T and points a finger at him. "Get me a direction and distance. I want to blow those bastards away." Then facing both of us says, "And get back inside as quickly as you can." We both respond simultaneously, "Yes sir."

Going outside the wire at night is nuts. Taking a jeep and driving around outside the wire at night is certifiably insane. I realize now that the reason the Colonel was studying my face in such detail is that he may be sending us to our deaths. We will be going deep into the "no man's land." It's a free-fire zone, and neither side needs anyone's permission to open up and blast away. It is an open invitation to any Charlie: "Here I am in my jeep." If we are attacked in that zone, it will be all but impossible to crawl back through our own heavily fortified perimeter wire. The perimeter is also heavily covered with claymore mines. But almost everything in Vietnam is nuts, and this takes us another ten notches further past insanity. I am glad I am going with someone I trust; I don't think I could do this alone; I doubt I could find the courage.

We step outside of Operations, and I tell the Captain, "I'll get the jeep. I'll be back in a minute." I walk directly to my hooch, which is only steps away, and grab my M-16. I walk out the opposite door into the motor pool area and grab our jeep. It fires instantly, and I drive around to the front side to pick up the Captain. He gets in and says almost in a whisper, "You ready for this?" I reply "Yeah, let's just get it done." I drive out of our section of Uplift and turn south on Highway 1. We drive just a couple hundred yards, where we reach the main gate that is closed each evening at 5:00 PM, blocking off Highway 1. We stop just inside the gate and are greeted by three waiting MP's who swing open the long heavy gate. All three shake their heads, as one quietly says, "Good luck." I very slowly, and as quietly as possible, pull away. As I do this, we hear the solid clunk of the gate close behind us. We are committed now.

I drive just a short distance down Highway 1, and then turn right and begin driving slowly along the barren no-man's-land between the outer perimeter wire of Uplift and the thick wood line of Charlie's back yard. It is surreally spooky. I am not worried so much about Charlie taking a few shots in at us as I am of someone in one of our bunkers unloading a belt of M-60 machine gun fire out at us. I drive to the general area of the suspected impact. We dismount and with a single flashlight we search for impact craters. Our conversation is limited to bare whispers. Our search takes much longer than I had anticipated. We cannot immediately find the craters; we have misjudged their impact location.

We move further to the west and further from our jeep. I think about retrieving it but decide against making any noise starting it; the engine noise will only give away our location to Charlie, and we have already been here too long. We finally come upon several small but rather elongated craters; they are only a few inches deep. We whisper to each other, and I hold the flashlight as the Captain uses the compass to determine from the pattern of the dirt and debris field the direction in which the rockets were fired. As to distance, it is an educated guess that the rockets, probably 122mm, were fired from maximum range, given the elongated craters. If they were fired from close range, they would have dropped straight in, and the craters would be more rounded.

Finished here, we walk as silently as possible back to the jeep, which is much further away than we thought possible. It fires instantly again, and I drive back toward the main gate on Highway I. I don't dare put the lights on. The MPs hear our approach and swing the gate open. Honestly, they are as relieved as we are. Capt. T brings this information into FDC. About a half hour later, a gun ship flies over the area to our south, spraying thousands of rounds on the jungle below, with pass after pass of machine gun fire. No one ever knows if this has succeeded, as we never venture out there to look.

I return to the outside wall of the mess hall and watch the last part of the movie. When it ends, I go to my hooch and lie on my bunk and fall asleep. Life goes on. Sometimes it's best not to think anything through too much.

Hooch Mates And Humor

Things for me now are not too bad at all. I feel I am in relatively good position; I like my no-leadership-required jeep-driving job, which keeps me off the guard roster and the everyday shit details of Army life at Uplift. Though I will only admit it to myself much later, the job actually entails much danger. I get along quite well with the Captain I work for, and I generally get along well with my new hooch mates, most of whom work in FDC. They are a sharp, bright bunch and usually maintain good humor, which is a necessity for coping with our life in the Army. We sometimes play a game in the evening where we pick out various Officers and ask the question, "If he weren't in the Army, what would he do in civilian life?" We of course are aiming at humor and are not necessarily kind in our choice of their potential civilian jobs. The Colonel is an appliance salesman at Sears, the Major is a bell ringer for the Salvation Army, and Fruit is on a permanent probationary status as a part-time stacker at a potato chip factory.

I think they are a little too tough on the Colonel, as I don't think he is that bad a guy. I remember that shortly after I arrived in Vietnam several of us "newbies" were sent to the mess hall to meet with the Colonel. It was a rather brief meeting, and the Colonel did all the talking. I recall almost nothing of what he said until the very end. He finally told us that "It's a difficult and troubling time in our country, and at this moment not all appreciate your service here. But later on, I assure you that you will feel proud to have served your country."

Well, I guess he was at least half right; I have never felt that the country ever appreciated our service here. As to being proud, I'm not sure. I have never ever been ashamed, but it's never been my style to boast about much of anything. On the other hand, I bristle at the many politicians who claim they served during the Vietnam era, when in fact they never spent a day here. Worse yet are those politicians who take the hawk position but never served a day anywhere.

I think the Colonel truly cares about our lives and has done what he feels necessary to keep us safe and alive. He once chews me out for not having my mosquito net properly in place, as malaria is widespread. My only complaint is that he should keep better control of Fruit. Fruit is mentally ill, a bully, and a coward, and he has done much to make life unbearable at Uplift. In difficult situations, good leadership is critical; are we to have a good leader or be made miserable by an incompetent bully? We deserve much better than the abuse that we get from Fruit, the Colonel should squash him like a bug.

Cardinal Rule Number II: Never Forget, It Can Always Be Worse

From time to time, I am assigned to take our Battalion Doctor on a day trip. He lives in Uplift just like the rest of us. He is an easy-going guy and not at all caught up in any of the military protocols and other Army bullshit. In fact, he is a draftee like most of us, except for the fact that the Army made him a Captain on his induction day. He is just counting down his days until he can leave this place and get out of the Army. He is easy enough to talk to, especially when we make our road trip house calls. He is not at all happy about having been drafted into the Army, but has accepted his situation and performs well enough, it seems. He just doesn't "believe in the cause," and like most of us, knows it is a lost one. He just doesn't want to die here, as he tells me more than once. He never drives north of Uplift towards Bong Son and LZ English. as he considers it far too dangerous. He is right about all of it.

On this particular morning as we get into the jeep, I ask the Doc our destination; he replies, "a leper colony near Quy Nhon," and he hands me the directions. My response is, "That should be interesting," and I begin the drive south. I can't remember the colony's name, but I do remember its residents, poor souls; what a dreaded disease. It seems that some order of Catholic Nuns is running the place; I wonder what Madame Nhu would think of this?

Surprisingly, the colony is easy to find; we drive only a short distance off the main road. While the compound is not luxurious by any means, and seems a bit austere, it is reasonably well maintained given what I am sure is a meager budget. The grounds are free of any kind of debris, be it paper or even a palm leaf. There are a few rose-colored flowers in a couple of gardens that border the fronts of some of the buildings, but maybe sparse is a better description. The gardeners or maintenance men all seemed to be resident patients. They must be, given that each shows signs of leprosy, whether some disfigurement of the face or missing digits on their hands or feet. Many displayed all of these signs, and a couple seem to be able to take only painful slow steps.

There are no military guards here, so we enter the grounds unchallenged. I guess, what would be the point of that? Charlie sure as hell wouldn't want this place. One of the gardeners points with his arm toward a faded off-white, almost gray building. We pull up next to another Army jeep that is parked in front of an unassuming building that has a faded sign that is unreadable. We assume this is the office. As we dismount, we notice that the other jeep holds a small olive drab sign with a small black cross; below that in black letters is the word "Chaplain," aka, the God Squad.

We are expected, so we knock and enter and are immediately greeted by an older Vietnamese woman who guides us down a short hallway to a large reception area. Here, we are greeted by two nuns who I assume must run the place. They are European and seem to have been here a long time, judging from their fluency of Vietnamese as they exchange a few short sentences with the staff. The Sisters speak perfect, though slightly accented, English with us and the Army Chaplain who has arrived just ahead of us. I try to place their accents; one sounds vaguely Canadian, the other possibly French, but I am not certain and do not ask. They seem unpretentious, though admittedly we are only with them for a very brief time. I would think someone who is running a leper colony is not likely to maintain an air of Queen Shit in the Moonlight. The Nuns offer to take us on the obligatory tour of the facilities. I am actually quite curious about the place; after all it's my first "leper colony".

The nuns take me, the Doc, and the Chaplain for the tour; the Chaplain's driver appears completely uninterested and stays behind. We are taken by a few of the wards, but they seem to hold only a few people each. All are adults, but their ages vary greatly. One of the nuns explains that some of them hold small jobs around the compound. At the last ward, we look in to see just a single patient, a young woman sitting up in her bed. She looks towards us and gives a pleasant smile. She is one very pretty girl. I very consciously give her a gentle wave back. And she returns it. The tour continues down the hallway, but I only go a few steps. Without saying a word, I turn around and walk back into her room.

She greets me with a smile as I walk towards her and take a seat on the chair next to her bed. She speaks no English, and my fractured Vietnamese is almost useless. Yet somehow, we make small talk; we exchange our names and our ages; she is twenty years old. I can see no visible signs of her leprosy and wonder what she is doing here. But only a moment later, perhaps sensing my unspoken question, she pulls her legs out from under a sheet that came up only to her knees. I see that her left foot is dark, scaly, and shriveled. It shocks me, and I force myself not to grimace. I think it must be terribly painful, but she does not appear to suffer from any pain. I look at her face and gently nod a quiet acknowledgement of her terrible circumstances. We talk a bit more, and then ask if I may take her picture. She is genuinely flattered by my request and so sits up straight in her bed and smiles a sweet smile; what courage. I take her picture and almost immediately I hear voices at the door. It is the entourage. I nod towards them and then gesture to her that I must go now; I smile and say good-bye. At the doorway I turn around and wave a final good-bye, and she waves back.

The nuns tell all of us, but I assume mostly for my benefit, that, "She had been staying at a Buddhist temple for quite some time, but they asked her to leave six months ago. So, she came here and we took her in." The nuns provide no other details of this event, her life, her family; they simply go on to the next subject.

We are led back to the reception room where we are each brought a piece of pineapple-upside-down cake. I look at the Doc who intuitively knows my question; he gives me a very slight nod, "Yes," and so we eat the cake. It is delicious.

Just as we finish, a small group of Koreans enters the reception room. There are three civilians and a Korean Military Officer as an escort. It is a surreal group; there are two young women who are dressed as the Korean version of Geisha girls. The group is here on a good will mission; to cheer up the lepers? Add bizarre to surreal; it seems so inappropriate. The Korean Geishas are immaculately dressed in bright beautiful robes, but their makeup is so overdone they look hard and whorish. They spot the camera that I am holding and they insist, almost demand, that I take their picture. I really don't want to, given their obnoxious attitude; I finally take their goddamn picture just to avoid making a scene, but now, talk about two Queen Shits in the Moonlight.

I leave the Doc to finish up his meeting and I wander outside where I am greeted by the Chaplain's driver. He tells me he loves driving the Chaplain around and that it has really provided him with some great benefits. I am thinking, "Me too, I'm away from the lifers most of the day," but I have completely misjudged him.

He now shows me a diamond engagement ring he picked up yesterday at some LZ that he and the Chaplain had visited. It seems that the Chaplain was making a "house call" to console some poor Army private who received his girlfriend's engagement ring back in the mail. It goes without saying, but what a terrible care package to receive in Vietnam. The driver tells me that he took it off the guy's hands for next to nothing; he didn't want the poor guy to have this constant reminder of a broken heart. If fact, the driver tells me this is the third diamond ring he has gotten since he started driving the Chaplain around just a few months ago. He is smiling ear to ear and tells me this is the best job he has ever had in the Army and that he will make a killing when he gets back home and sells the rings. I'm not even listening at this point as he continues to go on. It always amazes me how random life in the Army is. The Chaplain is working hard to make good souls, and his driver is working hard to make good deals. What a combo!

The Doc comes outside, we get in the jeep and I slowly drive us away from this place. It will take close to two hours to get back to Uplift, and most of the first part of our trip back is in silent meditation. I think of the difficult hill these people must climb every moment of their lives, and climb that hill in the middle of a war. At some point, we are stopped to let a convoy of trucks pass in front of us. As we wait, I ask the Doc what will happen to those people back in the colony. He stares straight ahead and silently shakes his head.

Steak Night

On a few rare occasions the powers that be attempt to do something special to boost morale. It worked once before, months earlier, when we saw the skin flicks inside our boarded-up mess-hall one night. That particular evening had been more spontaneous than planned and is most definitely not officially sanctioned. But Barbeque Night is an official Army-mandated affair that we actually have only once. The head mess cook, a rare good and decent lifer E-7, actually tries very hard to make good tasting meals. It is not an easy task, given the limitations of what is available to him and the distance it has to travel. But he makes a remarkable effort most days, and the food is often better than the stuff they serve back at Fort Sill; at least he never serves the dreaded creamed chipped beef on toast, aka "shit on a shingle."

We frequently have beef pot roast that is often served for both lunch and dinner on the same day. We have some cooks from the Northeast. They serve us Yankee Pot Roast for lunch, and the Puerto Rican cooks serve us Spanish Pot Roast for dinner. It is always a little tough either way. Sometimes we have spaghetti at lunch; when we later feed it to our Vietnamese workers, they relish the noodles. But from time to time, we have hotdogs for lunch and when we offer them to our Vietnamese workers, they refuse to eat them. When I ask one of the young Vietnamese women who speaks some English what is the problem with hot dogs, she replies almost angrily (dropping the "f" for "h"), "Me no eat, same - same my dick, hucking number ten!" They will only eat the rolls and ketchup.

One evening the head cook, a rather decent and caring career man and newly promoted to E-7, serves us steaks grilled over charcoal with baked potatoes; we are so stunned. We are even given two free beers. The steaks are quite good; it is one of the best meals we ever have at godforsaken Uplift. You might think everyone would be happy, laughing and joking, but it becomes almost melancholy as the evening wears on. We are most appreciative of his effort, but the more they try to make it like home, the more you miss it. I wish it were the usual forgettable "meal," on just another forgettable night and not one that reminds you of better things. But as it turned out, we never have "steak night" again anyway.

Up In The Air

As I was leaving our mess hall, having eaten the noon meal of Spanish Pot Roast (the Puerto Rican cooks were on duty and tonight we will have New England Pot Roast which is just as tough) Captain T finds me. He tells me we will make a quick trip up north to LZ English this afternoon and to meet him in the Operations Room at 1:00 PM.

I grab my flak jacket, helmet and M-16 from my hooch and then walk the very short distance to Operations. As I enter the room Captain T is laughing at the story another Captain is telling him. The Captain telling the story seems a bit offended that Captain T has told him he smells worse than manure. And as I get closer to both of them, I can smell it also. I say nothing but the odor is strong in the heat.

The other Captain is angry as he explains why he has feces on his clothes. It seems he was interrogating, with other Army personnel, a suspected member of the Viet Cong trying to get the usual information as to their numbers, locations and the names of the other VC. This Charlie had been caught as he and a few others had attempted to blow a small bridge, which was really no more than a glorified culvert. The Charlie denies he is a member of the VC and says he knows nothing. But the Captain is certain he's VC. Frustrated with Charlie's denials of any involvement with the VC, the Captain drags him from the interrogation room and tells him he is going to take him up in a helicopter and throw him out the door. As they approach the chopper, the Huey fires up and is turning its blades as the Captain attempts to lift and push the Charlie on board. It is at this point that the Charlie realizes that this was no mere joke but a threat that would be carried out. So frightened by the thought of being thrown from the Huey at a thousand feet, the Charlie loses control of his lower intestinal track. And as the Captain is lifting and pushing him on to the Huey, the Charlie discharges profuse and copious amounts of feces into his pants. The Huey never does leave the ground, as now the pilots are furious with the Captain for causing feces to be smeared around the cabin of the Huey. We never do hear what happened to the Charlie, but the Captain goes on and on as to how he tried to rinse his shirt and pants at the Officers Latrine, but only to be chewed out by the Major who was in there at that time.

At this point, I tell Captain T, I'll bring the jeep around to the front and I start to walk away. Captain T tells me "Good, I'm coming with you" and, as he steps away, tells the other Captain, "You really stink, you should burn your clothes".

Top Goes Home

It seems to come without warning, but I'm sure that there have been signs of what is about to happen. But I never saw it coming. Maybe it's because I am almost always on the road away from Uplift each day that I haven't seen the signs. Or maybe it is just his way, but Top finishes his tour and with little personal fanfare leaves us behind to cope on our own. I don't blame him, his time here was up and he went home, but it is a sad day indeed.

There is a small and brief ceremony when he leaves. It is held in the middle of the parking area of the motor pool, which is really the only place within our cramped part of Uplift where there is a little open space. I have driven the Captain someplace and we have returned just before lunch and when we drive into the parking area, the ceremony has just broken up. It must have been a very brief ceremony as Uplift is considered a forward area, and the High Command has forbidden any formation whatsoever, lest a rocket come in and take out a large number of GI's.

I have no sooner gotten out of the jeep when a friend approaches and tells me a little sadly that Top has just gone out the front gate in a jeep to start his way home. I only say, "That's really too bad. He was so good to us." But now my friend asks, "Did you see what just happened?" I tell him "No, I missed the whole thing." He points to a 1st Lieutenant standing next to the mess-hall; I think I recognize the guy. He is about to climb into the back of the truck that is headed back down to base camp at Phu Cat. From there he will travel to Cam Ranh Bay and then home. My friend continues his story, as he points to a trash can by the mess-hall. "They gave him some kind of commendation, and right after the ceremony was over, he walked over there and threw it in the trash can." I respond, "Nice job," and we both smile.

A couple of weeks earlier, I had driven the Captain up north, well past English, to interview the same Lieutenant; I think he may have lost his rifle in the bush, so there was some kind of investigation, as the Army really frowned upon lost weapons. I don't remember the details. But the Colonel did not like him even before that happened; consequently, he made him stay in the boonies until the very last moment. But throwing the commendation in the trash can was a great move, FTA baby, FTA.

With Top gone and his replacement nowhere in sight, Sergeant Patterson, as the next highest-ranking NCO, is temporarily made acting First Sergeant. Ol' Pat does an okay job of it, but he is not happy or particularly comfortable with his new and apparently unwanted elevation. He was happier just running his survey section and nothing more. He was high enough in rank and had been in the Army for so long, that he was not yanked or jerked around by too many. Besides, the battery clerk gets him through it, much as a good secretary gets a new boss through the first few weeks. Ol' Pat has no agenda, no vendettas or scores to settle. He isn't out to screw anybody, as he is a decent enough guy. In fact, the only thing that he does differently from the usual grinding daily routine is to have a small water tank very near to his hooch filled with water so he can take a private shower. I think he is more than a little embarrassed by his rather substantial girth and near 400-pound weight and doesn't like walking in the open to the NCO showers. Now it's just a half dozen steps away. Besides, the other lifers are equally happy he has his own shower now.

Fruit Goes Wild

But with Top gone and Sergeant Patterson only passing the time away and not about to buck the system, Fruit goes on a rampage. Top has been the antidote, but now that he's gone, Fruit spreads his venom everywhere. Captain Fruit, who is hated by the entire battery from the Colonel down to the lowest private, feels everyone is out to get him. But the hatred toward Fruit is simply caused by Fruit. It is so obviously self-inflected, but Fruit cannot see himself. Instead, he worsens his own pain by bullying everyone else: every Sergeant and every enlisted man. No one likes him, no one respects him, and he has not a single friend even among the Officers, as they know an asshole when they spot one. He drives people away from him; his self-created isolation is pure hell, but he does not change. He lacks the courage. Everyone hides from him if it is at all possible, but he of course finds them at some point during the day. Where is there to hide on a small LZ? He turns Sergeants against each other; some of them are a bit like Fruit, and they in turn lash out at the enlisted men. It is like a spreading disease.

Now For Some Charity

The end of June finally comes, and with it comes payday. The Army pays once a month and we are paid on the very last day of the month. We are not paid in U.S. currency per se, but in Military Scrip, aka, "funny money" or Monopoly Money. Some guys spend part of their pay on the necessities like booze, drugs, whores, and gambling, but then just piss the rest of it away. But most of us keep about thirty bucks and then buy a military money order with the rest of it and mail it home. Other than booze, drugs, whores and gambling, there is almost nothing else to spend it on, so why keep it here? It will only be lost or stolen. But every so often the brass decides we should "voluntarily" donate a small portion of our pay to some charity. To make our "giving" easier to do, a charity officer is selected to collect our donations. We line up for our pay, and a clerk from somewhere hands us the appropriate paperwork in triplicate, which lists our pay and its various deductions. We sign and are handed our copy and then our pay is counted out. It is at this point that we must step over to the "charity officer."

This has happened once before, at Fort Sill. I was a private first class at that time perhaps making $136 a month before taxes, and was pressured, as all of us were, to "donate" to a list of charities. I hated doing it. Sweet Jesus, we were paid so poorly and every dollar counted. But we were basically forced to donate at least a couple of dollars to one charity on a list handed to us. I donated two dollars to a Native American Orphanage located somewhere in Oklahoma. I remember an hour or two later a couple of Officers laughing, joking how almost every enlisted man had chosen the Native American Orphanage. They just didn't get it. We knew we were getting screwed over, so our sympathies went to the group that we collectively considered to have been screwed over even more than we were, the Native Americans. There are so few leaders here and yet so many bullies.

But this time, this mid-day on this last day of June, in the sweltering heat of South Vietnam, I say no. The charity officer, Captain Iowa, is taken aback. I know the guy a little bit, as I have had a few conversations with him as I have driven him on two or three short trips. I don't recall his name, but he is from someplace in Iowa, married with a kid, and wants to get home as much as any of us do. He is a tall, calm, composed, fair haired, good and decent guy from the heartland. I do not mock him, as he's a just and capable leader, kind of what you might expect from a guy from Iowa. But I repeat myself to him. "No, I'm not giving another cent. The Army and this place already take enough blood, sweat and tears from me." I say this calmly and evenly, with no anger in my voice, but I look him squarely in the eye as I do. He studies me for a moment and knows I will not back down. He simply says, "You're one hard son of a bitch," and smiles. I am slightly offended by his words, but I don't think he knows what to say and is trying to be humorous. Neither of us knows what's coming, but in just twenty days we will have another conversation. It will demonstrate how vastly different our views of the world around us are.

Such Tragedy

The summer heat is scorching and is broken only in the late afternoon by rather brief thunderstorms that seem to come from nowhere. I still drive the Captain all over creation. Occasionally, as we drive along Highway 1 back to Uplift, we are caught in those tropical downbursts. With no top on the jeep, we get completely soaked. But we can drive out of the storm and back into the sun and be completely dry by the time we get back into Uplift just before 5:00 PM. But as June turns to July, the thunderstorms in the late afternoon become less and less frequent, and now it is simply hot all day, sun up to sun down.

But there has been a terrible tragedy. I have just returned from a long trip, and it is a little after 5:00 PM as I enter my hooch. Everyone in the FDC hooch is oddly quiet, as if waiting for something terrible to happen, but it already has happened. But I get little information. As an NCO walks in, everyone stops talking. Something is very wrong.

I get some supper with a couple of guys, and I get bits and pieces of the story. The conversation is splintered with stops and gaps as someone either walks by or joins us at the table. But I piece this much together: Grandpa and a few others had worked the FDC night shift and decided to use their time off to make a day trip down to Service Battery at base camp which sits at the far end of the Phu Cat airbase. We send a truck down there every morning from Uplift to drop outgoing mail and personnel off, and in the afternoon the same truck returns with mail and any incoming personnel. There is a PX, a steam bath, a massage parlor, and a bar in the NCO club at the airbase. Everyone had a good time, but maybe too much time was spent in the bar. In the late afternoon, they stood just inside the main gate of the airbase, waiting for a ride north. A truck from the 173rd, with which we share a portion of Uplift, stopped to give them a ride for the trip back.

Our long and drawn-out conversation remains unfinished as the mess hall closes up. We return to our hooch, but no one speaks of the details. MPs arrive shortly, and different guys are called into operations for questioning. Finally, Grandpa is taken away for questioning. It is then that I hear the full story. On the return trip back to Uplift, as the truck was traveling along a long curve rounding a rice paddy, Grandpa fired his M-14. It is an older rifle that shoots a large heavy round. He was not shooting at anything in particular, only shooting toward the rice paddy. But the round carried a long distance beyond the rice paddy where the highway curves around it. At that same moment a teen-age girl rode on the back of a motor bike; the bike traveled in the opposite direction of the truck and was hundreds of yards away. It is cruelly unfair, but the bullet struck her in the head. She was killed instantly and fell from the motor bike onto the pavement of Highway 1. The local police are called; someone had noticed that the truck was from the 173rd. U.S. Army MPs are now called in; they drive to Uplift where they question the driver. He recalls a guy from our unit telling him he was going to take a few shots out the back of the truck. Their investigation doesn't take long. Grandpa is charged with reckless manslaughter and will be court-martialed.

Things in our unit continue to worsen. Fruit is still on a freewheeling rampage. By sheer chance, he spots me just before our evening meal. He is furious at some Staff Sergeant and sends me to find him. I do as I am told and find him in the NCO hooch. I tell the Sergeant that Fruit wants to see him now, but the Sergeant, another lifer loser, is furious at me for having found him. I protest that I am only the messenger, but he is seething. A month or two earlier, this same Staff Sergeant bitterly told me how about a year before, he had started Officer Candidate School, but after six weeks he quit because he thought the other candidates were so inferior and he didn't wish to be part of this. I knew it was a bullshit story; the truth was he probably couldn't make the grade and was most likely tossed out of the school. He has probably been in the Army a dozen years and hates it, but for much different reasons than we do. We reject the Army, but the Army rejected him, and this is his future. He is sullen and angry at everyone, even the draftees, who have no control over any of this.

A day or two later, I have to drive this same Sergeant north to English and then back. But as soon as we begin the trip, he complains continuously about my driving. When we finally get back to Uplift, he fires me from my job. Normally I would go see my Captain, but he has left that very morning to go on R+R, it will be ten days at least before he is back. I can do nothing. I am immediately put back on the guard roster and the usual shit details of daily life at Uplift. Life sucks here once again.

Grandpa is back with us at least temporally until his court martial. He has an Army attorney and he tells us of the serious charges he faces. I don't think he is a murderer, but he has done something incredibly stupid, the consequences of which are so painfully and so unduly tragic for that young girl and her family. I had liked him, he had already graduated from college and had started law school, he had a good sense of humor, he would be out of the Army soon, and he had a future and now this.

Big D and I and a few others reflect upon this event and the circumstances surrounding it, but Bitter John seems unusually quiet and says little. He normally complains, with such regularity that one can set the atomic clock to it. He cynically grumbles about our predicament, but much more often of his predicament of life in the Army. He conveys this in a somewhat humorous way, yet with such deeply held bitterness. I think for the first time, he finally sees that maybe he's not the only one in this god-awful Army in this god-awful place called Vietnam. None of whom the country we serve cares about. It doesn't last long and he soon reverts, but for a while he finally sees he's not the only one in shit, and that it can always be much deeper. He finally understands **Cardinal Rule Number II: Never Forget, It Can Always Be Worse.**

Corn-Fed Bare Blonde Band Stampede

There are no days off in the Army. Every day is a workday; the only possible exception is Sunday. Uplift is just big enough that there are some organized church services on Sunday morning. If you really want to go to one, the Army allows it. After all, it is Army Chaplains performing the church services; therefore, our attendance is officially sanctioned. I never go but a few guys do. Otherwise, it is a regular workday.

The war doesn't stop because it's Sunday and then start up again on Monday morning at 8:00AM sharp. There is guard duty every night in those bunkers on the perimeter; communications and FDC still run around the clock coordinating artillery bombardments. Charlie doesn't observe Sundays, neither do we, though for some reason Sundays are just a little slower. The only big difference that Sunday makes here at Uplift is that we don't bring in our Vietnamese day laborers. This means that there is a pause in the general shit details of our daily life on Sundays. This is really a nice respite if you're part of the group that gets stuck with doing them the other six days of the week. So, the smart thing to do is to lay low and not remind anybody that we aren't doing shit work details that afternoon. Generally speaking, the NCO's and Officers know the unspoken rules of Sunday afternoons. If you need somebody you know where to find them, but otherwise leave people alone for at least a few hours. The exception to this is of course Fruit. What a self-tormented AH.

I have just walked from my hooch to get a drink from the tall stainless-steel dispensers that stood on a small table just outside the mess hall. They are kept full 24 hours a day. I have the purple flavor, though its taste and its color have no correlation. But on my way back Fruit stops me. He orders me to dig the nearby, small two-man bunker a little deeper. There is of course nothing wrong with the bunker to begin with, but this has nothing to do with reason, only with him being a bully. What choice do I have but to do it? I retrieve a long-handled shovel from storage and begin digging the hard, red clay deeper. I probably work for a half hour alone; no one dares come near me, lest Fruit, wherever he is, sees them and also puts them on another shit detail. It is hot and humid; the work is no fun, and it serves no useful purpose.

Suddenly, I hear trucks entering Uplift. They have come through the southern main gate which straddles Highway 1. There are two trucks and a jeep that have turned left onto the road which runs right in front of our part of the LZ and leads to 173rd compound. The lead jeep is marked with large white letters that read "MP" and the two following trucks have banners that read "USO Show;" the 173rd is getting a show put on for them. This is my way off this shit detail.

I take the shovel with me and put it back in storage. Then I go to see Ol' Sergeant Patterson, who is the acting First Shirt, our temporary Top Dog. He is snoozing in his hooch just as I expected and hoped. I know he doesn't really want to be bothered by anything, so I ask him as a favor if I could walk over to the 173rd to watch their USO Show. He grants permission, telling me with a smile, "Get over there right now, that's an order." The man is at heart a decent guy; why would he say no? These USO shows are put on to boost the morale of the troops, after all. Now I have great cover if Fruit starts something later: I was ordered by the First Sergeant to attend a USO show. I cut out through the back of our compound by going through the tiny emergency Field Hospital right behind us, so as to not attract any attention, and then enter the 173rd's part of the LZ.

Hundreds of GI's have already gathered on the hillside that looks down upon a close-by plywood stage. I am among the last to arrive, so I stand very near the top of the hillside, but my view is excellent. The USO show has quickly set up, as it is not Bob Hope, Bing Crosby and Hollywood starlets. It is actually just a four-piece Rock and Roll garage band from someplace in the States that absolutely no one has ever heard of. I don't think the USO pays much to anybody, and I'm sure they haven't paid much to these guys. But for the band, maybe it sounded like a fun thing to do at the time they signed up. Maybe they were hoping for some exposure and a record deal back home. But here they are: a drummer, two guys with electric guitars and the lead singer, a tall, long-haired blonde gal from the heartland. I suppose a far more romantic description of this scene would be that they performed on a perfectly smoothed granite stage set against a natural amphitheater holding thousands of adoring fans. But the stark reality is that it is a scorching hot afternoon as they climb up onto a plywood bandstand facing 600 sweaty GI's who sit on the dusty red clay of the close by hillside in crappy Landing Zone Uplift.

The band is introduced and we give them a very warm reception, as we think this is going to be great. They do the first number, and some of us realize they are not that good. But we politely applaud anyway. They do their next number and we are hopeful that they are just getting warmed up and will improve, but they don't. They finish, and we politely applaud again. It's just not much of a show, though I admit it is far better than digging a bunker a little deeper. They do a third song and a fourth and a fifth. I cannot remember a single song they played or what she sang. They are so forgettable; it's not a fair thing to say, but they suck.

They do a couple of more songs, but they are starting to lose us. Thirty or forty minutes have gone by; they should wrap this up quickly before we start booing them. I am beginning to think that this afternoon's USO show is going to be some unmemorable footnote in history. And then everything changes so quickly... The blond tells us, "This next one is dedicated to all the brave men in Vietnam." We cheer, but it's not once but twice, as she then takes her top off. Oh My God! There is an audible gasp that must be heard a mile away. All six hundred of us suck in so much air that we surely cause nearby barometers to move several inches. We are paralyzed and cannot move. She begins to sing, but we are not listening, we can only stare wide-eyed at her ample, full, and luscious ta-tas. These are not what we might expect on some skinny flat-chested Vietnamese girl; no, these are corn-fed Iowans, State of Mainers, Idahoans. May God Bless Her, America, and the Constitution of the United States.

I have the presence of mind to look to either side of me, to make sure that I am not delusional and that I am seeing what I think everyone else is seeing. I am not delusional; every single GI is now staring bug-eyed with his mouth wide open, gasping for oxygen. But the mass paralysis that has affected every one of us wears off at the same moment, and we all, at the same very instant, begin to move forward as if lockstep. First it is only a step or two, but it then becomes a stampede for the stage. There are only about six MPs, and they are quickly overwhelmed as guys begin to mount the front of the stage. The blond screams, and she and the band run down the back-stairway, leaving their equipment behind, and jump into the USO truck. The USO truck pulls away from the 173rd with at least a hundred guys chasing it down the dirt road. I think to myself, "Someone should have filmed this. What a movie scene!" I walk back to my unit; it's getting close to suppertime. Wait till I tell Big D and Bitter John.

No Relief

Within just four days of this, Fruit leaves forever. There is no ceremony; he just goes, as his time here has ended. I am told by other Officers that he has tried to extend his tour here, but the Colonel would not approve it. To our great relief, a rather decent good guy is temporarily put in charge. He's a young Captain, and does not have much time left in the Army; he will only be with us for about six weeks more. He will have completed his time, then be discharged and then go home; lucky him.

We all perk up a little, but it is short lived. Only a few days later, our new First Sergeant arrives. We all take one look at him and immediately know, "what an asshole." He is of barely medium height and is slightly heavy; his hair is cut short on the sides, military style, but it is much longer on top and full of Brylcreem. He combs it straight back in an attempt to hide the bald spot on the middle of his head. It is so greasy it shines in the sunlight. His face is always red, like that of an alcoholic. It becomes abundantly clear within the first few days that he has limited education and is not especially bright. He must have sucked up hard, for he is newly promoted to First Sergeant. In fact, this is his first assignment as a first shirt, and he is going to show us all that he is in charge. God help us, another bully. His first name is Frank, and when we speak among ourselves, we always refer to him as Frank, or AH Frank, or Frank the AH. We had all lovingly and respectfully referred to our earlier First Sergeant as "Top" in recognition of his top position. He earned our love and respect and we displayed it. But AH Frank only earns our hatred and disgust.

It starts the very next morning, when he calls every man in every section who's not working to a mass formation. These mass formations are strictly forbidden in forward areas, as ordered by the very top General in Vietnam. There have been mass casualties when an incoming round landed in the middle of a formation, and now they are strictly forbidden. AH Frank cares little about that; he simply wants to bark orders at us. It's all about him. But he doesn't get far into it before Captain "Good" comes by and dismisses the formation. He takes Frank, who is livid with anger, aside and explains that these mass formations are forbidden by order of the Commanding General. We hear AH Frank whining, "How am I going to take command then?"

I try to stay out of his way, but that is impossible, given that I have no job to report to other than the usual shit details. But Frank is pleased, as it gives him some people to order about.

We Make Our Own Fun

Life goes on, even if it is miserable. I again supervise the Vietnamese day laborers and pull guard duty about three nights a week. As it is the same small group of guys who have guard duty, we don't necessarily become great friends, but we certainly get to know one another. Putting the same group of guys on guard duty over such a long stretch of time is bound to have some consequences. Each evening, once we reach the perimeter, each and every square foot outside of the wire is a free fire zone. If you hear something move, or even see a palm leaf falling from a tree, you open up. No permission needed, no questions asked, just open up. Whatever or whoever it was knew they shouldn't be there. You might use your M-16, but usually you would fire the machine gun as the occasional tracer round within its belt would illuminate its direction of fire with a trailing red arc. Or if you are not quite sure of what you think you saw or heard, you might just pop a hand flare.

These are not the bigger flares that one can shoot upward with the grenade launcher. The hand flares are just that: handheld, hand-launched small rocket flares with parachutes about the size of a handkerchief. They are encased in a simple aluminum tube about an inch in diameter and maybe ten inches long. The tube is open on one end, and at the other is a small metal cap that one can slap with the palm of a hand to launch the flare. The flare is propelled by a tiny rocket and then pops open and burns brightly as it floats down on its tiny parachute. They are simple to use and are kind of fun; maybe too much fun.

One evening on guard duty, during the twilight just after sunset, whether by accident or by design, the bunker to our left shoots a hand flare towards us. It gets most of the way to us but then the parachute pops open, which greatly slows it down. Its forward momentum is stopped, and it floats to the ground. It startles us a bit, as we were not expecting "incoming" from the next bunker, and we hear the guys in that bunker laughing loudly. We shout obscenities in their direction, and one of my comrades grabs a hand flare to shoot back at them. But I stop him saying, "Take the parachute off first." He's unsure about doing this, so he hands me the flare, saying, "You do it." It's not that complicated; just don't drop the thing as you're doing this, or it will pop open in the middle of your forehead.

I pull the parachute out of the open end of the tube, remove it, and then slide the small rocket back into position. Then, standing up, I hold the launch tube horizontally and aim directly back at the offending bunker. I tell my two comrades, "Like this," and I immediately slap the cap at the bottom of the tube. The rocket ignites and shoots the flare horizontally toward the bunker just up the hill from us. Without a parachute to slow it down, it flies by where they stand on the second floor of their bunker only a foot over their sandbag roof. They duck down as it comes at them, and now we laugh our heads off.

They are momentarily stunned but they quickly regroup, and in a few minutes, they send two rocket flares minus their parachutes back at us. My bunker mates now send a few back, the last of which embeds itself in the side wall of their sandbag bunker. Surprisingly, the plastic / fiberglass bags catch fire. We stop our missile assault as they stand outside their bunker and take their shirts off to beat out the flames. We laugh till our guts ache but notice that those guys are now shouting and pointing to just in front of our bunker. We smell smoke. One of their errant rockets has set the dry brush on fire just past our bunker, and it is spreading quickly, pushed by a sudden strong breeze. I begin to think of what excuses we can give the Sergeant of the Guard, but the strong breeze is the prelude to a fast-moving squall line which quickly puts the fire out. We behave ourselves for the rest of the night, and all is well in the morning.

Religious Preference

Another slow-moving week passes by, and AH Frank has finally found a way to have his formations. Each evening, immediately after supper but before darkness settles in, AH Frank conducts mandatory motor pool preventive maintenance. He makes everyone who is available to go stand around individual trucks or jeeps and perform preventative maintenance. Put the lights on, put the lights off, toot the horn, kick the tires, check the oil, check the battery for snow, etc., etc.

Though it's not technically a formation, it does violate the spirit of the prohibition of concentrating personnel. But it's all about Frank, as he paces back and forth yelling at us for 30 minutes. He begins to feel powerful, and he also begins to cultivate the hatred toward him.

A day or two later as I am supervising our Vietnamese day laborers on a sandbag detail, Frank the AH comes over. There is nothing to see except a pile of sand and a pile of sandbags, yet he searches for something. It is a sweltering morning, and I have taken off my shirt. He tells me I am out of uniform; I shrug my shoulders as if to say, get off my back. But he barks, "Dog tags, dog tags. You only have one dog tag." I look; he's right, you wear a pair of them on a stainless-steel chain around your neck. I don't know how I have lost only one. The only time you really need them is if "you bought the farm," and they need to identify the body. At that point, what does it matter?

AH Frank barks, "See the clerk and order a new pair." Honestly, I happily comply; it gets me out of the hot sun for ten minutes. I walk into the clerk's office and tell him, "AH Frank wants me to order a new set of dog tags." He is the same clerk I met on my first day at Uplift. He would be the Army's poster boy of what an Army clerk looks like. He's tallish, very thin, blondish, and wears glasses. I swear if you wear glasses as you enter the Army, they instantly make you a clerk. But he is liked by everyone and has been able to maintain his good humor despite having to work under Fruit and now Frank the AH. He laughs, "You're the second one this week." He puts a triplicate form into a typewriter and then begins typing as he asks, "Last name, first name, middle initial," then "service number, blood type?" At the last line, and without looking up, he asks, "Religious preference?" I start to answer "Ah…um…," but I pause the longest moment, contemplating possible answers and then say "Buddhist."

The clerk looks up, in quiet disbelief, but I smile and nod my head affirming my religious preference. Now the clerk's face displays a broad smirk that goes ear to ear. "Oh yeah, that's good, they're going to really love this." I hear him quietly spelling to himself as he types with just one finger, "B-u-d-d-h-i-s-t." He pulls the triplicate form from his typewriter and says joyfully "Sign your name here."

About a week later Frank calls me over at his mandatory nightly preventive maintenance in the motor pool. "See the clerk; your dog tags are in." As much as I now want to smirk, I look straight-faced, and I say, as if asking a question, "They're in already?" Frank the AH is enraged and his face is beet red; I sense he is close to a stroke. I am certain he feels I have somehow used the military code of justice and given him a "poke in the eye." His tiny brain doesn't allow him to understand how I could have legally pulled this off. The fact that he can do nothing about it causes him extreme anxiety. But he's dumb; it wasn't directed at him as much as to the whole state of affairs. Besides "When in Rome, do as the Romans do." And I am in the land of the Buddha.

His Rage

A couple of days have gone by, and on the third morning, I climb into the back of our 1-ton truck. The truck resembles a heavy-duty civilian pickup, but has a canvas side wall and roof over the front cab and rear body of the truck. It makes the morning run back down to the Service Battery base camp at the far edge of Phu Cat Air base. It is a motionless, scorching hot morning, and the dark brown heavy canvas that covers the back of the truck provides only minimal relief. There is something about the smell of canvas in the heat and never-ending oppressive humidity of Vietnam. You smell it as you near the truck and when you sit in the back of the truck surrounded by the canvas roof and sides it is almost overpowering. And the newer the canvas the greater the stench. It is a very odd and peculiar chemical smell of something rotting and once smelled it is chemically unforgettable to the brain; you will always recognize canvas in the tropics for the rest of your life. There are two wooden benches on each side that run the length of the back of the truck. I sit on the passenger's side but as close to the rear as possible, to get as much air as I can. Besides, there are already five or six guys inside the truck and they have seated themselves further in. I cannot remember why I was going down to base camp, only that it was necessary. I remember nothing of the trip itself, what I did once there, or even the return trip later that day. I only remember this ugliness. The canvas stench now evilly sets the back ground for what is coming next.

Seated further in from me in the back corner to my right on the driver's side is a Puerto Rican guy. Julio is just another Spec 4 like me, just another guy. I know him a little bit, and he is always decent and friendly. Julio speaks with a thick Spanish accent, but he is as dark and black as any man I have ever seen. At first glance one might think him to be just another urban black guy from Mobile or Baltimore or Dallas. But when he speaks with his thick heavy Spanish accent, it seems so out of place, you have to smile; Julio is a good guy and he will roar with laughter with you.

We are about to leave when AH Frank approaches the back of the truck and looks in. I briefly meet his eye, but he looks past me towards the others. He focuses on the Puerto Rican guy and then demands, shouting in at him, "What are you doing in there, **boy**?" I look toward Julio; he winces as if struck with a lash. But he maintains his composure and answers civilly that he has some errand that must be taken care of in Base Camp. But AH Frank is uninterested. He stands red faced, sweating in the broiling morning sun with his Brylcreemed hair shinning and he shouts into the truck, **"You get out of there boy!"** Now I wince as the words go by me toward Julio. The words spoken are so heavy with such deep-rooted profound hatred; it is as if they could snuff out life itself. If there were any last remote vestiges of lingering doubt as to what a true, complete and utterly vile piece of shit Frank is, they are now gone forever.

I look toward Frank and send daggers with my eyes, but he doesn't even see me, he is so focused on Julio. I now turn and look at Julio with as much sympathy as I can put on my face. Julio is seething with anger but says nothing. I am hoping that Julio will accidently drop his rifle, discharging a round that happens by sheer circumstance to hit AH Frank between his eyeballs and blow the back of his head off like a squashed melon. But it doesn't happen. Julio slowly stands and wordlessly makes his way toward the back of the truck and dismounts. As he passes me, I gently pat his back once, and Julio answers with a faintly heard murmur. Frank will never last his year here. Each of us carries an automatic assault rifle; it's only a matter of time and place.

Regretfully, it is not only some of the NCO's who are racists; sometimes bigotry raises its ugly head among the officers. I witness that one morning when the Captain who runs the communications section walks by a First Lieutenant who is seated in the front passenger seat of a jeep. The Lieutenant is waiting for his driver when the Captain demands to know why he doesn't salute Officers. Of course, the Battalion Commander, a Lt. Colonel, has ordered that there was to be no saluting within our section of Uplift. It is too crowded, and we would all be continuously saluting each other all day long as we bump into each other. But all that Captain Bigot sees is a Black face and not a fellow Officer. The 1st Lt. simply smiles and in a serious voice responds, "I always salute an Officer when I see one." Captain Bigot is about to have a coronary, but then sees the silver bars on the 1st Lt. shoulders. He walks away embarrassed, but offers no apology. Another Army AH.

Man On The Moon

The days drag on endlessly. There is the regular rotation of guard duty on the wire, the daily grind of the shit details of stringing new barbed wire as the old wire rusts away, and of course, there is sandbag detail. The highlight of the day, such as it was, is the Vietnamese day laborers. They are generally in a good mood and work pleasantly and compliantly despite the monotony of endlessly filling sandbags. For them it is not a bad deal. We pick them up in the morning and drive them home in the afternoon. We pay them each week, and we feed them each noon the same lunch that we have. As a bonus, every few days when the garbage cans are full, we load the garbage into the back of a deuce and a half (2 1/2-ton truck), and in the afternoon we take them and the cans of garbage back to their IDP camp a few miles down the road. The garbage is used to feed their pigs, and our workers are most pleased by this arrangement.

I often make this return trip with them, sometimes riding shotgun up front and other times riding and standing up in the back of the truck with the laborers. We usually take the truck convertible-style, that is, without its dark brown canvas top. It just makes it easier for all of us to get in and out of the truck, as we, or our day laborers can climb down the sides as well use the back tailgate. But the main reason is that if Charlie takes a few pot shots at us from the roadside, we want to be able to see him and fire back unobstructed.

As the workday ends one day, we load the cans of garbage into the back of the deuce and a half. Our day laborers climb aboard, and we begin driving south down Highway 1 to their IDP camp a few miles down the road. We have left Uplift a few minutes late, as there was a ton of garbage to be loaded, but we should have plenty of time to reach their camp and return to Uplift before 5:00 PM. We are forbidden to be on the road after 5:00 PM, as Charlie works the night shift, and a deuce and a half is a nice fat target.

All seems to be going well. We arrive at the IDP camp without incident; we have expected none. A crowd of onlookers has gathered round as is customary as our day laborers climb down from the truck. We drop the tailgate, and I begin to slide the steel drums of garbage partially out over its edge; two or three of our laborers now gently lower them to the ground. There are six cans, and it's taking a few minutes. But our buck Sergeant grows impatient. Normally an easygoing enough guy, he has simply been here too long. He enlisted for three years instead doing the two-year term of a draftee. It is a mistake that some have made when receiving their draft notice. He has already completed his 12-month tour in Vietnam, but like almost all of us he is seeking an early out from the Army. If you leave Vietnam (alive) with less than 150 days remaining of your enlistment, whether as draftee or volunteer, you are released from active duty on the day you return home. He doesn't want to spend another day more in the Army than he has to, but he has been in Vietnam too long. The place only embitters you, and the longer you stay here the harder you become. And some turn mean as they near the end.

Now our buck Sergeant comes around to the back of the truck and begins to shout at our day laborers to hurry up, but they are unloading the heavy drums of garbage as quickly as they can. I tell him to calm down, we're almost done, we'll have enough time to get back, but he won't even look at me. He shouts obscenities at our laborers and now does something mean spirited. He pushes the last two cans from the edge of the tailgate. They fall at an angle and of course spill their entire contents on the roadway. The onlookers now rush in to take the garbage; our day laborers get none of it. I see the shocked look on the faces of our workers, then their anger, then their look of bitter betrayal. I shout at our buck Sergeant, "What the fuck?" But he will not look at me. He walks to the front door of the cab, jumps in, and we drive away. I am ashamed of our conduct here; it would have been only another minute or two to finish unloading.

I had liked him and had even respected him, but all I see now is another bully. Screwing over refugees in a crappy camp? I am furious at him. There was no need for this.

We arrive back at Uplift at 4:45 PM, with time to spare; we could have easily spent five more minutes to unload. I am so disgusted that I jump off the back of the truck before it is even parked in the the motor pool. I speak to no one and immediately head toward the shower area to wash my hands.

I finish and then slowly walk back toward my hooch. But I run into Captain "Iowa." He says hello to me most pleasantly, despite my earlier refusal to contribute to his list of charities. He seems in particularly high spirits. He has just returned from the Phu Cat Air Base and tells me he has watched on TV the first man stepping onto the moon. I knew of our space program, but had not realized that today would be the day of the moon landing. I am momentarily buoyed by our country's technological milestone. I am greatly curious, so I ask him, "What was it like?" meaning in the physical sense. But Captain "Iowa" completely misunderstands my question. He stares away momentarily, as if looking at Mt. Rushmore for the first time, then looks at me and says, "I felt proud to be an American." I am stunned, then angry, and then sad. I say not a word, shake my head no and walk away.

From The Frying Pan Into The Fire

I have promised myself to change my situation here, but I am unsure how to do so. I recall how on a few occasions, when driving Captain T from Operations around, we would stop at a small base to check on things with a young buck Sergeant from our Battery who was attached to an Infantry unit. He would act as the go-between to call FDC to ask for illumination or even high explosive rounds. I ask my Captain friend if I can do the same thing. My timing is most fortuitous, as they are momentarily shorthanded, and the job is mine. It will take a day or two to set up, so he cautions me to put my things in order and be ready to go on very short notice. Then he asks a final time: "Do you really want to take this assignment?"

I guess you had to be there, but being so weary of the day-to-day shit and seeing no other alternative, I tell him yes and take the assignment. I will leave my Artillery unit to join the Infantry, to call in artillery fire when and where needed. Looking back on this, it wasn't as if I saw some grand future there, it was that I couldn't stand where I was. I guess it was leaping from the frying pan into the fire; but it was my leap.

I pack away a few things, mostly clothes, into a footlocker. I then pack my remaining belongings into my duffel bag. One change of clothes, some toiletries, and every soldier's best friend (besides your M-16), my poncho liner. A poncho liner is a very lightweight polyester blanket. It is printed on both sides in camouflage colors of various shades of greens and tans to blend into the jungle background. It is your sheet to lie upon, it is your blanket on a cool night, and it hides the dirt well, no need to see how filthy it is, as this is what you will sleep on. In the entire year that I spend in South Vietnam, it is never washed once. I guess the only personal items I bring along are my new Seiko watch and my new dog tags that read "Buddhist" as my religious preference. It's a small gesture, for sure, but to my pleasure, it does go up the ass of a few of the "lifers," especially AH Frank.

I have the noon meal with a few friends and say goodbye. It's nothing emotional, just see you later, a few jokes, and tell asshole Frank to go fuck himself. It's not like I am leaving for good, and I am certain we will all see each other again. Everyone wishes me well, and I am convinced that one or two (Big D for sure) would happily join me if they could. I sling my M-16 over my right shoulder and sling my duffel bag over the other and walk away. Big D shouts after me, "Always remember, FTA." I laugh and shout back "Adios MF."

I walk out the front gate of our unit and then on to Highway 1, which cuts through the most eastern section of LZ Uplift. Walking just a short distance up the road, I come upon two of the tracks (APC's) of the Mechanized Infantry Company that I am to report to. The second track has a "water buffalo" attached at the rear to be towed along with us. An Army "water buffalo" is simply an oblong water tank mounted upon two wheels. It is painted the usual drab olive green of the Army, but it contains the potable water we will drink for the next few weeks. Later on, this water buffalo will play a pivotal role in our young lives, especially mine. I report to the lead track; their greeting is nonchalant. I climb up on top of the lead track to join a few others already sitting there and introduce myself. I sit on the left-hand side of the track; and then a few more climb up to join me. My initial thought is that they seem a hard bunch, not at all unpleasant, but hard nonetheless. In less than five minutes the diesel roars to life and we slowly pull away from LZ Uplift.

We travel north for several miles on the relatively smooth pavement of Highway 1 until we reach a tiny and undignified crossroad. Here lies a small and probably unnamed hamlet of one or two very small shops and a few dwellings that cling to Highway 1. It is unremarkable, and I have previously driven by this spot a hundred times, barely noticing it. But we turn here now, at this crossroad to the right, toward the coast several miles distant. We leave the pavement of the highway to turn down a narrow twisting dirt road, with thick, choking bellows of reddish-brown dust that follow closely behind us.

There is trouble almost immediately. I doubt we have traveled more than two hundred yards when we encounter a tiny Vietnamese bus. There are a few motorbikes, which easily maneuver out of our way, but there is a series of small hooches with scraggly fences in front of them on the bus's side of the road. The bus driver has slowed to a crawl and pulled well over and then stopped to let us pass. He has moved the side of the bus to within a few inches of the fence, but this doesn't seem to be over far enough to suit our track driver. There is just enough room for the vehicles to pass by each other, but our driver is most fearful of land mines planted at the edge of the road, and as we pass this tiny bus, our driver stops our track. From my perch atop the left side of the track, I watch in disbelief as our driver reaches over and punches the bus driver twice in the shoulder very sharply. The bus driver, a young man, winces in pain. No one says a word, and we then drive on. A hard bunch indeed. I don't think we've won any hearts and minds today.

We travel east along this dirt road at an unhurried pace of 8 or 10 mph for a few miles, then turn sharply off the road, heading south now across areas of low brush and dry rice paddies, as the start of the monsoon season is still a couple of months away. There are several tread tracks, running north – south in the ground in front us. We follow along them, but always to one side or the other of these tracks. The theory, or hope at least, is that any land mine will be planted on a traveled path and therefore we always ride to one side, making sure we tread on fresh ground. My gut instinct is that it's a roll of the dice, but what do I know? We travel on for a few miles more, crossing a small shallow river. "Tracks" can swim; the driver moves a flat plate away from the top front of the track to keep the water from rolling up into the open hatchway that he protrudes from. The track, being a hollow aluminum box, floats with the treads providing the propulsion. There is little freeboard, but we float. Not fast nor pretty, but we sit up top high and dry.

Paradise Lost

We continue to push on at a steady 6 or 8 mph traveling south across the open grasslands and dry rice paddies. Our pace is unhurried, but is not leisurely as the terrain is uneven and bumpy and more speed would be bone rattling as well as dangerous. We ride in the open on the bare metal top of the track and one could easily be bucked off. Besides the other track is towing the water buffalo which holds our drinking water. It is mid-afternoon now, and the sun scorches us and the land. For many weeks now, the rains have been very light and most infrequent. The grasslands and dry rice paddies are pale yellow as they thirstily await the coming monsoon. After another couple of miles, we come upon a small cluster of hooches that cling to a small island in this sea of pale-yellow grass and straw stubble of the previously cut rice crop. This small island is actually just a raised area of earth in an ocean of rice paddies, albeit dry paddies. In the wet season this small hamlet will truly have the look and feel of an island, for it will be completely surrounded by water-filled rice paddies that will steadily turn green as the rice shoots grow tall.

The "island" hamlet is oblong in shape, perhaps less than a half mile in length and about half that in width. The island rises, much like a flat plateau from the dry paddies that surround it, to a height of perhaps eight or ten feet, but no more. All of the hooches are on the northern half of the island and are protectively shaded by the towering palm trees. The hooches themselves seem to be agreeably spaced, urban planning be dammed, they are perfectly scattered but close enough to each other as to create the strong bond of community. They are rectangular in shape and at first glance are seemingly identical. But upon closer inspection, each is slightly different from the others; be it some subtle difference in their size or height or even the pitch of their roof lines. But every hooch has a thatch roof that has been turned brown by the blistering tropical

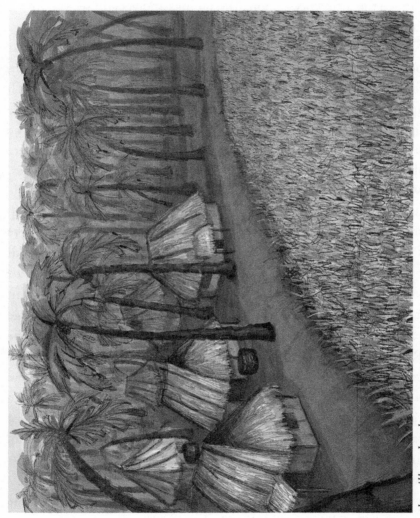

the village by the coconut grove

sun. Their sidewalls are nearly the same color, but darker due to the color of the mud and dried straw used in their construction. They look the way a large family might; all have dark brown hair, but one can see the differences among the siblings and yet still see the strong family resemblance.

At the southern end of the hamlet lies a large coconut grove that occupies fully half the island. The grove appears dense and lush, for here the coconut trees grow close together; not a single hooch appears among them to provide any break in their spacing. We take up our position at the southwestern side of this island hamlet at the point where the village ends and the coconut grove begins. Here the elevation gently lowers itself into the sea of dry rice paddies. We join two other "tracks" already there and now form a crude semi-circle just onto the very edge of the dry paddy. We will camp slightly higher up on the gently sloping edge of the island, where some palm trees provide us with some filtered shade. The coconut grove is to our east, our backs are to the hamlet behind us, and we look southwest out across the open rice paddies. But this is a joint action, for on the opposite side of the coconut grove sits a large platoon of South Vietnamese soldiers. The ARVN's (Army of the Republic of Vietnam), as they are known, hold the southeastern corner. We do not have a clear direct view of each other, but there is a path near the southern edge of the coconut grove and with a radio, communication enough to hold this end of the hamlet. Not far from the southern tip of the island, the open grasslands end, and the thick wood line begins; this is the direction that Charlie will come from.

"Charlie" is the nick-name we have given to the Viet Cong. Using the Army's "alphabet," with Viet Cong abbreviated as VC, which would be referred to as *Victor Charlie* in a radio transmission to ensure no miscommunication. But we have shortened that to just "Charlie."

Remove us and our "tracks," and this would seem a timeless tropical paradise. After the rainy season the hamlet would surely be a low-lying, palm covered island in a sea of green rice paddies. But it is not paradise found; it is paradise lost. And there is danger everywhere.

Life In The Bush

Living in the bush isn't so bad, at least not here. We are blessed with several weeks of sunshine, and except for a very brief shower or two thrown in, we are dry most of time. This of course makes life much easier, especially during the night; we can sleep and stay dry. Most of us sleep on the ground, but a few hang hammocks between the "tracks" and sleep that way. To me, it's a stupid move. You only have to see an artillery shell, a mortar round, or even a grenade explode once and you understand. When that shell explodes by ground contact, the metal shrapnel is often upward and outward. You want to be as low as possible on the ground or even under it. When the powder, the dry chemicals inside the shell, begins to burn, it is at an incredible speed and ferocity. Gases are the by-product of this combustion, but at such pressure that the steel metal jacket, i.e., the metal casing of the shell, is almost instantaneously blown apart. It is when this concussion wave hits you or the steel shrapnel slices into you that the damage is done. And even if the shrapnel were to gently fall upon you, it is red hot and would severely burn you. Sleeping in a hammock is for dumbasses. But for them, maybe it's a death wish. Not to worry, death is a commodity that is in plentiful supply.

As for me, I have gathered some straw from the village edge and lay my poncho liner on that; it feels luxurious and, on some nights, I sleep like a baby. I say "some nights," as sleeping and the amount and intensity of the VC's nighttime activities are in a direct correlation.

The food is mostly C-rations (the Army's official description is: rations, canned), some of which, to a man, we find intolerable. The two least favorite of all are the ham and lima beans, and the ham and eggs in a can. The ham and lima beans take first prize, though the ham and eggs does earn a rather commendable second place. This *ration* can only be described as evil, inedible, and unfit for human consumption. How did the Army come up with these combinations? The pork and beans are a universal favorite; however, the best meals, which we save for the evening, are these relatively new freeze-dried dehydrated meals in a plastic pouch. Simply open and add warm water for a hot meal. They are greatly preferred over the C-rations and come in several flavors, although we seem to have mostly chicken or beef. We take water from our "water buffalo" then heat the water in a small aluminum pot.

To heat the water, we carefully take apart Claymore mines, our "field cook stove," to remove the C-4 explosive, which is then broken into small pieces. We light the C-4 with a match or lighter, so it burns steadily in the open rather than lethally exploding when enclosed inside a mine. While this may seem a waste of resources, there really aren't any alternatives. There are no "cooks" assigned with us, and we have neither generator nor refrigeration. It is stinking hot, so by necessity, we travel very light. It is Spartan; it is basic, lean, and mean. But we are not without some sense of luxury. For dessert there are crackers with grape jelly and peanut butter. I sometimes take the cocoa mix and add heated water for an evening beverage. Living the high life baby, living the high life.

From my first full day on in the bush, we arise almost as a group. It's probably the fullness of the sunlight awakening us at about the same moment. Individually we make ourselves some kind of breakfast, most often some canned fruit or maybe canned pork and beans and maybe some coffee; I can't honestly remember. That done, we do a little housekeeping around the encampment. We burn up any debris and adjust any sagging sandbags around a couple of earth-bound machine-gun emplacements. Or, on occasion, we fill and stack new sandbags, as they don't seem to last long in the tropical sun. I do more than my fair share of the sandbag filling, much to the relief of my new comrades in arms. They are relieved and somewhat grateful that I unhesitatingly pitch in; it builds trust quickly that I am willing to pull my own weight. Everyone in every unit always wonders if the F'ing New Guy is going to be a help or a burden. It only takes a day or two and my "newness" fades away; I quickly become one of them.

We don't do a whole lot during the day. There is a radio watch, 24 hours a day, which we all take turns with, but beyond that there is little to do. A few of us pen a brief letter or two, and there is often someone playing a radio. There is only one radio station to listen to, the Armed Forces Vietnam Network playing the top forty. Mostly we just try to find some shade and stay out of the broiling and brutally intense tropical sun. Of course, the evenings and the near-unending nights are a whole other story. The action is invariably and almost exclusively during the night hours; the days, thank god, are the respite from the long nights. It's Charlie's big back yard; he works the nights; darkness is his friend and cover. He does not dare be seen in the open daylight, where an air strike, or much more likely an artillery barrage from a not-too-distant firebase, would be called in upon him. No, he's no fool.

Our one and only break from this daytime routine is the bath. Yes, the bath. At least every other day, but often every single day, we stroll into that tiny hamlet at the edge of the coconut grove for a bath. I would not delude you into thinking that we are a particularly hygienic group. It is more the offensive reading of our own collective "funk" meter that determines the frequency; simply, how bad do we stink? If you need to take a crap, you grab some toilet paper and squat behind some nearby bushes with your trusty black plastic Mattel Toy (M-16) by your side and hopefully have an uninterrupted, peaceful, and pleasant shit. There is, of course, no bidet. We live, work and sleep in our clothes in the tropics. With daytime temperatures usually approaching 100°F, it doesn't take long for us to stink.

Of course, one does not simply stroll into that hamlet for a bath. There are preparations, rituals, and protocols that are absolutely mandatory and faithfully observed. We cannot all go together at once. Some of us are needed to keep our encampment secure, so we usually go in two or three small groups, maybe four or five at a time. After that is sorted out, everyone who is going, and I mean everyone, loads up with ammunition. We take an ammo box from inside one of the tracks and fill up our "clips." The "clip" is actually a twenty-round "magazine," that being an inexpensive, spring-loaded, small black metal box slightly longer than a deck of playing cards. Back at Uplift, the occasional lifer would complain that it was a magazine, not a clip, as the clip is a small metal strip that holds the M-16 rounds at their brass base and is used to load the magazine. But none of us ever says, "Oh, my magazine is empty." We call it a "clip" and that is that. There is a bigger, 30-round magazine that is curved like a "banana," which we of course call a "banana clip;" it just sounds cooler to us.

The far more common size clip holds just 20 rounds, but they are known to jam when full; the last thing you want. So, you play the odds in your favor. I never put more than 18 into a clip. The "banana clip" is not widely available, so a few guys join two clips back-to-back with electrical tape so as to have a quasi-40 round capacity clip. The next step is to take an olive-green narrow cloth apron, which contains 6 pockets that accepts one clip each. This "apron" can be tied around your waist or slung over your shoulder. And then for good measure, you "always" put a full clip into your M-16. A few of us stick a hand grenade into a pocket, just for good luck. One last final detail about your M-16: I always keep a round in the chamber, but with the safety on, as does most everyone else. The safety is just a small pivoting lever right by the trigger grip. It is effortlessly and quickly moved by your thumb as you keep your finger on the trigger and squeeze. Otherwise, you have to take your hand off the trigger, pull the spring-loaded bolt back, which allows a round to be removed from the spring loaded "clip" (magazine). When the bolt is released, the round is pushed into the chamber. Then you put your hand back on the trigger. It takes no more than a couple of seconds to do this, but in that moment when you need to fire that weapon, a couple of seconds can be a lifetime. We are too scared to waste even that brief amount of time.

The final step is to open up a box or two of C-rations and pick out those dreaded stinking ham and lima bean concoctions. This was our "currency" with which we paid for our baths.

The Bath

We do not rush into the hamlet, but rather we slowly and calmly walk over and enter the hamlet. It is quite close by, only a couple of minutes away. We enter smiling and gently waving our cans of C-rations. We don't wish to panic anyone, lest somebody does something stupid that sets off an irreversible chain reaction. The village inhabitants smile back a little nervously--why wouldn't they, with a group of GI's walking in and each carrying an automatic weapon? But they quickly relax when we stop at the hamlet's one "public" well and by hand signals and gestures convey that we wish to have the kids throw buckets of well water upon us in exchange for a C-ration. I strip naked with two other guys in the center of the village, and we each cheerfully hand over a can of those God-awful ham and lima beans. We smile, or more likely smirk, as we hand over what we so poetically refer to as "Ham N'Mother fuckers" or "Ham N'Chokers." We think this quite the joke and chuckle out loud, the kids (and the villagers) having no idea what the lettering on those cans says, but they will soon find out.

The kids douse us with a couple of buckets of water that they pull from a simple shallow hole in the ground, the well having no stone or brickwork around it. We lather up with tiny bars of Ivory soap and then are doused again to rinse clean. The kids have a ball doing this, thinking this to be much fun, and they squeal and laugh in delight. They seem quite amazed by our penis size and our pubic hair, they themselves being hairless south of the border. I dry off and then put the same stinking clothes back on; as we all do. We now stand guard as the two other guys get their bath. Once finished with our baths, we wave goodbye and walk back the one or two hundred yards to our encampment.

We repeat this the next day, and it goes well. We skip the following day but then go back in the afternoon of the fourth day. It does not go so smoothly this time. As we hand over our can of ham and lima beans, the young boy of perhaps eight or nine brings his to a village elder, presumably his father or uncle. The elder looks carefully at the lettering on the can and though he cannot speak or read English, he does recognize that this is the same god-awful c-ration that we had given to the villagers twice before. He shakes his head and speaks probably one of the few English words he knows, a heavily accented "Nah, Naah" which we instantly recognize as NO! We of course protest. He won't back down and in fact, holding up two fingers, now demands double the price of the bath. We protest for the sake of protesting, but not a single one of us would eat the canned, vile red and green concoction, so we moan a bit and then hand over two cans. We finish our baths but leave a little pissed off, the friendly villagers not quite so friendly, now driving a slightly harder bargain. I'm just glad we are getting rid of the stuff.

This slight turn of events is the main topic of discussion that evening as we dine on "fresh" freeze-dried-dehydrated chicken stew, pouched. We cook it slowly over an open fire of small pieces of C-4 explosive carefully removed from a freshly opened Claymore Mine. Yeah, just finger-licking good. We feel we have been outsmarted by these ungrateful villagers who hold an unfair monopoly of shallow well water, which none of us would drink even with a gun pointed to our heads. Still, there must be something we can do to counter this. Somebody suggests that we trade off the canned eggs and ham. I drag out a couple of open boxes of C-rations. I point out that all the good stuff has already been eaten, and we have traded away, under unfair trading practices, all of the bad stuff except for the canned eggs and ham. It is arguably as bad as the canned ham and lima beans. I ask the rhetorical question of my comrades-in-arms: Is anyone going to eat this ever? I get a chorus of No's and shouts of "Trade it, Trade it." We are back in business.

The next day is a sweltering steam bath, and in midafternoon we return to the hamlet for our bath. We are not so warmly greeted, but we immediately show our new C-rations. We point out the different lettering on the cans' sides, telling them, "No. 1, No. 1." They don't seem convinced, and one of the elders points out that lettering for Ham (in Ham and Eggs) is the same as the Ham in Ham and Lima Beans. We insist it is No. 1. They accept the deal but do so suspiciously. We bathe and then quickly spilt.

We skip the next day, but on the following day (and we are really stinking), we return to the hamlet again, bringing only the canned eggs and ham. They are not pleased to see us. They know we have deliberately tricked them. They speak in angry tones, and after much gesturing, we understand they have fed the C-rations to their pigs. (Honestly, I think, poor pigs.) Since we insist on bartering with "pig food," the price of the bath is now three C-rations. We protest, and a couple of my comrades shout, "Fucking Number Ten," a serious curse and insult. In the end, we pay the extortionate price. Hell, it's not like it's coming out of our pockets; we just don't like getting screwed. I guess they don't like that either. It has taken less than a week, and we have worn out their welcoming hospitality.

The Second Night

The first night is remarkably quiet and peaceful, and I sleep on the ground upon my straw bed as baby would in a bassinet. I awaken well rested, relaxed, and at ease. Being in the boondocks in many ways is a much easier time than dealing with the day-to-day drudgery of LZ Uplift. Very simply, it is very much "less Army;" there's a lot less Army crap from the bullying desperate lifers. The professional Sergeants (NCO's) are always easily recognized; they just stand out as poised leaders. But there are just not enough of them. The rest of the Non-Commissioned Officers, the NCO's, are under-educated and incapable leaders, so they become bullies. Hence, they are universally despised and hated. They cling and hang on for dear life to the Army, as they can do nothing else with their lives. They stay in for life, ever so slowly being promoted, waiting for someone in front of them to retire or die so that they might move up. Of course, the Army, the Pentagon, the Defense Department, Robert McNamara, and LBJ consider this to be some cheap bargain by which to wage war. Wage war on the cheap? What a stupid concept.

But there are no lifer bullies in our platoon here in the boonies, not a single one, and that is why I find it so much easier. It's mostly Spec. 4's like me and some PFC's, one young Sergeant and one Lieutenant. So, for the most part, we are having an easy time of it, the days are sunny and pleasant, and though blazingly hot, they are dry. In the evening, as the sun sets, and as the heat dissipates, the palms and coconut trees seem to look greener. The twilight is tranquil, and as the dusk settles in, the view of this tiny hamlet clinging to the slightly higher ground by its coconut grove is postcard picture perfect. All is right with the world in the daytime ... the nights, however, are an entirely different world.

The trouble starts on the second night, and it begins with the sound of a single gunshot. The sound is not loud, as it comes from some distance away. It has a sharp, dry crack to it, undoubtedly small arms, and almost certainly rifle fire. It is about 10:00 PM, the sun is long gone, we are about to bed down, but now everyone stops short of whatever they are doing and strains to listen for what will come next. Our platoon sits at the very southwest edge of the hamlet. Just to our east lies the bottom edge of the coconut grove, the hamlet is directly and immediately north of the grove. Just past the coconut grove to the southeast sits a platoon of South Vietnamese soldiers, better known as ARVNs (Army of the Republic of Vietnam).

The sound of the rifle shot comes from the southeast, the ARVN's side of the perimeter, but it's not them. The rifle shot comes from well beyond the perimeter. It's Charlie, and from the darkness well past the perimeter, he shoots in at us. Although this is a joint US – ARVN operation, we maintain separate camps, albeit close to each other. Unless we are patrolling together, we barely interact during the day. We are separated by less than two hundred yards or so, with only a partial and rather limited view of each other, but in the darkness neither one of us would dare try to walk over to the other. In the darkness it's a no man's land, and either group would shoot first and ask questions later.

We wait for ten minutes and hear nothing. But as soon as someone says, "He's gone," there are three quick cracks of rifle fire again coming from the south, slightly closer in now and nearer toward our side of the perimeter. The ARVNs open up with a short burst of machine gun fire. We watch the red tracer rounds race outward in a slight arc toward the low horizon. There is no return fire coming back at us. We stand with our M-16's aimed in the general direction that the sound of the rifle shots came from, but we don't shoot. Our firing angle would be a little too close to the ARVN's flank, and nothing is worse than getting hit by friendly fire.

A few minutes pass, when one of the ARVN's pops a hand flare off to the southeast. It shoots skyward, and then pops open burning brightly, if briefly, as it floats to the ground on its tiny parachute. We see nothing, but I suspect it illuminates us as well. A half hour passes, then a couple of dry cracks of rifle fire, but now directly to the east of the ARVN position. Charlie sticks to the east and southeast side of the perimeter, the ARVN side, which has better cover and he knows to be the weaker side. This goes on for another hour until finally Charlie quits for the night. It is harassing, and we get no sleep for several hours, but no damage done. Still, I am sure Charlie is pleased.

From this night on, we are probed and sniped at every night. The probing and the sniper fire generally come from the south-southeast; the topography is the main reason. This tiny hamlet and its coconut grove that we occupy are surrounded by dry rice paddies and grasslands on all sides, but the dense wood line is quite close to the south. The rice paddies are dry, flat, and low except for the slightly elevated earthen berms that divide and form the maze of paddies. The berms offer some measure of protection. But to the south and southeast, there is just a narrow stretch of grazing grassland probably less than two hundred yards wide and then a wood line of thick brush and trees. It is not jungle, but it is thick, lush, and green, and it provides excellent cover, especially if Charlie shoots a few rounds in at us and then moves left or right to shoot a few more. I doubt you could see anybody in that thick green maze of brush and trees in the daylight; you definitely wouldn't see anybody in the pitch black of night.

And so it goes, night after night, an Asian version of a Mexican standoff. Neither side gets too close, but everybody hopes the other will make some mistake.

Each night the intensity and the duration of Charlie's probing and sniping picks up. In the dark of night, he can't really see us in any kind of individual way, just the general location of our position. But I must assume he takes much satisfaction in harassing us for half the night, and he certainly must hope that a stray round or two will cause casualties.

Each day the inhabitants of the hamlet become less friendly. It's not just the crappy C-rations we try to con them with for our baths; they just want us to go and leave them alone. We are not at all certain which way their sympathies lie, with their government or with the Viet Cong? But I doubt it's with the hopelessly corrupt South Vietnamese Government. I don't think they support the VC either, except at the point of a gun. The poor peasants of the countryside are on the bottom rung, and neither side is going to do much to change that. To them it may as well be 20,000 BC. The wealthiest peasant might own two water buffalo, which he uses to plow his rice paddies. He lives in a grass and thatch hooch and sleeps on a grass mat. Saigon is some very far-off place that doesn't know he even exists. The countryside may as well be called Charlie Town. The government has a tenuous hold during the day only; at night it is Charlie's town.

The Second Week

By the beginning of our second week, each and every night now has a seemingly unending scheduled period of several hours' duration of sometimes fierce exchanges of fire. Neither we nor the ARVNs suffer a single casualty. We cannot be certain, but we don't think Charlie has suffered either, as he does not seem at all discouraged, given his perfect attendance at the nightly shootout. He does not let up.

That night's main event starts at the usual time of about 10:00 PM, but for some reason seems only halfhearted and is over well before midnight. Just a few pot-shots of rifle fire here and there, to which we return double and then some. By comparison, the night before, the exchange had gone on nearly to dawn. Still, we find it somewhat difficult to sleep, as we keep waiting for things to pick up. We finally drift off and, in the morning, we awake to find heavy clouds, and before too long it begins to rain. The rain is light; it's just off and on showers that last most of the morning. We build makeshift tents out of ponchos we stretch from the sides of the tracks and just hang out underneath them trying to stay dry. The showers bring the bugs out, which we swat at. It's a miserable day.

By midafternoon, the skies brighten and the sun pops through, turning everything steamy, but I console myself by thinking that at least we will have a dry night for sleeping and my straw bed will be dried out by then. An hour or two later, when I go to check on the state of my bed, I find that it is gone. The villagers have come and raked up the hay and taken it back to their hooches. I wonder whether they do not wish to appear to the VC to have provided aid and comfort to the enemy (us). In any case, I am actually more offended than angry, the welcome mat having literally been abruptly pulled out from under me. I accept the situation for what it is, which ain't fair, but tell me something new. I still have my poncho liner, and I just sleep on the ground that night after another of Charlie's rather brief and lackluster performances. Though the ground is harder, I sleep comfortably anyway. I guess you can get used to anything.

Pay Day

The next day is cloudy, but at least it doesn't rain, and it is actually just a bit cooler. But the days, and for that matter the nights, are starting to run together now, and LZ Uplift seems a hundred years ago. I guess I have started to become a boonie rat now.

In the very early afternoon, a Huey circles low and slowly overhead. We have not called for one to come, and we are not expecting anyone, so we are clueless as to why it's come. We cannot raise the Huey with our radio, as we don't have his frequency. He hovers overhead and then drops a purple smoke canister to the ground, I guess to check wind direction. But there is no wind, so he lands close to our tracks. A Captain jumps out, and as he walks towards us, I recognize him as my battery commander, Captain Good. He greets me almost laughing, as I am shocked by his appearance here. I suspect he is somewhat shocked by my personal appearance too.

He hands me some mail and then tells me it is July 31st, payday. The Army pays you on the last day of the month, though none of my comrades get paid this day. They must have made some alternate arrangement for their pay, but I have not; in fact, I don't even know the date. As to my actual pay, it's almost $6 a day, plus $2 a day for combat. Of course, there's no time off, unless you count sleeping on the ground; but I do love the food. I tell the Captain to hold my pay, even though I have no money at all on me; it is of no use out here. We shake hands; he jumps back into the Huey and departs. I think he had found an excuse to take a chopper ride and did so. I return to my comrades who joke about my personal mail delivery service, and I laugh with them.

The afternoon is uneventful; we don't bother with the bath that day, as it seems pointless to put the same dirty clothes back on. We have our evening meal, the good stuff, the freeze-dried chicken stew in a sealed pouch again. We play some cards in the gathering darkness, mostly passing the time until the highly probable, predictable nightly shootout begins.

The Long Night

The shooting starts around 11:00 PM, a little later than usual, but as it does, we quickly realize this is not just three or four guys taking a few pot shots to harass us. This is a lot of small arms fire. In the pitch black, you can't see anyone shooting at you, so you can't count the number of shooters. But over time, you gain a sense of the number of shooters by sound. It's not terribly accurate, but you quickly learn the difference between three shooters and a dozen. And tonight, this sounds like at least several dozen, and they are well spread out. This time it is not just on the ARVN's side of the perimeter.

A day or two earlier we had moved a couple of tracks just a bit closer to the ARVN's side to better support them, though it is not so necessary tonight. We open up with machine gun fire mounted on the top of the track. Every fifth round is a tracer, the red arcs of their flight guiding the gunner as he sweeps across the inside of the wood line. The downside of tracer rounds is that they give away your firing position; Charlie gets to see exactly where you are. The hand-held flares won't quite reach Charlie's position. To counter that, we use the grenade launcher, "Thumper," to shoot parachute flares over Charlie's head to illuminate him. It goes off with a significant kick and a loud "thump." The round shoots skyward, where it "pops," ignites, and slowly floats down, suspended by its parachute. But we still cannot spot any Charlies.

This exchange of fire is fierce for some time, but a light breeze starts to drift the flares back towards us over our heads. We stop shooting the flares, as we do not wish to illuminate ourselves. So, I am told to call in to request artillery illumination, which can put bigger, longer lasting flares further in over Charlie's head. I call Uplift for illumination just to our south; they already have the co-ordinates. They plot a firing angle and charge size and then contact an artillery battery about five miles north of us. It only takes two or three minutes and we hear the rounds "pop" open; these flares ignite much higher and burn much brighter. It's not daylight, but it is bright. The small arms fire momentarily stops on both sides; we stare intently, looking for some kind of movement, but Charlie doesn't flinch.

As one flare is just beginning to lose its intensity, another round arrives over Charlie's head; it "pops," and another flare ignites and slowly floats downward. The timing, long since practiced, is perfectly executed. It's an eerie sight, a pitch-black night in the bush, broken by the overhead sound of a loud "pop" followed immediately by the ignition of the flare, which burns so brightly that one now sees not just the shadows but the actual differences between the shades of "green" of the palms and coconut trees, brush and grasslands. As the "older" flares die out, their off-white parachutes are silhouetted against the night sky by the "newer" flares; to call it surreal is an understatement. However, we still cannot detect any movement of Charlie.

As I watch the perfectly timed illumination flares pop open one after another, I wonder if it is too perfectly timed, just too regular, too expected. I call back to Uplift and request to have the timing of the flares slowed down by about 20 seconds. A calm voice replies that the timing should be perfect; I reply that it is, but maybe we can catch Charlie off guard in between the flares. He understands immediately. "Yeah, good idea." It takes about a minute and half for the adjustment, then as the last flares burn out, there's a pause of pitch black, then a flare "pops' open and it's almost daylight again. We try this for several minutes but cannot catch Charlie off guard; he is not easily fooled.

We call off the flares but ask the battery to stand by. Several minutes pass. and the firing starts up again, but as soon as it starts, we request illumination rounds, same co-ordinates. They arrive in less than a minute, and now finally some Charlies are very briefly spotted running along the tops of the berms of the rice paddies closest to us. In fact, we see 40 or more Charlies standing on the tops of paddy berms firing in at us. There are only 25 of us. One can easily do the math; we are outnumbered nearly two to one. The firing on both sides intensifies instantly.

Charlie loves a knife fight. The VC have no air force, they have no helicopters, they have no tanks, and they have no howitzers. Charlie cannot fight from a distance without these kinds of weapons, so he gets in close. If he gets in close enough, you will be most resistant to call in a suicidal airstrike or an artillery bombardment on your own position. Charlie always plays his best card, his ace card: "Get in close." Charlie, now spotted, immediately drops out of sight, and he knows what's coming. Now that we have a definite target, we waste no time, and we request a few rounds of "HE" (high explosive), same coordinates. But there are some anxious moments caused by some delay. I inquire about the delay, and I am told that FDC is attempting to contact the very nearby ARVN unit. I explain that the ARVNs are with us and under fire from Charlie as well. That issue is now cleared up, and in just half a minute, I get a response on the radio of "Shot," meaning, "On the way." From the same unseen firebase about five miles away, the cannoneers fire their 105 howitzers, sending four rounds of HE towards us.

In many ways I greatly respect the "cannoneers." The "gun bunnies," or "cannon-cockers" as they were affectionately called, have in my opinion the worst possible job. I know some would disagree, but most would agree it is lousy duty. There are four to six howitzers in a battery that is often placed in a small encampment called a firebase that can be in the middle of nowhere. Anyone needing support within the firing radius of about 7 miles is immediately aided, be it by illumination, smoke, or high explosive. The "cannoneers" respond day or night, scalding heat or monsoon rain, hour upon hour if need be. The 30 pound-plus projectiles are hand loaded into that howitzer; it is physically tough work that can last hours at a time. Even if you are off shift, you aren't going to get much sleep with the guns going off. Many of these guys go deaf after a year of this. Though the battery can defend itself, they are sometimes placed in isolated locations. If need be, the howitzers can shoot shrapnel rounds at very close- to point-blank range. But if Charlie is that close, things are looking grim, and more than a few of these firebases have been overrun. I was glad I was not on the guns.

As to those thirty-plus-pound projectiles coming our way, they exit the muzzle of the howitzer at a velocity of 1600 feet per second, the HE round covering that five-mile distance in about 20 seconds. You don't want to be under this. Though a 105 round is big enough that you might see it on a bright clear day, one would never see it passing by in the darkness. The rounds announce their arrival as they explode just above the ground to spread their lethal shrapnel and cause as much bodily injury as possible. They explode about one or two hundred yards out from us, slightly close, but safe enough. Anything much under 100 yards is beginning to get close.

All firing stops and everything is now ghostly quiet. We watch and listen but see and hear nothing; Charlie has left the building.

Neither the ARVNs nor we suffer a single casualty. But I wonder to myself what it must it be like for the villagers living in this tiny hamlet. Of course, we never ask them. But some nights must seem hellish to them, especially given the fact they have no control over any of this. They didn't go to war; the war came to them. I am certain that they wish we would just go away, as just our presence alone endangers them. We are conscious of the hamlet and its inhabitants, but only as a very distant second thought.

The next morning the ARVNs sweep through the nearby wood line, but they find nothing. It appears Charlie got away clean.

Afternoon Interlude

Our Lieutenant leaves at mid-morning on a chopper for some meeting with headquarters. He returns in the early afternoon and brings with him some supplies and clean clothes for us. They are not our personal uniforms per se; they are used but freshly laundered uniforms from a variety of different outfits, judging by various insignias sewed onto the arms at the shoulders. You simply go through them till you find something that fits. I wonder if the guy who wore this is dead, or did he finish his tour and go home? Now with fresh clothes and more C's, we head to the hamlet for baths. We even bring some good stuff like chicken noodle soup. I open my can up with a p-38 (a tiny can opener) to show the kids and elders; they spot the noodles and smile. We temporarily mend fences, if only for the day.

We return to our encampment, and every one of us is in a good mood now. We are freshly bathed, and we are wearing clothes that don't stink. Though we are not at all fond of C-rations, there are now many small cans of peaches or pears among them, and these are always welcome. Everyone has gotten their mail that was brought in on that re-supply chopper, which they now read. I do not receive any, but I was not expecting any, as my old outfit still holds my mail. It is a cloudless sunny day and exceptionally hot, yet the humidity seems a bit lower and there is a slight breeze as the afternoon wears on. It is, in so many ways, a very pleasant afternoon in the bush. As my comrades-in-arms, my fellow boonie rats, sit or lie in the shade, they read their letters from home and snack on tiny tins of peaches. They eat with their fingers, and though the tins are at the ambient temperature of 98°F, the peaches are nonetheless so delicious. Life is, at least momentarily, very good indeed.

Though they have long since readily accepted me, I have no mail to read and so I feel a bit like the odd man out. So, on this hot afternoon, with little to do, I walk by myself, alone, back into that hamlet. It is just about 4:00 PM.

Of course, I string the olive drab cloth bandolier holding six full clips over my shoulder and bring along my constant companion, my M-16. Collectively, we give the M-16 many nicknames, "little black death," "widow maker," and "Mattel Toy" among others. It is not very long and is rather light, weighing only about 8 pounds. Being

the couple by the ancient temple

made of aircraft grade aluminum and black plastic, it very much resembles a Mattel toy gun.

The little village is still and quiet this hot late afternoon, its inhabitants waiting for the heat to dissipate. I do not carry my weapon in my hands; I sling the M-16 on my right shoulder, this being a much less threatening position to any inhabitant of the village. I walk past the well where we bathe, through the village until I near the back side of it. I don't dare venture out past it, where the rice paddies begin. I keep back a bit and stay in the shade of the tall palm trees. I sit on the remains of what seems to be a very ancient stone- and masonry-like foundation that sits about two feet above the ground. I suspect that this tiny village was once more substantial, for just to my left, some thirty feet away and built of the same material, are stone-like masonry steps.

The steps are quite broad, being very generous in their depth, and are at least 30 feet in length. Their pitch is shallow, and they rise softly to a large masonry-stone platform only a few feet above the jungle floor. There are no sides or walls, but I see two or three short, small sections of columns that perhaps may once have supported a roof. But these columns rise no more than one or two feet, if that, and their tops are jagged as if broken uncleanly. The place looks a thousand years old. This ancient remnant sits easily on the most prominent place of this village; I wonder if this was once the floor of an ancient temple. If nothing else, it is well shaded, as the palm trees lean over the open space above its floor to freely grab the sunlight. And this spot, being about eight feet above the very nearby rice paddies, not only offers a great view but also catches what breeze may move across them. What better place to sit on a hot day?

But now, on the very top step sits a rather elderly couple. They wear the "black pajamas" so common among the peasants of the countryside. They sit serenely together looking out across the rice paddies, neither speaking a word to the other. But their body positions, their body language, is that of a couple sitting next to each other as if they are in love. And I think, good for them.

Though I sit silently and take in the same view of near and distant rice paddies, I remain further back from them. I do not wish to crowd them with my presence, so I keep back a respectful distance. I sense a unique moment, that by sheer luck of timing and place, I am somehow privileged to participate in. I know my weapon violates this moment of time and place, but I would not dare to be without it. I have no sense of any immediate danger, but I know full well I am in the jungle, their jungle, and it can change in an instant. In the distance, to the northeast toward the ocean, I see a single white crane. He is many hundreds of yards away. I watch the crane as he takes a few ungainly steps in a distant paddy, his brilliant white feathers standing out sharply from the dried yellow straw of the previous rice harvest. There must be some water in the paddy as he then bends and reaches with his long neck and beak to gather something to eat. As ungracefully as he might walk, he nevertheless carries himself with great elegance.

A long moment passes, and I watch as the elderly man slowly and silently turns his head to face me and with what seems to be incredible grace, he gently nods his head in recognition of my presence. I study his face; he seems both ancient and young. I nod quietly in return. He studies me for the longest moment and then gives me the most peaceful of looks. He nods again but ever so slightly and then slowly turns away to look upon the paddies once more.

When I look back upon this, I see the clues, but then and there I do not. I wish I could have read them better, to see what might be coming; but maybe you're not supposed to know. As I look back on this moment from five decades later, it is my realization that he was reading my future and was telling me: "You will be all right."

I sit calmly, placidly in the shade of the tall palms looking out over rice paddies and I drift far away. I daydream of living here; I travel no distance but I feel I have time traveled back a thousand years without ever moving an inch. It seems familiar, yet ancient. What has it been like over the centuries? Did I have water buffalos to pull my plow through the rice paddies? Did I have a wife and children? Forty minutes go by and then, perhaps because the heat is slowly lifting, I drift back to the present. It startles me more than just a bit to realize that, as I was daydreaming, the elderly couple has gone. Though their absence causes me no urgent alarm, I am uneasy, for I have overstayed. I know I must get back to the tracks. Why tempt fate? I stand and with purpose in my step, I briskly walk back through the hamlet to my company. I am safe.

It is now just before 5:00 PM; my comrades-in-arms are just stirring. They begin to stand and we now begin to joke about the uniforms we wear, whose nametags tell of other people we know nothing about. "Oh, I knew that guy; he went on R&R to Hong Kong and never came back. Better be careful because he's AWOL." Or, "That guy caught the "black clap," he went to that special hospital in Japan, but he's never going home." We joke, we laugh, and we are good. The sun gets lower in the sky, there is at least another hour of sunlight, but it has cooled off a bit. It is a most pleasant evening. It is now about a quarter to six.

Charlie's In The Schoolhouse

It all changes in the blink of an eye. We hear heavy machine gun fire very close in to our left, the southeast. Almost immediately, an ARVN soldier runs from their side of the perimeter shouting at the top of his lungs a very heavily accented "VC!" "VC!" For the briefest moment we think his side is being hit, but as he is shouting, he points repeatedly to our southwest. We look in the direction he points to and now follow the tracer rounds of the machine gun fire. It fires not in at us, but out toward another tiny hamlet less than a third of a mile to our south-southwest. We watch as three Charlies, each with an automatic weapon, run across a clearing and then duck into a small single-room schoolhouse. This daylight appearance of Charlie so close by is shockingly brazen. We have foolishly relaxed far too much, the ARVNs, fortunately are doing a better job of protecting our collective butts. We move slightly to our right just past the tracks, to watch this play out.

The ARVN machine gun stops as the three Charlie runs into that small schoolhouse. The building is built of poor-quality masonry, I am sure. It has the usual brown thatch roof, but the walls are painted a pleasing off-white. It is easily the most prominent building in that hamlet.

And we wait; but it is not long at all. If I were Charlie, I think I would wait for the dusk, which is coming shortly. But perhaps fearing we might come into that hamlet before that happens, he doesn't want to be trapped in the schoolhouse. So, before we can get ready to go, the Charlies run out the front door. We stop our preparations and now watch three guys, dressed in black pajamas, run toward the east in a slight zigzag to a thick clump of brush and bushes, approximately halfway between the schoolhouse and the deep green maze of the wood line. They run with their rifles in one hand, ammo pouches tied to their waists, and as they do so, the ARVN machine gun opens up, sending a hail of bullets toward them. We watch the tracer rounds; they are off the mark, but it is difficult to hit a moving target at this distance. All three Charlies safely reach the fat clump of bushes and disappear into them. The ARVN machine gunner stops firing, but then sends a repeated short burst of just a few rounds towards that clump of brush. He's good; he keeps the pressure on.

And Buddha Sends His Angels To Sing

This whole scene, start to finish, from its opening as the Charlies duck into that tiny white schoolhouse of that distant hamlet, to its closing as I fall, hitting hard upon the ground, plays itself out in probably just six or seven minutes. Maybe it's not even that long, but there are moments when time seems to crawl to a stop. It holds there for the briefest instant, a nanosecond, then with excruciating slowness picks up speed, then jumping to light speed in the next instant.

I play the tape of this event over and over again in my mind, and I even dream of it time and time again. And as I play it, I wonder what it was like for the three Charlies as they ducked into that tiny white schoolhouse. I suspect that at least one of them would say, "Oh we're in deep shit now." I wonder what they spoke of, who decided who would run first from the school toward that fat clump of bushes. I wonder what they spoke of when all three made it to that point.

We stand as a group-- I am center left-- as we stare transfixed, looking southwest upon the fat clump of bushes now about a quarter of a mile away. We don't wait long. It seems like only a minute, and now two of the Charlies jump from the clump and run zigzagging to the east seeking the protection of the deep green maze. It seems such a callous understatement to say they run as if their lives depend on it, but in this awful twilight reality, their lives are in great jeopardy. The machine gun starts up immediately. It is joined now by another M-60; they shoot heavy rounds, a few of which we see as tiny puffs of dust as they impact the earth. The second Charlie shoots a couple of rounds over his shoulder as he runs. But it's just for effect, as he is wild; no aim is taken, the shots far, far off the mark. I imagine that Charlie sees that wood line as being a mile away; the reality is that it is a little more than a hundred and fifty yards from the fat clump. Still, quite literally under the gun, it's a very long 150 yards. You *almost* want to root for them. Shockingly, most remarkably, they both make it. They simply vanish into the deep green maze with not even the slightest quivering of a palm.

We watch speechlessly and now glance quickly at each other, shaking our heads slightly with half grins of amazement and disbelief. But we all know what's coming next. May some God of any faith have mercy on that third and final Charlie. All eyes now concentrate their focus upon that fat green clump of brush and we wait. It grows eerily silent; it is a death watch. Ten seconds, 15, 20, what goes through his mind? He knows what he has to do; he knows what's coming when he does. Thirty seconds, 40, his heart must be racing, 50 seconds, the adrenalin surging through his system, one minute, one minute 10 seconds, and he breaks from the fat green clump. By his second step, he is already running at full speed, but the machine gun had already started firing at his first. He runs very fast in a straight line directly toward the deep green maze. He must hope that his speed in a straight line will give him better odds through the hail of bullets than trying to zigzag his way across that open field. I think I would have run in a straight line as well.

We see the occasional tracer rounds, their red arcs just behind him to the west as he runs at full stride to the east. To say that we see the occasional tracer round grossly understates Charlie's predicament, as only every fifth round fired from the machine gun is a tracer. The amount of steel flying toward him through the air faster than the speed of sound is almost incomprehensible. How does he keep ahead of it? But he is young and lean and appears to be extremely fit, given the speed generated by his strong lower limbs. He never stumbles; each stride seems precisely planned and perfectly executed.

He almost gets halfway............ and then both Charlie and time stop at the same moment, as if hitting some invisible, impenetrable barrier. Time holds everything in its presence for a decorous long moment, but then starts to move once more, but now at an immeasurably slow pace that crawls along as if we are watching a movie a single frame at a time. We watch, open mouthed, when Charlie stops, thinking he has surely been hit. We watch the tracer rounds catch up with him and then go past him, as the gunner has moved ahead of him when he stopped. I want to take a breath, but I cannot. Charlie now turns to face us, and we are stunned when he raises his rifle to his right shoulder. He steadies his aim with his left hand clasping the barrel and with his right-hand squeezes off the first two rounds. He is so good, so very, very good. He doesn't waste any time, but he will not be rushed by the chaos around him. Charlie's discipline is extraordinary, and He goes for the kill.

He could have fired wildly with a burst or two on automatic, but that just wastes ammo, of which Charlie has little to waste. Every rifle jumps upward just a bit with the recoil of each shot, and when fired on automatic, your rifle will soon be facing skyward. No, fire no more than two or three rounds at a time and stay on target.

We stand somewhat spread out and with relatively good spacing between us; after all we're not that dumb. But from where the lone Charlie stands about 400 yards back, he must see a fairly-tight group of guys standing too temptingly close together and not even moving. Just aim for the middle of the group, even if the rounds drift a little to the left or right, so what, it's a nice fat target; you're bound to hit something. All it's going to take is some guts and discipline; and he has both. But unknown to me, as I am the tallest, he takes aim at me.

I hear the ARVN's machine gun start up again, but as close as it is to me, the sound seems surreally soft. I watch, in slow motion, as the tracer rounds go by Charlie on either side of him. The bullets seem to travel so slowly, I think I can make them out as they go by him. Charlie pauses for the most minuscule moment and then fires three more single shots, pauses another brief moment then fires two more single rounds. This scene is seared into the memory banks of my brain, and for the rest of my life I watch this over and over again.

But now time speeds back up, accelerating from a dead crawl to light speed, as if to make up for this interlude and set itself back in the correct position of its passage.

It is often said that you never hear the shot that hits you, and I think it must be true. The physics alone requires that you must yield to its logic. The muzzle velocity of the bullet as it leaves the rifle barrel is almost twice the speed of sound. Of course, the bullet immediately begins to slow down as it travels through air, with friction and gravity finally winning and pulling it to a stop on the earth. I suppose if far enough away, the sound would catch up with the slowing bullet, but not at this distance; we are too close. But we are just far enough back that there is some delay between the time we watch Charlie squeeze that trigger and his rounds arriving. And understand, the delay is but one or two seconds.

We have foolishly concluded that we are just outside the effective range of his rifle; we have foolishly concluded that he cannot be that good a marksman. Certainly, we have concluded that with all of the machine gun fire going his way, he could not have the guts to stop, let alone the discipline to so precisely fire off those rounds. But oh, does he ever take us to school.

I hear the first two bullets go by the left side of my face. They are only inches away; so close I could have easily touched them with my fingers. It is a soft, barely audible, high-pitched singing sound, as if sung by an angel. And Buddha's angel sings to me in a whisper, "You must get down."

I hurl myself, chest first, toward the ground to be as flat as possible upon the earth. As I begin to fall, I now hear to my right side another soft, barely perceptible, high pitch singing; Buddha's angel singing in a soft voice again, "You must get down." I will myself to fall faster than gravity will allow so as to get below the third and final volley. But I feel a sharp, painful, solid thump very high on my chest as I hit the ground. I lie still for the shortest moment then raise my head just a few inches to watch Charles the Third disappear into the palms of the thick green maze. And as I do, I bring my right hand to my upper chest and I feel the blood.

In the years since, I play this tape over and over. I dream of it repeatedly. And in my dreams, I see everything with such brilliant clarity. There is no haze or fog of war; the colors are clear, true and bright, the greens of the jungle are so vivid. I see Charlie standing in his black pajamas, the blackest of blacks, and their contrast with the green palms is striking. In my dream I begin to look closer in, and as I slowly zoom in, I clearly see the red tracer rounds pass on either side of him, but he seems unfazed. I look closer yet and I start to see his face. He is a young man; his skin is clear and the color of creamy coffee. I look closer still and I begin to recognize him. I see him squeeze the rounds off; he will not be rushed. I look even closer, and now more of his face is revealed to me. I see no hate or anger, nor is he cold-blooded; I see only his stoic purposeful determination. The dreams never vary; they always end exactly the same way. He lowers his rifle from his face and I am so deeply astonished, shocked and saddened ... I see me.

I know instinctively that I have not been shot; it cannot be so. I refuse to believe it. It doesn't hurt enough; there is not enough blood, though I cannot explain to myself the pain or the bleeding. My comrades-in-arms still lie flat on the ground, but now one or two begin to raise their heads. We slowly begin to stand, myself included, and as I do, I reach inside my shirt and pull bloodied dog tags out. I see the words "Buddhist" and "O POS" glisten with red blood. I grimace as I see this; I cannot understand; I am invincible. But as I look past them, toward the ground where I had fallen, there lies an answer I want. I convince myself that I had fallen hard upon a coconut husk; its dark brown stiff fiber had scratched me quite deeply at the top of my shirt, which is now bloodstained. But I look closer at my wound; it is elongated, as if a jagged piece of metal had torn the skin. I will not accept that a piece of steel did this; Charlie cannot touch me. We all slowly rise, some more slowly than others, but we all stand. No one has been hit, not even a scratch upon us, save me. A couple of guys gesture toward the red stain at the top of my shirt, but I wave them off. "It's nothing, I'm good." But as I look back on this event in my life from fifty years ago, I admit I was hit by a ricocheting round. Back then I do not allow myself to accept that fact; for I am 21 years old and I am invincible.

There is a collective yet delayed sigh of relief. We stand in shocked disbelief that no one took a round; we all know we have come a little too close. Someone says in a poignant yet understated manner that is shaped by awe and respect, "That Charlie is good." There's a long moment of silence, and then someone else starts laughing, which then quickly spreads until we are all laughing like this is the funniest thing ever to have happened to any of us. But we all know we are lucky as hell.

We make our evening meals; we joke and talk about this day and then bed down. Charlie leaves us alone this night. Maybe he figures he has been as lucky as hell as well. I catch the radio watch between 1:00AM and 2:00AM. It is uneventful, and I pass it off to the next guy. I wrap myself in my poncho liner and lie upon the ground of that dry rice paddy. I think about this day and those Charlies. They are brave beyond the pale. They never give up; we will never win this war. But I am tired; I gently rub my bruised and bloody chest and then sleep like a baby.

Go Get Charlie

The Lieutenant leaves again in mid-morning to go to HQ, and he returns in the early afternoon. The day has been uneventful, though we do keep a sharper eye out for Charlie. His brazen daylight visit and its brief, but far-too-close-for-comfort firefight are still very fresh in our minds. Shortly after his return, we are informed that HQ has ordered us to take the small village a few miles to our east. It is from this village that Charlie seems to come and go to with such ease after his nightly firefights with us. The village lies directly on the coast. The plan is that one unit will come down the coast from the north, another one down from the west. We are to go to the southwest, as if leaving the area, and then turn east to the coastline and go north up the beach to block Charlie's retreat. There is a marshy area behind the shoreline, so we must travel far enough south to avoid it before turning east to reach the coastline. We will then finally turn north to reach the village and close the "back door" on Charlie. We have unquestionably the longer distance to cover.

We are not asked for any input, and none is offered. I now wish I had had the sense to ask to see a map of this area, but I think I was still too new with this outfit for such a question. We simply shrug and start making preparations. Some of the ARVN's will stay behind to secure their encampment as well as ours, and some of the ARVN's will ride with us. The four tracks that will go naturally include the command track, the one I ride on. We do radio checks and double up on our ammo belts. One or two guys will carry a grenade launcher. It really doesn't take that long; we could have left in thirty minutes or less, but you don't want to have to do this in the darkness of the middle of the night. And the plan calls for us to leave in the early morning darkness.

An Ominous Sign

At around 2:00 PM that afternoon, someone goes to the water buffalo to retrieve water for an early dinner and discovers that the tank is bone dry. I don't know who was supposed to watch it, but they have really screwed things up. Things take a turn for the worse when we radio in for a chopper to bring water to us, but none are available at the moment. A "water buffalo," especially when full, is quite heavy and is beyond the safe lift capability of a Huey. This will require a heavy lift chopper, like a Chinook. These are far less common than Hueys, and because they are always in demand, reservations must be made and prioritized. But it's getting too late in the day. They would have to fly in to pick up the empty tank, take it to be filled, and then fly it back out to us. There is not going to be enough daylight left to do so. They will not fly into a "hot" LZ at night just to bring water in. Our mood turns sour; we rummage through the C-rations and find a pitiful few can of peaches or fruit cocktail; at least they are wet.

The evening slowly turns dark, and as it does, Charlie starts his harassment again, nothing too fierce, just some sniping in every now and then. It's probably just a few guys moving slowly left to right, in and out, right to left. Charlie stays safely back. He is not looking for a fire fight; he is simply quite content to harass us. It gets quiet for twenty minutes, then a couple of quick dry pops of AK-47 rifle fire. About fifteen minutes passes, then a few more dry pops from a different direction. It goes off and on all night. No one manages to get any sleep; I know I don't. Finally, around four AM, we slowly get up. We grab our 16's and our ammo pouches and put on our steel helmets. We also put on our flak jackets; we hate them. It's like wearing a heavy vest, much like an old-fashioned life jacket worn by sailors. Our abhorrence is due to their weight and bulkiness in this heat and humidity. It won't stop a bullet, but it will stop most flak, and that could save your life, so we wear them.

Night Journey

At just after 4:30 AM, we climb up onto the top of the tracks. And despite the very early hour, the air temperature has risen steadily over night; it doesn't seem possible but it's already hot. The diesels roar to life, and we leave the *relative* safety of our encampment by the coconut grove and head southwest across the dry fields and rice paddies. We are "going outside the wire," though in our case we have no wire between us and Charlie. But there is nothing subtle in our departure; I think every Charlie within five miles has heard us coming or going. The diesels are not silent, nor is the clanking of the treads, nor the squeals of the bearings they ride on. The world must have heard us leaving, but part of the plan is to move to the southwest, heading away from our actual destination before turning east back toward the coast, a faked retreat. In the end, I don't think we fool anyone.

I sit on top of the track on its right-hand side, about halfway back. On the left-hand side sit another column of guys; one or two more sit in the middle. Everyone rides up on top; it's just safer this way, but it is very crowded. Nobody dares ride inside; after all, a "track" is just a diesel-powered aluminum box with tread tracks instead of wheels. It resembles a small tank, but there is no gun turret; there is no steel armor; it's just an aluminum box. If the track hits a land mine, you don't want to be inside it. The only one inside is the driver who sits up about chest high through a hatch up front.

There are probably 10, 12 maybe 13 of us sitting atop this bucking noisy beast. The other rule of track riding, perhaps the more important one, is never to sit sideways with your legs dangling over the sides. No, it's not the fear of getting a leg caught in the tread track at all; it's the land mines again. If the treads run over a mine, the shrapnel, the fragmentations, will most likely cut your legs off. So, we sit on our haunches with our legs crossed underneath us; we hold onto the track with one hand as we cradle our M-16's with the other. It is uncomfortable just sitting that way, and it gets worse once we start moving. But it is marginally better than walking, and certainly faster.

We travel in a single column, and we are last in line, as we are the "command" track leading from the rear; it's how the Army does it. Unlike in a daytime operation where we would keep a fair amount of space between us, this night we follow closely behind each other so as to stay together at least visually. But the down side to this, especially on a night like this, is that we eat everyone else's dust, sand, and diesel exhaust. There is no moonlight, so in the darkness, other than the general shape of things, it is difficult to see the terrain in front of us. And what may appear to be reasonably flat in the darkness is often much rougher than it looks. We ride across dry rice paddies, up their berms, and then back down them. Often, we hit them at an angle, so we buck and tilt and bounce and quietly curse and hang on. We would probably curse out loud, but no one wants to chance getting a mouthful of dust or sand by opening his mouth. We are already thirsty; it being fourteen hours since the water ran out, this greatly exacerbates our plight.

We don't travel that fast; the terrain does not permit it, especially at night. If we travel any faster, we will easily lose guys falling off the tracks. Which means a stop to get them back up on top; we would only lose more time.

We finally clear the last of the rice paddies and move into the wood line. It's not true jungle in the classical sense of vines hanging from every direction, but a maze of brush, thickets, and trees. The ground seems a bit more level; at least there are no berms to run into. But we are constantly being swatted and thrashed by the unseen branches, which cause considerable moans and curses.

We now begin to make several brief but unplanned stops. We seem to lose our bearings in the wood line; it blocks our view of the more prominent landmarks. We are losing time, falling behind schedule. There is no such thing as GPS yet, just a compass and line of sight, a tough gig in the darkness of a moonless night. At some point we must have turned east back towards the coast, but I know this only by the fact that terrain changes from the woods back to open grassy plains and that the horizon directly in front of us begins to turn pinkish. Dawn is coming; we should already be at Charlie's village, yet we are miles from it.

We now seem to be traveling slightly downhill; it is difficult to ascertain in the feeble light. We seem to level off for a bit as we head toward the pinkish hue, but then shortly begin to climb some steep dunes. Judging by the amount of sand in the air thrown up by the churning track closely in front of us, we must be getting very close to the coast. The sand is choking; everyone spits tiny particles of sand from their dry mouth. Now we are going down a long and steeply inclined sand dune and we begin to pick up speed. We abruptly level off and in the gathering light now see a gray coastline.

We turn north and our driver guns the engine; the track's diesel now gives off a much happier tone, running at steady rpm's on relatively flat terrain. We ride very high on the beach where the scrubby brush starts to grow, far from the edge of the surf line. In fact, I have only the barest recollection of the immense Pacific but a stone's throw away. But the beach is not where we're going. We are rushing to catch up with two other units to take a village from Charlie; everything else is a far distant second. The adrenalin pours through our systems like a dam bursting; we focus only on that distant hamlet on the beach several miles away, not yet in sight.

We race northward up that coastline in a single column, but we *race* at about 20 mph, no more than that. If we hit any kind of dip or bump, the track will easily throw us off. There are no guard rails, seat belts, or safety harnesses; you are sitting cross legged on your butt only an inch from the track's edge holding your rifle with one arm and hanging on with the other arm for dear life. It's more than a little precarious. Our attempt to reach Charlie Town before the sunrise is in vain. The sun rises over the vast Pacific, and for the last two miles up that beach our four, olive drab "tracks" are silhouetted directly against the big orange and pink ball rising from the sea. We are so pathetically laughably, easy targets; we would not even be rated as amateurs.

Our entry into the hamlet is stunningly anticlimactic; the other two units have already taken it thirty minutes earlier without any firefight. We have arrived so late at a party, that most of the guests are now about to leave. We dismount from our tracks, and I almost immediately bump into a 2nd Lt. from my old artillery unit. He recognizes me before I do him, and we are both surprised to see each other in the same operation in the same tiny VC village on the coast. But he is in a very somber mood; he asks if I remember another 2nd Lt. Vonn from our unit. He tells me just days earlier, Vonn and another guy were walking together in another Charlie Town when one of them kicked a Coke can which triggered a hand grenade. Their leg wounds are so severe they may lose their limbs or their lives. I silently ask myself, "Who the hell kicks a Coke can in a Charlie Town?" It is just so easy to get hurt here; you don't have to try very hard.

The Stone Age

Many of the hooches of this tiny surfside village are completely constructed of palm fronds, which are woven to make the thatch roofs and sides. There seems to be little mud used in the construction of the side walls. Here on this beach, there is only white sand; the needed mud from the distant rice paddies is not close by and is a little heavy to carry. Besides, the dunes shift in the wind, and anything too upright would soon be buried or blown over. Hence, the hooches here are far less erect than those back at the coconut grove. They don't stand as tall, and their corners and roof lines are much more rounded. Though the hooches are behind a dune of rather modest height, they are not at all far from the actual beach. These have been deliberately built lower and rounder to withstand the strong winds that must, on occasion, sweep in from the vast Pacific, which is but one or two hundred yards away. Nearby, on the ocean side, small wooden fishing boats, having been pulled back from the tide, sit resting on the sand in the very early morning light. In some ways, there is a sense of much less permanence here, almost a nomadic feel, as if the entire village could easily pick itself up to move up or down the beach. I wish I could have taken pictures. But our purpose here is not to make a documentary; it is to make war.

The other units have already swept completely and thoroughly through the entire hamlet. Each and every hooch has been entered and tossed; there is nothing here. No guns, no ammo, no medical supplies, no anything. And the one other big thing that is also missing here: there are no young men. In fact, other than two very ancient old men, there is not a single male in this entire village over the age of 12. In "our" hamlet by the coconut grove, there were a few young men, some fathers, some village elders, and a somewhat more normal representation of the population. Alas, there are no men; they all have safely fled. After all, it's a Charlie Town. Of course, we were supposed to block the back door, but we arrived far too late for that. No one from the other units gives us any shit about that, in part because they took the hamlet so effortlessly, but I think mostly it is because they know how far we have come in the darkness over the worst terrain. They are probably very glad they didn't have to do it themselves.

Nonetheless the bottom line is undeniable: Charlie got away clean, and we got to capture a bunch of women and children. There is always a yin and yang; there's always a sequence of events triggered by an earlier event, or in our case by the lack of an event. Our failure to close the back door, our lack of an event, must

the fishing village on the Pacific

somehow be balanced. An unseen hourglass has been tipped, and now each grain of sand dropping through ticks the time away. Though we linger here, we should not, for we have not the slightest clue of what awaits.

We walk through the village to see it for ourselves. We may as well, hell, it seems it took us half the night to get here. The hooches have already been emptied out. The women and the kids stand outside in the open, which is where we want them to be. This is absolutely necessary for **we need to see all**; if not, a pitiful and wretched outcome is most probable. Most of the women hold kids in their arms. As we pass by, they say nothing; most will not meet our eyes. They have dour expressions on their faces and look past us. As we near one of the hooches, a young woman holding a baby breaks her sullen expression to give a brief but the most hateful of looks. I don't blame her. But she seems just a bit too fidgety as we pass her, and I pause. Something seems off.

I am now more curious about what may be in her hooch. I walk slowly to its opening and, still keeping her in my sight, I stop at the very edge of its doorway. I pause momentarily and look back toward her; she sends daggers with her eyes, the intensity of which now alarms me. I move only one step past the doorway and stop; it is darker inside; my heart rate immediately jumps. From just inside the doorway entrance, I turn and look back at her. Her eyes send pure hatred, and her facial posture is that of a woman about to scream. The alarm bells sound in my brain. I turn back to look inside the hooch, but pause a long moment to let my eyes adjust to the lower light. In these brief seconds, silently using my right thumb, I move the safety of my Mattel Toy from semi- to fully automatic.

I now step deeper into the darkness of the hooch, and as I do, I see a shadow move. I freeze instantly…my heart is pounding so hard that it is audible…I hold still…but cannot detect any further movement. My right hand tightly grasps the trigger grip, my index finger against the trigger only awaiting confirmation of a target. My adrenalin gland pumping out its high-octane additive to my blood stream, my heart quickly pushing it through my system. I wonder who will die here. I take another half step… I see the shadow move… it is then that I realize I am causing the subtle changes of the shadows as I move from the doorway.

There is zilch here. The hooch has already been tossed and thoroughly searched, and I see nothing to alarm me. In fact, I see very little at all. It is just a plain, rustic, country peasant home of thatched roof and sides. It is almost barren. A few grass mats, very few clothes, some wooden cooking utensils, an iron pot and pan. It's 20,000 BC. I touch nothing, and I step out, for I feel I have violated her enough. I feel her eyes upon me; I look toward her and shrug; she holds the blank look on her face, but at least she doesn't give the hateful look again. It is an immense understatement to say that we are both relieved. But when you hear of stories where someone has thrown a hand grenade inside an "empty" hooch "just to be sure," now you know why. I am glad I did not throw one.

Now What?

The Pentagon has a mindset that if we "bomb them back to the stone age," we will win this war. But this hamlet is at the stone age; bombing it back to the stone age is fruitless. They will only hate us even more. But to argue or even consider that bigger philosophical debate is pointless. What do we do here and now? We have taken a hamlet of women and children; so, what are we supposed to do with it and them? Is it to be search and destroy? We could burn the village to the ground and move the inhabitants to a camp, but to what end? There are far too many refugees living in their own country; why make more? We could occupy it, or at least set up camp at its very edge, as we have back by the coconut grove. But then you cannot occupy every stinking place everywhere all of the time.

In the end, we do nothing at all. But none of this is anything we have any input into; someone higher up the chain makes the decision. They will call this action a success, and we will leave. But it causes me to wonder; why did we bother to take it at all? Take this village only to hand it back; what was the point? The South Vietnamese government's hold on the hamlet is tenuous at best during the day; this evening Charlie will have firm control once again. We will get back up on our "tracks" and leave the Charlie hamlet by the sea, whose name sadly I don't think any of us ever learned. It didn't seem important at that moment, though later on in my life I truly wish I knew its name. Our departure is without fanfare, almost nonchalant, almost like a collective shrug of the shoulders. For all our trepidation of the night before and nighttime maneuvering itself, our entry was anti-climactic and our departure even more so. All this for nothing?

We climb up top, the diesel fires up, and now in single file, our four tracks leave the hamlet. The sun is now getting much stronger, and though it is still quite early in the morning, it has rapidly warmed up. The day gives every indication that it will be scorching hot; the air is utterly, totally, completely, absolutely still. We leave the same way we came in; we enter back onto the beach and head south. But now we ride almost at the water's edge at a relaxed, even pace of perhaps 6 or 8 mph. It is as though we are taking the tourist route home.

But alas, the sands continue to drop through the unseen hourglass; each grain counting down the time.

No one speaks of it, no need to jinx ourselves, but we all are relieved that our luck holds again, not even a scratch upon us. We are invincible; Charlie can't touch us. Our formation is again single

the village of women and children

file instead of all spread out, to lessen the chances of hitting a mine, of course. Each track follows exactly in the tread tracks left by the track in front of it. If the lead track doesn't hit a mine, then none of those following behind will either. But who the hell wants to be first? And we are last in line, the "command track" leading from the rear. Hell, who wants to be last? The problem of being last is that all of your help is moving away from you if you come under fire. Last sucks. The only difference from our night journey is that now, in the full light of day, we keep generous spacing between the "tracks," as we have clear visual contact with each other.

The Perfect South Pacific Paradise Beach

Now in the bright morning sunshine we are able to look more closely at our surroundings, especially given our leisurely pace as we move south back down the beach. To our right, the inland side, I see, higher up on the beach, the tread tracks we left in the sand at the top of the beach just an hour or two earlier. We always seek the un-trod ground, always avoiding the "traveled lanes," for fear of land mines. So, we ride very low on the beach, nearly at the water's edge; Charlie would not waste a mine here. But up past our earlier tread tracks, there is tall grass and scrubby brush which slowly gives way to a marshy swampy area, with a few mangrove trees clinging to each other. This is the area that we had to travel so far south from our encampment to get around; sweet Jesus, I am glad we did not try to come through that in the pre-dawn darkness. To our left, the surf rolls in from a pale blue Pacific, but I begin to notice that the farther south we travel, the stronger the surf becomes. There is a convex curve in the beach that was unnoticed in the weak early light during our rush up the beach this morning. But as we round the apex of this curve, the surf immediately grows exponentially. It is an astonishing feat of Mother Nature; it is breathtaking. At the same time, the upper beach gently gains in elevation, the grass and brush thicken, the mangroves disappear, and a few palms start to appear. The surf grows higher still, but the phantom hourglass continues to empty, unhurriedly and steadily giving up its sand.

We travel south another half mile, and the waves are huge now. They are at least 15 feet high, and some push higher. They are immense, perfectly and purely formed, magical beasts. Where do they come from? I say aloud to myself as much as to anyone else, "I love the beach." Still, the guy sitting right in front of me says, "What?"

I do love the beach; it is my earliest memory. I am perhaps two years old, and I am lying on a blanket (I assume), and just to my right is a house of some unclear shape. But I am certain of its green color and that I lie in its shadow. I know this as an absolute certainty because just a short distance to my left I see brilliant sunshine striking the off-white, yellowish, tan sand. I do not sense the sunlight striking me, but I do see it close by. Right in front of the off-white sand, I see blue water in slow motion. I am most pleased and comforted by this view. Even then I know that life can be as good as a day at the beach.

I move further ahead in time, and I am now three and a half years old. I am at an ocean beach and I stand ankle-deep in the water. The gentlest of surf rolls in, and the water rises to my knees; it stays there momentarily, and then rolls back toward where it came. As the water goes back out, I feel it pull the sand around my feet and toes; this is fun. I want to go deeper, but my mother has hand-made my bathing suit from white terry cloth, and I am baffled by her decision to make a bathing suit from a towel. I quite honestly think she's dumb, because when you get out of the tub, that's when you put the towel around yourself; you don't wear the towel into the tub? (Of course, I am yet unaware that we live at the poverty line.)

I decide to go deeper into the water; if my towel bathing suit gets wet then it's her fault. I walk out until the water is waist high, whereupon I am knocked flat by the next incoming wave. I am surprised by this but quickly stand up. I don't take the wave's knockdown as anything personal; it was actually fun, and now I know what waves can do. Later, when I walk out of the water onto the beach, my towel bathing suit is very heavy and it pulls at my waist. It now probably weighs half my weight, and it is hard walking. I think this situation to be most stupid. I want to take it off, but there are other people around, and I know I shouldn't.

I move ahead, and now I am four and a half years old. I have become quite wise with the ways of the world. I have completely given up on my parents; they are both idiots. But a rather elderly lady has driven us to a more protected beach where it is low tide and I can see the stony mud flats left exposed by the receding tide. At first, I do not see the rationale for going to the beach at low tide; it doesn't look as neat and clean as it does at high tide. But the elderly lady, reading the distain on my face, walks me down to the mud flats and urges me to toss a stone. I do as I am told, and where the stone hits the ground, water squirts from the mud. She hands me a plunger that one would use to unclog a drain. She now directs me to push down where the "squirt" came from and then pull the plunger up. I follow her instructions and up pops a clam. Oh, so this is what you do at low tide! And now I know, high tide or low, day or night, anytime is always a good day at the beach.

"What?" It's the guy just in front of me again. I heard him the first time, but he has raised his voice this time to make sure I can hear him. I repeat myself; "I love the beach," but now I raise my voice to be heard, not just over the diesel and the clanking tracks, but also over the booming surf. He gives me a slight shrug of yes, and then looks away. I wonder if he is just half asleep, but then I think maybe he's just having a bad day in the Army. Let's face it; every day in the Army is a bad day. But the surf is booming; it starts as distant thunder, then rapidly becomes quite close. The boom created by these huge waves dropping onto that beach is not like a single thunder clap, but rather a slightly softer continuous one. It is as if Mother Nature has her hands on a mammoth grand piano playing a wondrous chord on the deep bass keys and holds her foot to the sustaining pedal. You feel these notes as much as you hear them. And just as the bass notes subside, she hits the keys at the top to provide a clearly audible sustained "hiss". Then only the briefest moment later, she again plays those low chords ......

This is unquestionably the most spectacular beach I have seen or will ever see. I say this with all the conviction and wisdom of a twenty-one-year-old. As I look back on this moment, I know I was probably right. As we travel south the beach becomes broad and now is thickly lined at its top with scrubby brush, tall grass, and the occasional struggling palms which seem to lean in a multitude of directions. In places the jungle seems almost to reach the beach but then abruptly gives way to sand dunes that reach far inland. And then the jungle reaches out back to the beach. I raise my head and look south; the beach stretches in a long gentle arc for unknown miles. I now look east. The visibility and my view are limited only by the curvature of the earth; the Pacific is so flat and undisturbed; it might aptly be labeled "blue infinity." But now, I attempt to fathom the immense waves.

Something far offshore, perhaps an unseen storm, must be pushing these huge combers in, but as carefully as I scan the distant horizon, I see nothing; it is absolutely cloudless. There is no wind in any direction; it is unequivocally dead flat calm. And yet, huge combers pound the shore. I look out to where they are first seen. They seem to subtly arrive and are barely perceptible but then steadily grow for the first three quarters of this final short leg of their thousand-mile journey. It is in the final few hundred feet that they grow with incredible swiftness into pure, perfect, fifteen–foot magical beasts of Pale Blue liquid glass.

It would seem silly to give these waves any acknowledgement of a living, breathing personality, but they are alive. They tell us that they are not fearful, and that they actually feel majestic and rather proudly so. But I concur: they are and they do. The clarity and transparency of the water are extraordinary. As the combers climb high, there is a moment where I can see through them to the still relatively low sunlit horizon behind them, they are the softest, palest shade of blue.

The Pale Blue Beast reaches its final zenith then falls forward smashing into the sand. There is a low frequency faa-whooomp-sss as thousands of tons of seawater fall from a height of fifteen feet. I swear I see a bounce of the beach after every wallop, which I can feel through the aluminum body of the track. You cannot help being pulled into and observing this epic battle of the immense raw power of the Great Pale Blue Beast smashing against the unyielding primordial, tropical, sandy Rock of Gibraltar. You wonder how long this battle has raged: yet another, Asian version of a Mexican standoff. Nonetheless, there is an unfathomable, unquestioned purity to this battle.

We drive further south, in and out of the mist caused by the Pale Blue Beasts crashing against the whitest sand I have ever seen. There is no wind to disperse it. We feel the mist upon our dry faces, then smell and taste the salty brine. We are so parched that each one of us is licking his lips to gather what little moisture has landed there. Now the scraggy, scrubby brush and ragged grasses and palms thicken; they grow along the edge of the abutting but unearthly tall sand dunes. We come across the occasional, random pieces of driftwood, yet they seem perfectly placed. The beach seems ancient, untouched, and so unspoiled I imagine it to have looked the same a thousand years ago. I envision myself as Robinson Crusoe; I pick the spot where I build my grass shack in the shelter of palm trees, and I pick the two coconut trees where I hang my hammock. I wonder whether the gods would allow a barrel or two of rum to wash in onto the shore, after all they have provided unlimited coconuts from the nearby groves. There is such a sultry look and feel here it almost seems sexual.

We pass through Paradise, not knowing that the sands continue to fall through the unseen hourglass. The sand's flow is deliberate, it is constant, nothing can slow or stop the grains of sand. Our fate was sealed hours ago.

We finally reach the point where we see our entry point onto the beach from earlier this morning, which now seems a month ago. We drive slightly past this point so that we will tread upon new ground, and then slowly turn west moving away from the beach. We pass through this broad strip of brush, tall grasses, and scraggly small palm trees now to face the tallest sand dunes I have ever seen. They are at least ten stories tall, and they are so steeply inclined I wonder whether the tracks will be able to climb them. We pause momentarily, then the first track begins its unhurried climb up the steep dunes. Slow and steady is the key; to gun the engine will cause the treads to throw huge amounts of sand. Only when the first track nears the top of the dunes does the second track begin its climb up them. We purposely keep generous spacing between the tracks, as Charlie would find us too tempting a target all bunched together halfway up a long steep sand dune with so little maneuvering room.

The first track disappears over the top of the dunes and as the second track nears the top, the third track begins its climb up them. Now the second track disappears over the top of the dune, the third track climbing slowly but steadily up the enormous dune. As the third track nears the top, we, now alone on the beach and the last to leave it, pause one final moment, and all dozen of us turn to take one last look. I say quietly a final time to the guy next to me, "I love the beach." He nods his head yes, but it is as though he is half dead, as if my words are barely registering. I wonder again whether he cannot see this Eden or is in some sort of "shell shocked" state. The diesel revs, the track lurches slightly, and we turn *going off the beach* and begin our climb up the sandy Gibraltar.

I sit on the right-hand side of the track with my legs tucked under myself. I cradle my M-16 with my right hand as I grab hold of the track with my left, and as I do, I see my deeply tanned arm with a new watch on its wrist. It is of course the self-winding Seiko, which I so proudly bought at the Air Force PX in Phu Cat for $12.50. I am so impressed with my own impeccably, albeit quite accidental, good taste; I smile to myself anyway. I see the second hand, it moves in precise one second intervals, sweeping evenly around the dial face; it too is ticking away the time. It is just shy of 7:50 AM on a clear, sunny, cloudless morning in early August at a perfect South Pacific paradise beach. Little do I know it is 30 seconds to hell.

The third track has disappeared over the top of the dune. We are now momentarily isolated and alone, and it is suddenly the most eerie of feelings. We make our slow progress up the dune and almost to the halfway point; I turn to take one last and final look. From our slightly higher elevation, I see above the broad beach line, and the immense Pacific now seems a deeper shade of blue.

I never see that beach again. We leave behind an unnamed, untamed, primordial beach, an ancient place of epic proportion and epic beauty, one I will remember as an Eden with faultless clarity, in such vivid, remarkable detail. I know I could never go back, as it would never be the same. How could it?

One might wonder about my obsessive need to paint the picture of this faraway place, in which I spent 30 or 40 minutes. I cannot let go of it, this place, this beach, this moment in time, so deeply imprinted into me that it is now part and parcel of my DNA. This surfside Edenic interlude is the first, last, and only good thing to come of this day. I could not let go of this even if I wanted to, for I must keep it, maintaining the balance of the equation, to balance off a seemingly unendingly long ordeal. It holds the yin and yang in equilibrium.

In my view, Hell is opportunistic in its nature. It waits with all the patience of eternity. Never give it a chance; don't go off the beach. But we don't know this.

I turn back around and now look forward, up toward the top of the dune. The phantom hourglass is nearly empty now; just seconds left, just a few more grains of sand are yet to pass through it. We are so naively unaware of what is coming.

We are all in a good mood. Nobody got hurt this morning in our unit; our luck holds. It will be a much shorter journey back to our encampment by the coconut grove. We will not have to go as far west as we did in the darkness of last night. We will take a shortcut back; the daylight affords us good line of sight. We will call for a chopper to bring us some water. We haven't eaten since yesterday afternoon, so the dehydrated chicken stew will taste good. Maybe I'll write a letter this afternoon.

We continue our slow climb up that long and steep sand dune … now the last single grain of sand drops through the hourglass… our fate is delivered and hell is unleashed.

A Little Taste And Flavor of Hell

I have only been facing forward for a few seconds when there is a loud and powerful rattle-your-brain explosion. It comes from the other side of the sand dune. We are so stunned. There is an almost instantaneous towering black cloud of smoke, sand, pieces of metal, and tread tracks that has risen from behind the sand dune. At the same moment, I see the shock wave hit the top of the dune, and it lifts the sand from it as if a strong gust of wind has just blown across the dune.

I hear the Lieutenant shouting, "Go, Go, Go," but our driver has already instinctively hit the gas. The diesel roars in a terrible anguished scream, the treads grasp at the sand and churn wildly, throwing sand far and high behind us. The track skids slightly sideways, bucks, and then rears back. We all immediately begin to slide backwards. I tighten the grasp of my left hand on the track to stop my backward slide. Most annoyingly, the guy in front of me does nothing to help his cause, and I must now hold both of us on the track. Our driver eases up momentarily on the throttle to allow the treads to gain some traction and this lets the track settle itself just a bit. But then he hits the throttle hard again, and the diesel roars once more in terrible anguish as it churns its treads wildly, throwing sand back into the air. The track bucks again as if to throw us off its back.

I grab harder still, but the guy in front of me still does nothing to help. The world is blowing up in front of us, and I am stuck sitting here. I don't think I can hold us much longer as the track begins to accelerate up the steep dune. I think about jumping from the track to the ground, but I am not certain I can clear the churning treads from a seated position. Once on the ground, I would have to run in the deep sand up the dune, and I am not sure I could keep up, not knowing how far we would go. I decide to hang on for as long as I can. I wonder how many Charlies are over the hill. I wonder how close they will be. I truly fear the Charlies will be very close.

It is probably only a minute more, and our track clears the top of the dune, but only just barely, as I hear shouts of "Stop, Stop." The track lurches to a halt and we jump from it to the ground. We look down from the top of the dune in shocked disbelief at the smoldering track on its side. Just over the berm of the sand dune, the ground is shaped like a huge shallow bowl. It is nearly two hundred yards across; the pitch of its banks is far less severe than the ocean side of the dune we have just climbed. On the far side of this bowl sits the first track, at the very edge of the grassy plain, and beyond that I see the dry rice paddies. Its crew is running down into the bowl. In front of us part way down the bowl sits the third track, and its crew is running to the bottom of the bowl where the second track lies on its left side, part way over onto its top. It is missing its right tread and some of the wheels that support the tread. There is thin wispy black smoke coming from its right side, and lying in a crude semi-circle of perhaps 215 degrees are seventeen bodies. Some of the guys toward the back and especially on the left side I can see moving slowly, while those on the right side lie still.

Our eyes dart from side to side, and it takes some moments to register, but there is not a single Charlie to be seen. We begin to run down the slope of the bowl to help out, but the Lieutenant shouts for us to stay back: "Hold the perimeter, stay on the hill." Only he and our medic run down the hill. So, we stay near the top of the berm and spread out slightly. We can only watch.

With my eyes, I follow the tread tracks of each of the three tracks. Everyone had stayed in line. Why had the second one been blown? Was it a bit heavier than the first, was it an inch to the left or right, or was it just a crap shoot??? Someone wonders aloud, could Charlie have planted this mine when he slipped out the still open back door, knowing we would have to return this way? Why didn't we close the back door?

I look for footprints in the sand leading from the wrecked track, but I cannot pick any out. I wonder from the size of the crater by the track whether Charlie has used an unexploded artillery round, perhaps one of ours, or perhaps something bigger. Even though the track weighs over 20,000 pounds, it appears to have been so easily flipped over. No, they didn't run over a hand-grenade. But for all we know, maybe Charlie buried that mine the day before or even the week before. But all of this is conjecture, and all unanswerable.

We see our medics scurrying from man to man, applying and wrapping bandages, performing a crude field "triage." It is a French word meaning "to sort" or "sift." The French field surgeons of World War 1 would "sift" or "sort" through the casualties, sifting out the dead, the dying and the wounded. The dead could not be helped, the wounded could wait at least a while, but the dying might be saved. And surely the Vietnamese, being a French colony for so long, and at war for so long, would know this "triage." We see the Lieutenant shouting into a radio, asking for medevac choppers. We can only watch from atop the dune. Oddly, I never once look back over that high steep dune toward Eden but am held transfixed by the scene unfolding at the bottom this vast sandy bowl. Paradise and hell lie next to each other, separated only by a mammoth sand dune.

Where is the medevac? Our expectation is that the Huey with its Red Cross painted on its sides and nose will instantly appear, but of course that is not possible. But still, it has been 30 minutes. Uplift is not that far away, and there is a small field hospital there with a medevac chopper. And somewhat farther to the north at LZ English, there is a much larger base with plenty of choppers. Finally, we hear the familiar "chomp, chomp, chomp" of a Huey, its blade beating the air. He is coming hard, but he is slow and laborious; we cannot fathom this until he lands. It's not a medevac, but a Huey full of freight. He has heard our call and come, but he can only take one or two.

We will take anything we can get, and two of the smaller walking wounded are put on board. He lifts off slowly and heads northwest. We are disappointed, but only momentarily, for a minute or two later we hear again the "chomp, chomp, chomp" signature of a Huey. We see the bright Red Cross on its nose. A Huey's blade makes a very distinct sound when it is pushed to the very limit to make speed. We hear this, and then we see him; to say that he is coming hard is an understatement. He flies so very low and so very fast. He flies barely over the treetops, but so quickly, at 135 mph, that any Charlie on the ground would have little time to react to fire a few rounds off at him. To give you some perspective, imagine standing on a sidewalk as a truck passes by you at 135 mph.

Now the medevac clears the last of the coconut trees at a frightening speed and drops towards the ground like a rock falling, but in an amazing display of airmanship, the pilot lands as softly as a feather. He lands close to the turned track, and no time is wasted. He is barely on the ground when the worst of the wounded are loaded. He takes off in less than a minute, briefly heading toward the ocean and then turning tightly to the northwest. He makes haste, and he is so good. A third Huey comes in almost immediately, though not a medevac, and lands just a little further east of the track. It is not at all a gentle landing and seems more than a little sloppy. A few guys are carried on, and now some of the walking wounded are put aboard, but I can see from my somewhat distant position that the Huey looks crowded. The Huey strains to lift, it gains about two feet of altitude and only a little forward speed, but then smacks the ground hard but evenly with its skids, bounces slightly and comes to a halt. It has become scorching hot in this shallow bowl of white sand, and the air is thin.

The Huey tries again to lift off. It gets a couple feet off the ground moving forward slowly then drops, hitting the ground, then bouncing back into the air, and then hitting the ground again, and then stops. They need to take someone off the Huey; it is painfully obvious that it is dangerously overloaded. Is the pilot stubborn, pressured, or breathtakingly stupid? He revs the Huey's main rotor; the blades beat the air, the sand swirling about. He now lifts about three or four feet making slow forward progress but cannot maintain it and now smacks the ground very hard, bounces, and pitches forward. Though the front of the skids are curved upward to deter catching a branch or digging into the ground, none the less, the Huey's momentum now causes it to pitch clockwise as if to tip over on itself. We watch in horror and I hear the collective groans around me. The Huey's pitches its nose down, and its tail lifts all in the same motion. Time crawls to a stop once again and we watch as time moves forward one picture frame at a time, the anatomy of a slow-motion catastrophe.

The Huey is slowly rotating on the front of its landing skids; there must be near panic for those aboard. I see the main rotor blade adjusting to the pilot's input; the blade tilts slightly backward. This is an attempt to brake the forward pitch down; it also keeps the front of that rotating blade a few more inches from the ground. The result of any hard contact of that turning blade, at over 48 feet in length and rotating more than five times every second, would be catastrophic. The Huey's forward rotation stops and pauses, with the front of the rotating blade seemingly only a few feet off the ground; it now settles back on its skids squarely but quite hard. I whisper to myself, "fucking A, fucking A." I want to walk down there and, at the point of my gun, yank the pilot off to lighten the load, for he is going to kill them all. Let the co-pilot fly them out.

He revs the Huey again; he slowly lifts and very cautiously allows only the slightest movement forward. Loaded this heavily, the blades can only lift so much and move forward at the same time; if you "pitch" the blade to provide forward propulsion, some of your "lift" is used. He heads towards the coastline lifting ever so slowly and gaining some speed. He makes a cautious bank and a wide shallow turn at an elevation of 50 feet and heads west, perhaps to English or Uplift. The last obstacle is the tall coconut trees, some of which reach 80 feet in height. I pray Buddha to intervene, the Huey's skids brush the tops of the trees, and I see the palm leaves thrash violently in his prop wash.

A minute or two later the final Huey arrives. The last to be taken out are the ARVN's, the South Vietnamese soldiers from our encampment by the coconut grove. Several of them were jammed packed on that second track for some reason, but all were seated at the back of the track, and probably all on the left side. They limp and are banged up, and several wear red blood-stained bandages, but they don't seem too bad. Blind, shit luck had placed them on the safest place of that track. We stare at them with envy; they have the kind of injuries we would all like to have, just banged up enough to be put on that chopper and get off of this beach and leave this barren sandy hellhole behind. It is the infamous "million-dollar wound." Everyone dreams of getting a little piece of shrapnel in the buttocks; you get to leave this place and they throw you a medal, too.

The last chopper leaves and it grows momentarily quiet.

And The Shock Settles In

The Lieutenant shouts and waves us down from the top of the dune. The driver takes the track down near to the wrecked track, and we walk slowly behind it. Because I was the highest on the sand dune, I am the last to reach the blown track and stand at the back of the group. The heat at the bottom of this huge sand bowl is sizzling. As I arrive, the Lieutenant is telling us that HQ may want to try to salvage the wrecked track. But salvaged or abandoned, we must strip it as best we can to make it as light as possible and to leave nothing behind for Charlie. He shouts, "Now somebody get inside and start throwing the ammo out."

Our young buck Sergeant takes a wrench from inside but silently moves away from the rear hatch so as to open a plug to drain the diesel from its tank. He pretends he is busy, but he will not help organize anyone to enter the track. He is a kid like the rest of us, but he shouldn't be wearing those stripes. The Lieutenant then raises his voice, "Somebody get inside the track and start passing the ammo boxes out." He is standing by the rear hatch door as he says this, but nobody moves. I am standing behind everyone else, and I am a little surprised. He repeats himself more loudly, and still, no one moves.

The track is still smoldering, as wisps of black rise in several places, and no one wants to go inside it. Why would they? We are breaking down. The Lieutenant is about to scream his order a fourth time, but sensing the verge of our breakdown, I walk through the group and simply say, "I'll do it." I don't know what the matter is with everyone, but no one seems to be able to function.

I step through the open back hatch into the bowels of the track. It is an oven. The drab olive-green color of its paint readily absorbs the sun's rays. They hit directly from overhead, as well as the rays that are reflected upon it by the brilliant white sand walls of the huge bowl the track sits in. The aluminum body of the track effortlessly passes the heat through it; the inside of the track is easily 130°F. Everything inside has been tossed into a mound on the left side wall, but I quickly spot what we need to take with us: hundreds of metal boxes of M-16 ammo, boxes of machine gun belts, boxes of grenades. The track was probably carrying close to a ton of assorted ammo.

I know I will not last long in this heat. Upon entering the track, I immediately begin to sweat profusely. With both hands, I begin to grab ammo boxes and throw them through the hatch opening, and I work as fast as I can. I work bent over at the waist; it is a most uncomfortable position, but I push on. I am dying of thirst and quickly failing in the heat. I remove at least half of the ammo boxes, perhaps a bit more. I reach for one more box but can do no more. It is at that moment I see my watch again; I am stunned that it's only 09:10 AM. It has been only an hour and twenty minutes since the track blew up.

I look toward the Lieutenant, and he sees that I am spent. He reaches his arm in to clasp mine and quietly tells me in a voice that's both sympathetic and grateful, "Come out of there." I exit the track and stagger a few steps away. As I do, I hear him screaming at the rest for someone to get inside the track and help out. Someone finally steps up and moves inside the track to toss out more ammo boxes; we are finally functioning as a unit again. I grab my rifle, ammo, and helmet, which I had left by the track door, and then step further away.

Perhaps fifteen or twenty minutes go by, and three Hueys now land on the grassy plain just at the western edge of the sand bowl. The brass from HQ have come out to see for themselves the situation here; suddenly there is no shortage of choppers. As I look up toward them, I recognize a Captain from my artillery battery. I walk up the gentle slope to the grass plain; he sees me and greets me warmly. He is a short black guy from Alabama who did not get along so well with our white Lt. Colonel who was also from Alabama. So, he went from artillery to infantry, but then so did I. I tower over him by at least 10 or 12 inches, but as short as he is, he is powerfully built much like a small tank. I know he can be a tough hombre if need be. He nods in the direction of the blown track, and we both turn to look down into the sand bowl. In a rather decent and dignified manner he places his arm around my shoulder and quietly asks: "Are you alright?" I tell him I'm okay, and I am taken by his decency.

I notice a canteen on his hip and I ask if I can have a drink of his water. He becomes quite distressed and apologizes to me. He tells me with genuine anger in his voice that earlier in the day someone asked for a drink, but when he gave them his canteen, "The asshole drank it all." He nods towards a small group of officers as he says this. I respond, "He was a real asshole for leaving you dry."

Moments later, the brass decide they have seen enough. They get in their Hueys and take off. The Captain and I say goodbye and wish each other well. He will stay in the Army for life, and I will hang on for dear life until my time is up. I never do see the Captain again.

HQ has decided to try to salvage the blown track and will send a heavy lift chopper to try to carry it out. The first track will stay at the edge of the grassland and guard the crippled track as it lies overturned, still smoldering, at the bottom of the sand bowl. What poor bastards, to have to stay here in this heat. But by the end of this day, I will wish I had stayed here with them, for I do not yet know what awaits me. We are to return to our encampment by the coconut grove.

The Return To The Coconut Grove

We begin to climb up on top of the tracks, but the metal body, painted the dark drab olive green of the Army, is so painfully hot from the sun we can barely touch it. Every one of us takes his flak jacket off and places it on the top of the track to sit on it, so as not to burn ourselves. The diesel fires, and we head north leaving hell behind us… but a hellish presence follows us.

Our track takes the lead position. The third track now follows in our wake some 40 yards back. We are coming out of our collective state of shock, but we turn mean, and we are ripe for vengeance. The heat is terrible as we ride across the open grasslands; there is not a lick of shade anywhere near us. It is easily well above 100°F. The air is finally beginning to move, but only barely so, at one or two mph; what little there is, feels like a stifling, searing heat. We push on at eight or ten miles per hour. It is most miserable. We carry no water with us, there is no water back at our encampment… and evil still follows us.

Two ARVN soldiers travel with us, one a sergeant, the other a corporal. They both speak fairly-good English. They are both pleasant, decent men, and they serve as our interpreters. But I must presume that they feel bad about this morning's events. The ARVN Sergeant spots two men dressed in black pajamas to the west near the wood line. He thinks they carry rifles. We immediately wheel the track left, and the driver guns the engine. But as we close in, we see that it is only two elderly farmers with bamboo sticks herding a single cow. Several guys now lash out and curse the ARVN Sergeant for crying wolf, but I do not join in. I feel he was honestly trying to help.

The track wheels back to the right, and we continue to the north at eight mph. Every one of us is simply spent and empty, we are so defeated by both the elements and the events of the day. We have lost our discipline, and now we most dangerously let our legs dangle over the sides of the tracks. We risk great harm, but we are too beaten to care. Finally, the coconut grove comes into sight and we pull into our spot minus two tracks… and evil still follows us.

Left Dry, Alone, And On Our Own

As we climb off the tracks and begin to move toward the shade of the palm trees, we suddenly notice that the Lieutenant looks like tepid shit. He is pasty white and feverish and he calls the medic to him. The Lieutenant lowers his pants and shows the medic the spider bite he got last night, on the inside of his right thigh. We hear the medic saying, "Oh shit," and we all gather around.

It is enormous; there is a raised and reddish brown, perfectly circular area of inflamed flesh. It is nearly six inches in diameter and in the very center is a tiny white spot. My first thought: He needs to go now. I don't know how he has gotten through this morning. The medic tells him that he can do nothing for him here in the field. The Lieutenant doesn't want to leave us alone, but most of us tell him, "Not to worry, we'll be fine." He still resists going. I then speak up: "The sooner you go in, the sooner you will be back. You won't get better here." He has newfound respect for me since this morning. He nods and says, "You're right." We call for a chopper, and it seems a Huey is there almost instantly. He limps on board, and we shout after him, "Send water." and he emphatically nods yes.

The Huey leaves, and we are now on our own. I assume that HQ will quickly, if not immediately, send out a replacement for our

Louie, but they never do. In the end, we spend the next couple of days on our own. Leadership among the Officer Corps is a random, hit or miss affair, so it is hugely gullible and naïve to think that our welfare and our lives count for much. Nobody gives a damn. We are cannon fodder. The Army Brass cannot grasp this and is clueless about the terrible morale of its enlisted men and women. But, then again maybe they do. And then wonders why they will never win this war.

It is now 12:30 PM on a clear, sunny, cloudless afternoon in early August at a tiny South Pacific coconut grove. We are leaderless. Welcome to paradise lost and hell on earth. And I will soon learn **Cardinal Rule Number IV: Never Yield To The Lord Of The Flies.**

As awful and as gut wrenching as this morning has been, you would think that this day could not possibly turn worse, but it does. Unknowingly, I am only mid-way through perhaps the longest day of my young life. Things for me personally will become most terrible yet. It's **Cardinal Rule Number II: Never Forget, It Can always Be Worse.**

It is now 22 hours plus since the water ran out. The heat is draining our souls. We rummage through the C-rations hoping to find some tiny can of fruit that will yield at least some juice. But we find nothing like that; the closest alternative is grape jelly or peanut butter, and nobody wants either. It is at this point that four or five guys announce that they will get some coconuts from the nearby grove. Honestly, I don't think they seem smart enough to do that correctly. But I say nothing; maybe they will surprise me. They return in fifteen or twenty minutes loudly joking about their accomplishment. But I was right, they have brought back 5 or 6 coconuts in their thick brown husks; without a small ax or a large machete they will be most difficult, if not impossible, to open.

Now, Lord Of The Flies

And so, it begins. The unseen one sits among us now and he works his craft. We sit in a loose circular group under some filtered shade in the airless, sweltering heat. My comrades-in-arms now begin to try to open the brown husks. One has a small knife, and he attempts to cut through the husks, but he only gets the knife temporally stuck. He then uses a heavy stick to try to drive the knife through the husk, but he fails miserably, and someone shouts, "Idiot." He in turn responds with an angry "Fuck you."

The frustration mounts, and the name calling starts. Someone else grabs a coconut and begins to smash it against the open hatch door of the track, to no avail. Another guy throws a coconut with great ferocity against the track body thinking that this will surely crack it open. But the coconut bounces wildly and hits another guy on his right shin. Almost immediately, I see a small blood stain through his pants. I grimace at his pain. He lets loose a torrent of swears and curses directed in a very personal manner toward the thrower. They almost come to blows, and we must separate them. And the coconut lies on the ground unopened. Everyone, in this terrible heat and dissatisfaction, is calling each other a fucking asshole …and everyone's thirst builds. Somebody then shoots a single round through a coconut with his M-16. A small trickle of wetness seeps through the husk, they attempt to drink this but dislike the moldy flavor of the brown husk. And finally, everyone gives up.

Cardinal Rule Number 1

I let ten minutes pass, and then I stand; I put my cloth bandolier of M-16 clips around one shoulder and then place the strap holding my "Mattel Toy" around my other shoulder. I speak to no one and quietly and without fanfare or notice walk slowly away from our encampment toward the coconut grove. I do not invite any of my comrades to come with me. I don't want them with me, as I feel they are far too unstable and will cause and do far more harm than good. I will get a "green" coconut, one that hasn't grown its thick husk. These green ones have not matured enough to have developed any of the edible white meat inside them, but they are full of "juice" and are easily cut open. Doesn't everyone know this?

So, I begin the short walk from our encampment... but the unseen hellish presence follows me now. He will soon work his craft again. What is wrong with me, why can't I sense what's coming...

And in my desperate thirst, I foolishly and most stupidly break **Cardinal Rule Number I: Never Go Into The Jungle Alone.**

The Woman In The Coconut Grove

The grove is close by. It is far in neither distance nor time. And yet as I look back on this, it is a world away. A very odd, distorted, almost unfathomable place where both Paradise and Hell have no actual boundary and yet invisibly touch each other. There is no storm where they meet, no thunder or lightning, no whirlwind or great vortex. They simply meet, their boundary for lack of a better description is not visible, it cannot be seen, or heard, nor can it be smelled, or tasted or felt or even 6th sensed; for your senses cannot detect it in any manner. For detection requires that the unseen, unknown, un-sensed boundary must be perfectly straddled with each leg firmly implanted on either side. And how does one find oneself straddling the unknown, the unseen, and the un-sensed? It is a fate about to be, a fate about to be changed, a where and when, a place and time, some crossroad, some fork in the road of life. And it is at this moment and place, the moments and places both being both right and wrong; this touching of both Paradise and Hell is known, felt and fully sensed, and is instantly recognized and you are terribly sickened.

Best to keep a strong grasp in Paradise, if not, Hell will surely pull you in. For each side, with powers beyond this world, pushes, pulls, with extreme pressures and temptations; there is only one rule here, **Cardinal Rule Number V: Never Straddle The Boundary; Be On One Side Or The Other**.

I walk steadily and evenly from our encampment into the coconut grove. I do not rush, and though my thirst is desperate and urgent, I confidently know what I want to get and that I will have it shortly.... but he follows me closely now.

I walk east along the small narrow path that connects our position with that of the ARVN's. The southernmost edge of the coconut grove lies at exactly the halfway point between our camps. It is at this point that another small narrow path now runs perpendicular from it to the north and into the heart of the grove. I turn here and walk perhaps six or seven dozen steps into the shaded, soft, oddly lit luminosity filtering down through the high canopy above. There are mixes of odors here, I smell the decay of leaves, palms, wood, husks, but it is not at all unpleasant. It is simply earthy, organic, woody, with the occasional wisp of something sweet. Some of the younger coconut trees grow tightly together, only two or three feet apart, along the path. They grow as straight as an arrow skyward, racing each other for the tropical sunlight high above them and the ground is deeply shaded here.

Farther down the path, for one reason or another that only Mother Nature could explain, one tree finally wins out, and it now shades out the competition. As those trees die out, the winner now leans over to grab the sunlight. And what was once "straight and narrow," now becomes "fuller and curvy," the "classic looking" coconut tree. Farther in, the coconut trees are more widely spaced, and without the need to compete for the tropical sun, they grow much stouter, if not shorter. I know not whether this was planned by the villagers or it is simply a different species, but with a long bamboo stick, one can reach the green coconuts and knock them from the tree. I quickly find the tree I desire and, most fortuitously, there lies under it a very long and slender bamboo pole. All is as if it has been planned, arranged and predetermined.

It is very quiet, and the light from above is not clean and clear but seems surreally whitish. But nothing seems amiss. I have not the slightest premonition…and yet… I sense I may be watched. I hold still, almost frozen, not even taking a breath, and listen closely but I hear nothing but the ambient soft background of the coconut grove. I wait the longest moment, but pick up no vibration. Now I silently look completely around me with piercing eyesight, but my blue eyes, with better than 20/20 vision, can detect nothing; I see only the green maze and the trunks of coconut trees bathed in the soft white light. Still, there is the slightest inkling of which I cannot read…

But I waste no time. I cannot believe my good luck in finding the long bamboo pole and think that someone from the village on the far side of the grove must have left it here. It is only much later that I consider other possible reasons for the fortuitous find of the pole.

The coconut tree of my desire is to my left just two steps away. I grab the long pole and, now facing east, I begin to poke at the green coconuts high above. But within the seemingly briefest spacing of time, my peripheral vision detects movement to my right. Passed down eons ago from our ancestors that lived in another jungle, our collective human brain learned to survive in that jungle by detecting movement first and only then focusing on the object. Better to detect the movement and be wrong about the tiger that is not there than not to detect the movement and be eaten by the tiger that is there. The hairs on my arms and neck stand in alarm, I sense a terrible danger, and I turn immediately, though I know it is already too late. But as I turn, I instinctively know it is not Charlie; for he would have already shot me dead.

She stands but two arm-lengths away, squarely facing me. The woman is not young nor is she elderly, but I would guess at least 15 or 20 years older than I. The eye contact is immediate and is not kind. She begins to speak in a most unfriendly tone, and as she does, she makes repeated gestures to the coconut tree and herself while shaking her head, "No." I have learned perhaps 30 or 40 words of Vietnamese, hardly enough to possess much fluency, but I quickly grasp her meaning. "The grove, the trees, the coconuts are mine, no you cannot take them, now go."

I respond *"No, no, no, Mama-san. Di-di, Mama-san, di-di"* (go, go). I turn back to the coconut tree and continue with the task at hand. But she is not to be dismissed, and she moves with me, taking a half step closer. She begins shouting, her voice angry now, as I attempt to knock a coconut loose from high above; but it remains stubbornly attached. I just want to get a coconut and then leave; she can have the rest of them to herself. She continues with her verbal assault; it is non-stop. I attempt to appease her, displaying my index finger and telling her *"One, one, just one Mama-san, just one."* I make a gesture with my hand that I wish to drink the juice; I bring a phantom coconut to my lips as to drink it, but it does no good; her verbal torrent continues.

But now she pushes things. She steps close in and reaches to take the bamboo pole from me. I cannot allow this; I do not trust her so close; she is becoming wild. I instinctively step back, and with the same motion, I bring the bamboo pole down towards her, gesturing as if to slash her across the shoulder. I shout, *"Get back Mama-san, get back, di-di mau Mama-san, di-di mau"*. (Go quickly Mama san, go quickly.) She stops in her tracks for a moment, and I take that brief opportunity to move around the tree, but she comes right after me. I cannot allow her; I will not allow her to come so close. I hold the bamboo pole with my left arm and with my right hand I grab the M-16 that hangs by its strap from my shoulder and I swing it upward to point it at her chest high. I shout, *"dung lie, dung lie."* (stop, stop). She stops and even shuts up, if only briefly.

"Don't make me do this Mama-san, don't you make me do this." I gesture with my rifle for her to move back, and she does until I get her back around the tree. I take a brief look at the coconut tree, and now, holding her at gun point with my right hand, I begin to hit the coconut with the bamboo pole using my left arm. It only takes two or three solid pokes and the coconut drops to the ground with a soft thud. Finally. You would think it would end now, but this only enrages her more, and she begins screaming at me again in rapid-fire Vietnamese.

I want to tell her that I am sorry for taking the coconut, but that I am in desperate need of its juice. I have had no water since the previous afternoon. We have had a horrific and deadly morning. I have no money to pay you for it. I risk my life to help you. I don't want to be in this fucking place. I hate the fucking Army more than you do. But you have a thousand coconuts, you will not miss one, I must have it.

But there is no time for this, there is no way I can communicate this to her. And given her rage, I don't think she will listen or even care. I am sure she sees me as some brutal alien invader who is stealing her coconut. And she is right.

Now if I can just pick up that coconut, I will get out of this coconut grove from hell. My eyes dart toward the coconut on the ground, it lies but six feet from me. I make small, slow side steps towards it, but she moves with me and moves closer to me as well. *"Don't you dare Mama san. Don't you dare."* and I shake my head emphatically no. In spite of her lack of English, I am certain she understands me.

I still hold my M-16 on her and now bend at the knee. I keep a fixed stare on her, but with my peripheral vision, I can see the coconut, and with a slow and even motion I grasp it with my left hand and hold it to my chest as I stand. I try to speak in an even voice, *"We are almost done Mama-san, just let me go,"* and as I say this, I slowly step backward. But she follows me now step by step. She is screaming once again at me, gesturing violently with her hand.

"Don't do this Mama-san, don't make me do this, don't you push me Mama-san." But I am backing up blindly, and I have no idea what I am backing up to. I desperately want to look around me, but I don't dare. I do the next best thing, I glance quickly at my feet to see where they are, but it is a mistake. She lunges at my chest striking me and the coconut; it falls from my grasp. Oh god…

And now in a loud whisper, *"You mother fucker Mama-san, you mother fucker".* There is no way out of this. She, I…We have turned down a terrible road which has no outlet. You already know how this will end. She will not yield the coconut, I desperately need it, and there is no middle ground. I know some of my comrades in arms would have already greased her when she had lunged.

She stands silently six feet from me, and now with my left hand free of the coconut, I bring it to the front grip of my rifle. I know I have a round in the chamber. I made sure of it very early this morning at 4:00 AM, and I know it is still there. There is a soft, yet audible "click" as I pivot the tiny lock by the trigger grip from "safety" to "semi." She now begins a new and furious torrent, screaming unintelligible Vietnamese at me. I know somewhere in me that I should walk away, but I cannot. I will not leave without the coconut. Outside observers would find this scene unfathomable, this terrible crossroad at the edge of hell, but they do not stand where I stand. I stand with one foot in Paradise and one foot in Hell; I perfectly straddle the boundary; there is only one rule: you cannot stay here, chose one or the other.

But there is a sickening momentum now; the current is so strong that it carries things along even against their will. I try in desperation to stop this flow, for I already know the terrible outcome, but it's too late now, and both she and I know what I am going to do. I hold my rifle steadily upon her; it is aimed directly at her chest. I want her to know that I must have that stinking coconut. I want her to understand that I will kill her for it. So, I plead, *"Don't make me do this Mama-san, don't make me do this."* But she will not stop.

I want her to know that this is her last chance. With my right hand, I pull the spring-loaded bolt back on my rifle. As the bolt moves backward, it ejects the round that is in the chamber; it pops out of the side just above the clip (magazine) and drops to the ground. She watches intently, even as she continues her torrent. I let the bolt go. Its spring slams it forward now, and as it does, it catches the next round that sits at the top of the clip and pushes it fully into the chamber. Now we both know, with an absolute and terrible certainty, "little black death" is ready.

But this only increases the intensity of her abuse toward me. I aim at her; I see her face and her mouth; I see from it the spittle splaying forth. Her rage and hate are surreal. It cannot be about a stinking coconut, but she continues. My left voice tells me this is murder, my right voice tells me get the coconut. I step backward, she steps forward, and she will not allow me to leave. I stare into hell and hell stares back. Neither side flinches. I hold my finger to the trigger…and… now my life is changed.

And I Feel The Hand Of Buddha

I don't know how long he had been standing there. I did not see him coming, I did not sense his approach and surely, with her raging, I could not have heard him. But by the gentlest touch, I feel his hand on my shoulder, and it is angelic. And with his other hand, he ever so gently and forgivingly raises my M-16 above the woman's head. It is as if a thousand pounds are lifted from my back. The hand of Buddha pulls me from the boundary. He saves two lives. His benevolence towards me is as a soothing balm. He is one of the

South Vietnamese soldiers from the other side of the coconut grove. He may have been with us this morning, riding on one of the other tracks. If he wasn't, then his friends were. Either way, he knows the pain.

He speaks sharply to the woman, but only a few words. Her response is nearly as brief, but her voice is still full of rage. The ARVN reaches into his pocket and throws a tiny coin onto the ground by her feet. She quickly picks the coin up and then immediately berates him; she wants more money. The ARVN screams back at her, but she curses him. I fear all that has happened is that the ARVN and I have simply traded places, but without any resolution. She bitterly continues to complain, though I am so relieved by the intervention of the ARVN soldier that I no longer hear her words.

The ARVN stoops and then picks up both the green coconut and the single M-16 round. He smiles benignly as he hands them to me. I take them, in a wordless exchange, but nod my head gratefully. The ARVN very gently pats my right shoulder twice and nods his head, his serene smile telling me, "It's okay now." And then gestures for me to leave, as he attempts to step away, but the woman blocks his way and continues to send her torrent of hate and anger at him. She will not stop. Does she want to die?

I am so deeply shocked and so overwhelmed by the totality of this morning's events I can barely think and function. But years later as I think back to this moment, I am now so greatly indebted to the humanity of the Buddha. Imagine carrying the weight of a cold-blooded murder over the years and decades.

I stand motionless for a short moment. I must will myself to move. I put the bullet into my pocket and, holding the coconut to my chest, I begin walking back along the path back to the tracks. I just want to get out of this coconut grove from hell. Why risk another encounter with this tiny village's lone banshee, who is hell bent on suicide? I hate this place.

The Long Afternoon

I return to the encampment, but I speak to no one. I find the knife still sticking in a brown husk. I pull it loose and then hack away at the top of my green coconut, finally twisting the blade into it. The kid from Detroit, possibly 20, asks if I will share it. My harsh response even shocks me: "How about I shoot you instead?" He whines, as if he is deeply offended. But I don't respond; I walk a short distance to the base of a palm tree and sit against its trunk. I take a drink. It is wet, but it is devoid of any taste. There is no pleasure in it. Maybe the price was too high, but I cannot possibly drink it. I hold the coconut for a very long moment, then stand, walk over to Detroit and wordlessly hand him the coconut. He is dumbfounded, and he begins to say "What the...?" I have no response. I return to my position at the base of the palm tree and I sit in quiet despair.

The time passes with agonizing slowness. Too much has happened this day for me even to begin to think through any of it. The heat is near unbearable; I wonder when they will bring us water. On June 21st, the sun reached the Tropic of Cancer at 23. 4 degrees above the equator. In the past six or seven weeks, it has slowly made its way back to the south. We sit here at about 14 degrees above the equator, and the sun has moved just past us. But it still blazes almost directly over our heads, and it scorches Binh Dinh Province as if we were placed an inch from a mammoth heat lamp. There is not a single cloud. The air will no longer move.

It is now 2:00 PM, and finally we hear in the stillness of the unrelenting, oppressive heat, the sound of a helicopter in the distance. It is miles from us, but its pitch is low, heavy and its approach moves slowly. We instantly know it is not a Huey in a hurry. It must be a big Chinook coming for our "water buffalo". We are momentarily buoyed, but then so deeply disappointed that our hearts sink. It is a heavy-lift chopper, a "sky crane", but it has not come to take the water tanker for refill. It has come to lift out the blown track. The Army's priorities at this moment are so gut-wrenchingly perverted.

The "sky crane" is the oddest of birds. There is the smallest possible fuselage up front, which will hold the two pilots and little more. Behind and above are two massive engines that power a six-bladed prop of great length, and that is it. There is no dead weight; it is designed only to lift very heavy payloads. We watch it hover over the very distant sand bowl for several minutes. It slowly lowers itself to within twenty feet of the ground and holds. They must be trying to attach the carrying cables to the track, but all we can see is a sandstorm. It is probably ten more minutes at least when we hear its pitch rise. It now attempts to lift the track from the sand bowl. The sand-storm created by the massive props beating the air grows a hundred feet high, and the "sky crane" vanishes behind it.

We can hear this battle of chopper blades vs. gravity for several more minutes, but still, we see no helicopter. I wonder at what pace this goliath gulps fuel, but that may be the plan. The more fuel it burns, the lighter it becomes. After another couple of minutes, we see the "sky crane" rising above its self-made sandstorm, the crippled track dangling beneath it. He keeps going up and then slowly turns and heads southwest at a rather modest pace. I hope he gets higher, for he is a fat and slow-moving target.

About a half hour later, the track that was guarding the blown track pulls in. Those guys look absolutely awful, as if half dead. But they look at us with the same disbelieving faces. We are their mirror image. I guess they hoped that by some miracle we had found something to drink and were eager to share it. But as dangerously dehydrated as they are, there is nothing here for anyone. We must look terrible; our collective condition only discourages them further. They park their track under some palms and then immediately lie on the ground in the shade. We must all wait. It is now just before 2:45 PM. The sun and the heat will not relent; it's probably nearing 110°F, the humidity is crushing us to near death. When the air temperature nears that of the human body; the body attempts to regulate its temperature by sweating. As this moisture is evaporated into the air, heat is released cooling the body down. But at this moment we are in an environment where the ambient air temperature is dangerously far above that of the body. This nightmare scenario is cruelly worsened by air which will not hold any further water vapor. Our sweat will not evaporate, we can only get hotter until we die. Death by heat stroke is most unpleasant; hell, we won't even be awarded Purple Hearts as we were not wounded.

By 4:00 PM, we are becoming fretful that we will not get any water today. If we had not lost that track to the land mine, we could have sent a pair of tracks in with the water buffalo earlier today. It would have taken several hours to go back to Uplift, fill the tank and return, but we probably would have completed the return trip by now. The concern now is that if it gets much later, there won't be enough daylight for a chopper to make the round trip with the water buffalo. They won't risk flying into a hot LZ at night just to bring water, and I cannot blame them. We will just have to tough it out one more anguishing night without water. But the next day will be beyond terrible; I don't see how we will live through it.

One On One, Again

Another half hour passes and we hear the unmistakable sound of a Chinook coming our way. The Chinook is massive; it is the Army's biggest helicopter. It appears directly, but only briefly, over the "water buffalo" and then peels off to the south turning in a big loop. The pilot radios in telling us we must move the "water buffalo" further away from the hamlet because the pilot could see the thatch roofs of the nearby hooches starting to lift away.

Our universal reaction is, "So what? Blow them over." Given the last 24 hours, we have little sympathy for anyone. But our radio operator adds that they won't take the water buffalo otherwise. Given my life changing, gut-wracking encounter with the woman in the coconut grove, I am the most motivated and determined of any man here to get us water. I shout, "Okay, let's push it farther away." I rally five or six of my half-dead comrades. "Come on, we can do this." I lean against the tank and I PUSH! The others join me, but it is surprisingly heavy even empty, and it is difficult to push across the rough ground of the scrubby plain. It seems a Herculean effort, and I cannot understand the heaviness of the dry water tank, but looking back the task is so difficult because we are so weak. We are at the edge of heat exhaustion if not heat stroke. We push it for nearly two hundred feet until it stops hard against the first berm of the dry rice paddies. Now the Chinook comes back around and starts to lower itself, but then peels off slowly to the south again. There's no need for a call from the pilot. every one of us, me included, could see the thatch roofs of the nearest few hooches begin to lift away.

Everyone is now completely pissed off. There are several shouts of "fuck'em." I'm not sure if they refer to the pilots or the villagers. I fear they mean both. But I am determined that we will have water tonight; I will not yield: this has to be done. I shout, "We can do this; we can do this. We just need to get a running start."

The berm of the rice paddy is nearly two and a half feet high. It is very steeply pitched and almost rectangular; it will be like trying to roll something up a huge stair tread. More to the point, we are weak, tired, and dehydrated, and we are running out of time. We pull and push the water buffalo back away from the berm a short distance and then attempt to get a running start to get over the berm. We barely get halfway up, but we can't hold it, so we let it roll back down. Now we push it farther from the berm to get a longer running start. We try again and fail again. We try a third time and fail. I know we don't have much left. I shout "Okay, this is it, give me everything, it's now or never."

We grunt, we groan, we curse under our breath, and we hit the berm hard. There is a moment when we almost stall at the top, but I will not be denied, and I shout, "Keep it going." We go over the top ever so slowly, but then pick up speed on the way down the far side, and we push it another fifty yards out into the dry paddy. Now all eyes look to me; they seem to think that I have hooked a water buffalo to a Chinook many times before. Maybe because I am the tallest, they think I will be able to reach the Chinook's center hook more easily. But there is no time for discussion, I just climb onto the top of the water buffalo like I know what I am doing, and I grab the large steel ring that sits on top of the tank. It is this hoop that holds the ends of four steel braided wires that run from each corner of the water buffalo. It would seem intuitively obvious that I must slip this steel ring onto a large hook that projects about a foot from beneath the center of the Chinook. But in the hurried pressure of bringing a Chinook into a "hot LZ," the execution of this task becomes immensely difficult.

A Souvenir For Life

The Chinook comes around immediately and slowly lowers itself to just over my head. The noise underneath the Chinook is deafening; the downward prop wash which supports this behemoth above me is thunderous. I stand on the center of the top of the water tank and hold the steel ring high above my head. The steel wire straps, leading away from the ring back to each corner, form a pyramid that I now stand inside.

Just above and in front of me, I see a small glass window on the bottom of the Chinook. The window slides open to one side, and then I see the head and shoulders of the Crew Chief appear. His uniform is dark green; it is clean, almost pristine. He wears an olive drab helmet; a small mic extends from its side. I cannot hear him, but I do see his lips move as he speaks to the pilot, who sits far forward in the cockpit and is completely blind as to what is happening directly underneath the helicopter. I make eye contact with the Crew Chief, and I lock onto it, never once breaking it until near the very end.

The hook on the bottom of the fuselage is high and in front of me. The CC's (Crew Chief) lips move, and the Chinook slowly backs down to me, but it drifts to my right, out of reach of the steel ring I hold. I see the lips of the CC move, and the Chinook moves forward slowly, stops, then backs down to me but drifts to the right again. They try again and again; too far right, too far left, then perfectly centered but far too high. They grow frustrated, and the minutes and the daylight are ticking away. The roar of the engines, and especially the wind noise coming from the massive blades above me, are so ear-piercing, that it seems I stand in complete silence.

I watch the lips of the Crew Chief move, but I hear no words. The ever so slow drifting right or left or up and down of the massive Chinook only inches from my outstretched arms, feeds the brain a false reality of a silent, slow-motion world. In my peripheral vision, I can just see to my left my comrades in arms some distance away, but they must perceive me as standing in a hurricane. After several more failed attempts, the CC points his finger at his watch on the opposite wrist and shakes his head. They are running out of time... and it makes me livid.

I will not be defeated. Perhaps my earlier experience with the hamlet's crazed suicidal banshee in the coconut grove was preparing me for this moment. She would not let me go with a coconut; I will not let them go without this water buffalo. Buddha, being a tough master, trains me well, for he requires discipline. I give the Crew Chief the most incredulous look, and I nod my head yes as in *yes, we're running out of time because you were late showing and yes, you're an asshole if you leave now.* But most emphatically, I refuse to break my eye contact; I will not let him go.

If there was one universal grumble about the flyboys, it was that some of them were just a little too clean, just a little too far above it all. Don't get me wrong; I unequivocally state they had as much guts as anybody else, and some had more. But it was their lack of perspective, or at least their detached perspective, about what it is like on the ground that caused the rift. They might do well to spend some time in some isolated crappy firebase or spend a little time here in the boonies. Spend a few nights here, sleep on the ground, eat crappy c-rations, squat and take a crap behind the bushes, and hope that your fellow flyboys will bring you some water.

I stare at the Crew Chief with great intensity, almost glaring. He wears a perfectly neat and clean flight uniform; it is a deep dark olive green in color. I wear someone else's uniform. It is the same washed out, sun-faded uniform I put on days ago; it is dirty and sweat-stained, and I'm sure it must stink. It bears the name of some other guy who has either gone home or is dead. I hold my stare fixed and hard; *respect me flyboy, respect me. Don't you dare quit.*

I have been holding the steel ring above my head the whole time, but now I stretch the straps tightly and move the ring backwards and forwards, as to say, "Come on, come on." I know he reads my face, and I think I see the faintest smile. His lips move to speak some silent words into the mic. A moment passes, and then he holds his right index finger upward and gestures three times with it as if to say, "Okay grunt, let's try it again."

The pilot now slides the Chinook backward and downward, but it is too fast and too hard. I duck, but I still feel the underside of the fuselage brush my head, and I must lie down on the top of the water buffalo tank as the Chinook passes over my body; any lower and he will crush me. I see the Crew Chief's face clearly; we are now so close. I watch his lips moving rapidly as he speaks into the mic, and I now hear him screaming "Lift, lift." The Chinook now abruptly reverses its course. I look over my right shoulder, and now I see the hook coming rapidly back towards me. I have a sense of how Charles the Third felt; I must stay disciplined, I cannot flinch, nor will I be rushed, but this is the "now or never" moment of my young life.

I scramble to my feet and stretch the straps as hard as I can, and the steel hoop catches the hook. Alas, I am now airborne as the Chinook now jerks the water buffalo from the rice paddy; I must get off *now*. I jump forward and to the left. I am at least 12, maybe 15 feet or more above the ground. As I fall, I feel the water buffalo rush by me. I am midair as its left wheel brushes against the back of my head. I land on my feet, but hit the ground very hard, as the baked clay of that dry rice paddy has the consistency of concrete. The pain in my knees is off the charts, and I then fall forward landing on my chest. My comrades all cheer and rush toward me. But I am in such pain I cannot stand; as a group they pick me up and carry me back to the shade of the palm trees. We will have water tonight.

I don't actually recall the Chinook returning; I am in too much pain. But I guess an hour or so later the Chinook returns with the water buffalo full, and someone else unclips it from the hook. It's anticlimactic at this point. It is so much easier to unhook the ring. We have our water.

Years later, my knees bother me greatly, the pain a memento of this day and place. But the reminder is not necessary, I will never forget this day. And I will walk with a limp for the rest of my life; it is my souvenir for life. After all, I have foolishly and most stupidly broken **Cardinal Rule III: Never Get Brave – You Will Always Get Hurt.**

The evening, and for that matter the night, is quiet and mundane. We do rehydrate ourselves, and we finally eat, now that we have water to cook with and water to wash it down with. And Charlie leaves us alone. If I had been Charlie, I would have hit us hard. We and the ARVNs have taken 25% casualties; we are undermanned and leaderless. But Charlie leaves us be, not a single shot fired into us that entire night. The only thing happening in the darkness of that night is that one of us pops a single hand-held flare around 2:00am; he is suspicious of some perceived motion, but there is nothing to be seen. The flare provides modest illumination for a minute or so then goes dark as it burns itself out. It drifts backwards over us and probably lands near the hamlet's hooches just yards from us. It is a most insignificant event that should easily be forgotten, but the next morning that burnt-out flare starts a chain of events whose cruelty haunts me to this day. The evil presence still patiently sits among us and will work his craft at his next opportunity.

Lord Of The Flies Part II: Why Are We Gassing Children?

We awaken to a new day. It has cooled off significantly overnight, and there is the slightest bit of breeze blowing from east to west. A breeze early in the morning, even as weak as this one, is an extreme rarity. What good fortune, and we take it as a virtuous omen, though unknowingly, we should not. For whatever reason, Charlie had left us alone last night despite our being so undermanned and leaderless. I make no understatement: Most of us are happy to see the light of day. We made it through the night unscathed, we are alive, and we have water. We arise as a group as the sunlight wakes all at about the same moment. We make a bit of breakfast and drink some instant coffee as we now have plenty of water. We sit in a small group now, as opposed to being more spread out as we were days earlier. But there are just 18 of us now; the day before there were 25 of us.

There is some banter among a few of us, but it is a much, much more subdued group this morning for obvious reasons. Still, we have made it through a terrible ordeal, and there is a glimmer of hope that we will be okay going forward. We are down one track (APC) and its complement, we are too undermanned and leaderless, and unless we are reinforced, they will pull us back into base camp. I doubt we will be sent on any more missions to take any of Charlie's villages. We just have to get through the next couple of days and nights and we will be fine. Life will be okay once again.

But it is not to be. The evil presence still haunts us and most patiently waits for the next opportunity. And soon, I will be again kicked in the gut by **Cardinal Rule Number II: Never Forget, It Can Always Be Worse.**

Just behind us, to our west, we see about a dozen or fifteen kids from the village playing with the tiny spent parachute flare that was fired into the air just hours earlier, in the dead of night. The burnt-out flare is still attached to its parachute, so the kids roll it up and then throw it in the air. The oldest kids are about eight years old, no more than nine, and the youngest are about three. A steady but very light breeze catches the parachute and carries it slowly across the dry rice paddy that we had pushed the water buffalo across the day before. The breeze moves so slowly, the kids only walking, easily keep up with the drifting parachute. The children and the families of this tiny hamlet are far too poor to buy toys, but this tiny parachute makes a great one. We watch them for a while; they laugh, shriek and joyously scream their heads off. They are having a ball throwing it into the air and then chasing it as the wind, as weak as it is, carries it. After the hell of yesterday, we laugh along with the kids. We are having a good time as well.

But now the evil presence works his craft. The My Lai massacre had occurred a year earlier, though almost no one had heard about it other than the American unit that committed the atrocity. And hostile, volatile, bloody Binh Dinh province, where we are now, has had its own massacre only weeks earlier, although it is unknown to us. One may wonder how such things happen or are allowed to happen, or the bigger question: if started, why doesn't someone stop it before it spins out of control? I don't have good answers. There are many contributing factors, but one thing is always common: bad leadership or no leadership at all. **It's Cardinal Rule Number IV: Never Yield To The Lord Of The Flies.**

The Madness Of Vietnam: The Day We Lost The War

Cardinal Rule VI: Never Do Kids, For There Is No Bottom

Behind me, as I watch the kids of the village play with most of the others, one of my comrades has grabbed the "Thumper", the M-79 grenade launcher, aka, the obese single barrel shotgun. I now hear the loud "thump" of the grenade launcher as a round is discharged just over our heads out toward where the children of the village play.

I take a quick look around and see the guy who fired the M-79 round. He is smiling, so I assume he means no malice and has only fired a parachute flare so that the kids will have another toy to play with. He has aimed the round low, with no attempt at height at all, so that flare will burn on the ground and not in the air. Still, I think this a little too risky and unwise, as the flare will burn with great heat, and a child could be seriously burned. But I hope the kids will wait until the flare extinguishes itself before they grab its parachute.

The round, about the size of an elongated fist, bounces once or twice as it hits the ground and then rolls to a stop. I watch and wait for the flare to ignite itself, but it never does. I watch the round intensely, now thinking it's a dud. But then I spot a thin whitish wisp of vapor that can just barely be seen dissipating from the canister. I scream, "NO," but the kids, squealing with delight, run after it as fast as their legs will take them and never hear my shouting.

The older boys, perhaps 8 or 9 years old, reach the invisible cloud of gas together. They are so winded by their running that they take in huge lungsful of the gas and almost immediately cry out. They don't know what has happened to them; they cannot understand what they have done wrong. They scream as if tortured and then turn running blindly, rubbing their eyes as tears run down their faces. The bigger boys now collide head on into the younger kids rushing to catch up to get to what they think is the parachute. But heads smash into other heads and many of the kids collapse to the ground. Some of the kids struggle to their feet, holding their heads in great pain with their hands, some now have blood running down their faces. A few of the kids are unable to stand but manage to get on their hands and knees and begin to crawl back toward the hamlet. One tiny kid never gets up. He lies near that canister breathing in its poison. The reaction of my comrades is mixed. Half laugh out loud, but this is only funny in the way that a sick and twisted Three Stooges film clip is funny. The rest of us are sickened.

I am filled with an excruciating rage. Why the kids? They are not much more than babies; they are the only innocents in this madness of Vietnam. My first thought is, I will kill the guy who has done this. I now directly face the laughing, smiling asshole who did this. He is less than 25 feet from me. He belly-laughs as these kids scream. He is an incredibly sadistic bastard. I wonder whether he was always a prick. For him, the fun is not so much in the killing; his pleasure is in the torture.

I sit on the ground, as my knees are still too painful to stand on, but I hold my M-16 in my lap. I now turn it in his direction and, at the same moment, I know I will never get away with shooting him; the Army will court-martial me. Beyond him, I see our young buck Sergeant who I suspect is no older than I am. He smiles guiltily and shamefacedly at me, for he knows this is terribly wrong; but he should not have those stripes. He should have stopped this, but he lacks the courage.

Now the sadist opens the grenade launcher and pulls the empty cartridge out, and re-loads with another round of gas. He is going to gas the kids again. I cannot, I will not allow him to do so. I stare at him, and he watches intently as I now point my rifle directly at him. I then move the safety the two clicks from off to semi to auto. The index finger of my right-hand now rests against the trigger. This motion, this gesticulation of my fingers is not lost upon him, for he stops his laughing. It's easy to be a bully with a weapon in your hand, but now we both have one, and I am not a four-year-old little boy. He stares back at me and reads my eyes. He sees the boiling rage. I don't blink. He knows I will shoot him if he fires into those kids again.

He now points his weapon in my direction. From a distance of about 20 feet or so, that tear gas round will punch a hole in my chest big enough to drive a truck thru. But this only increases my resolve; I do not flinch. If I die protecting these kids, then so be it; if I die in Vietnam for this, then for what better reason? The sadist stares back in anger but reads correctly the hardness and hatred in my face. There is an outwardly long moment, but I do not turn away. I do not lower my face; I do not yield. Then he unloads the round from the grenade launcher and places it on the ground. He shrugs his shoulders and gives me a goofy smile as if to say, "I was just having fun." I now look back at the dry paddy where a single child lies; I see another small child from the hamlet leading an elderly farmer to him. The elder stoops down and picks the limp boy up into his arms and carries the child back toward the hamlet. There is only silence now. I look toward our medic but he does not offer any aid. He and our buck Sergeant disgust me nearly as much as the sadist. I ask the rhetorical questions to myself: How much blood do you really want on your hands? How do you go home after a day like this?

I think most of the rest of the unit is relieved that this didn't go any further, though no one has come up to me and said thanks for stopping this. But I am also certain that a few grumble that it is just gook kids, so what's the big deal? But no one dares to challenge me.

I never saw myself as any kind of hero, or even particularly brave. I never got a medal or a commendation for this, but one doesn't stop an atrocity in order to get a medal. I was just too angry to let this go on. Nothing more, nothing less; probably just a young fool desperately clinging to some last bit of decency and humanity before all was lost; desperately trying to save myself. But I could not let this go on. You don't do kids, because once you start, there is no bottom. And though I did not think of this at the time, my yin and yang were gravely out of balance from my encounter with the woman in the coconut grove; without my knowing it, perhaps this expunged a small portion of my karmic debt.

But the life lesson here is this: Find the courage to go against the grain. Find the courage to go it alone. If you take a stand like this, be prepared to stand alone; you may not ever get any backup. I didn't. Maybe the stakes were too high for another man to back me; after all, I and the sadist were pointing very lethal weapons at each other, and both of us had their index finger snug to the triggers. Who wants to die in that crossfire? So, I must stand and bear this weight alone. But I was on a knife's edge; enough bullies, enough travesties, enough cruelty. So, I sat, hoping he would shoot, so that I might shoot him. How deadly this game? How awful this morning?

I owe nothing to those children, except humanity. They are powerless, being bullied by the sadist with the power who takes great pleasure in the egregiously and unspeakably cruel and dirty trick he is playing upon them. He is about to do it again. Who will stand up for them? Who will defend children?

I look back at this moment five decades later. After I recently told this part of the story to another veteran, he responded a week later telling me, "If I were a betting man, I would have bet against you. You shouldn't be alive." I thought about his reaction to this part of the story for many days, and in the end, I decided he was probably right.

I don't remember much of the rest of the day; only that it was rather somber. Earlier that morning when we first awoke, there had been a tiny glimmer of hope and the possibility of a little happiness because we had made it through the night unscathed. But that has all been destroyed with the gassing of the hamlet's kids. No one speaks of that morning's terrible event that day or the next. And no one, but no one, dares to give me any shit about spoiling the fun; if anything at all, some silently respect me. But who knows, maybe all they see is another nut with a gun and a death wish? I hate this place; I hate myself for having gotten us the water, I hate myself for having enabled this conduct. I hate myself for being here.

For these last few days, I have been living life at a thousand miles an hour. To what end? If you're not careful, this place will eat you alive and you won't even know it.

That night is uneventful and the next day our Lieutenant returned. He is much improved, though he still looks pale and has lost some weight. He must have been quite sick. We never go back into that hamlet to swap c-rations for baths with the kids we had just gassed; how could we? This war is lost. Why would anyone in that hamlet back us in fighting the Viet Cong or North Vietnamese Army when we have gassed their children?

By the next day, we have been pulled back to Uplift. Skeleton crews drive the tracks back to the LZ, towing that water buffalo behind them. The rest of us are picked up with a Chinook, and we ride back in silence to Uplift. I had planned to stay with the infantry as it is more to my liking than the artillery battery I was in previously. But after the gassing of those kids, I know that at some point I would probably shoot the sadist (or he me). When I tell people that I hated Vietnam, they have no idea. Yeah, yeah, I know, I came close to greasing some woman over a stinking coconut days before, but it was not for the fun of it.

About 12 months later, it is August again, and I am back home in the US. My mother returns from her office job in the very late afternoon. As we have supper together, she tells me that everyone in her office is talking about how they feel about Vietnam. She tells me that someone said, "Your son was in Vietnam, what does he say about it?" I ask my mother what her response was. She responds, "He says nothing, nothing at all." I reply to my mother, "That's right Momma, I say nothing at all."

After the gassing of the kids, I console myself, telling myself that though these kids will not trust us now, that is a good thing. Better that way, better that they keep away from us, as the more time they spend around us, the greater the risk of tragedy. I hate this war, I hate Vietnam, and I hate the Army. And for decades, I bury this memory as deeply as I can. I repress this memory, into the deepest part of my being, somehow fooling myself that this event never happened. It is not until 2005, while doing relief work in Indonesia following the earthquake and tsunami, that I go into a coconut grove with a young Indonesian co-worker to get coconuts to drink. The memories are stirred and eventually break through to the surface. You never ever truly forget these kinds of things.

Five decades later, a PBS documentary covering the Vietnam War airs. Near the end of the story, a veteran is interviewed and he recalls another grim travesty. And he states words to the effect: "If there is one thing I could do, to make this war better, it would be to shoot the man that committed these crimes." I know what he means.

The Return, Back Into The Frying Pan

The Chinook lands at Uplift in midafternoon, and we pile out. I say nothing to my comrades, not even a good-bye. I limp as I walk alone back over to my old unit and head to my old hooch. It seems odd coming back here. I have been gone only a few weeks, but the break with my old unit seemed so complete.

There is a new Executive Officer (2nd in command); he seems young for a Major. I guess "Shaky" must have rotated out during my short stint with the infantry. I don't think Shaky got his medal and he was never going to make light colonel, not in this Army, screwed up as it was. He wasn't one of them, and they were never going to let him join the club. As I near my old hooch, I salute our new major (though I am not required to), and he returns it smartly. He asks, as he looks over my rather worn and weather-beaten uniform, where I have been, and when I tell him, he seems favorably impressed. He seems much more professional then the last two XO's we've had. I get to know him better later on. He is a lifer, but at least not a bully.

I enter my old hooch and find my old bunk, built of 2x4's and wooden ammo boxes. It still lies unoccupied. I guess I'm home. I find my footlocker and dig out some clean clothes, though they are a bit musty. I walk over to our communal shower and bathe; it has been many days, and the warm water and soap feel good. I dress and then head to our mess hall, as it is just about suppertime. I don't remember the meal so much, but it seems luxurious to be seated at a table instead of on the ground, even if it's paper covered plywood and a hard-wooden bench with no back. I am one of the first to arrive for dinner, but I take my time and linger, and soon I am joined by old friends. They look at me as at a ghost that has returned, and they tell me it seems as though I have been away a very long time. They are right; despite the fact that it has been only a few weeks, it seems like years to me as well.

I ask what has become of Grandpa. Bitter John and Big D tell me that he was court-martialed down in Quy Nhon, but they know nothing of the details. There is a strong rumor that he has been sent to "LBJ," but it is never confirmed.

The Army has its military "stockade" or prison located at Long Binh, in Dong Nai Province. With hundreds of thousands of Army GIs in South Vietnam, there are bound to be some who commit a crime that requires incarceration in a military stockade. The stockade, the prison, a.k.a. the Long Binh Jail, very quickly became known as LBJ, in a less than complimentary reference to President Lyndon Baines Johnson. Long Binh Jail was a little-known but sad legacy of Vietnam. It held tens of thousands of Army GIs over the years and had a notorious hellish reputation. The year before, there had been a terrible riot there that lasted days, including the murder of a prisoner by fellow inmates who beat him to death with a shovel. If Grandpa has gone there...

We change subjects and talk of happier things. There will be a movie tonight, and Big D tells me he has some really great joints and we can get stoned before it starts. The lifers will get drunk and we will get stoned, and so it goes at Uplift.

The next day was probably taken up with meaningless shit work details, I don't remember, but I do check the guard roster and I am back on it for that night. That didn't take long. Time drags on; the days are filled with work details around our part of the LZ. Nothing has changed. Those of us who don't really have a particular job or skill that is needed become part of the sub-group that does the grunt work around the compound. It is mostly replacing sand bags, restringing barbed wire, guard duty, and any crappy detail that pops up.

I am back to supervising our Vietnamese day laborers, but it is a much different situation from before. They are still the same poor, struggling peasants of the countryside, but I have changed. We are not quite the same friends we once were, as I have a much harder edge and now look at them with a bit more suspicion, wondering if their sympathy leans toward Charlie. I am still kind and respectful to them, but now in a much more distant way. Trong is still the foreman and has not seen me in some time; he still wears his "pork pie" hat. He asks where I have been, and when I tell him he looks back at me in disbelief, as if looking at a crazed person. He says, as he shakes his head, *"Beaucoup Charlies, beaucoup Charlies."* He is, of course, very correct.

In the evening it is again the near perpetual guard duty in one of the bunkers on the perimeter. But my bunker mates on the line find me to be a bit of a pain in the ass, especially the first couple of weeks. On my first evening back on guard duty, while there is still a bit of daylight, a nearby bunker shoots a burst of machine gun fire. I am sitting on the floor of the top bunker, and I scream at my comrades to hand me my rifle and for them to open up. But they shout back, "Calm down, it's just the next bunker test firing. What's the matter with you?" But I cannot help myself; in the boonies when one hears live fire, it's the real deal and not anybody test firing for the hell of it. My time in the bush has changed me, and I now wonder if I have not become one of Pavlov's dogs? I must fight this.

AH Frank is worse than ever, the never-ending sandbags details, and the ever-constant rhythm of another night sitting in a bunker on the line. At times I truly regret not having tried to stay with the Infantry unit I had been with. It was far better than this drudgery.

Hot Showers

I do find a way to vent at least a little of my frustration, though it is quite by accident. And I do get a little help from one of the cooks. One little job that is done daily, come rain or shine, is to fuel up and light the gasoline heaters that warm the overhead water tanks. There are two shower shacks placed next to each other, one for the enlisted men and one for the Officers and NCO's. The shower shacks are just a rectangular shed-like building with a doorway opening at each end, but with no actual door. There is a concrete floor, and the sides are just horizontal boards widely spaced apart; this provides some privacy and ventilation at the same time. Overhead are perhaps a dozen showerheads that are operated by simple brass valves, the kind you can buy in a hardware store back home for 79 cents. There is no hot or cold-water feed to make any adjustment with, but the water is never cold or that hot, not even on the hottest day of the year. On top of the tarp-covered roof is a large free-standing steel water tank. The water flows from here into a couple of copper pipes that feed the showers in a long loop around the shed. It is nothing fancy and the water pressure is low, only being gravity-fed just a few feet above your head, but it works.

There are about twenty guys from Service Battery stationed with us in Headquarters Battery at Uplift. They deliver the 105 rounds to a couple of our nearby firing batteries, but also drive the water tanker truck that is used to fill our water storage tanks, be it for the cooks or for the showers. Just inside the water tanks that are over the showers is a crude gasoline immersion heater used to warm the water. It is clever, though a bit dangerous. There is a gas tank next to it that feeds a small valve that allows gasoline to enter the water heater a drop at a time. You ignite the dripping fuel with a long stick and then adjust the valve to control the size of the flame. Everyone on the guard roster has this duty every so often, but usually only once a month. So, it is easy enough to forget to do.

It is my turn on this particular day. Usually, the water tanker driver fills the water tanks right after lunch. That done, we then fill the fuel tank with gasoline and then light the water heater, so that by the early evening the water is quite warm. But I forget to do it for some reason and I am reminded of it when one of the guys going on guard duty that night takes an early shower and finds the water a little cool. I apologize to him and he forgives me, but I hustle over there to light the burners, though it's rather late to do so. The next morning Frank the AH chews me out at breakfast, complaining that the Officer's showers were cold. I suspect it was the lifers more than anyone. He tells me that I am to do the job again today and that I better do it right. He walks away most pleased with himself. I finish my crappy breakfast, but before I can leave, one of the cooks I know sits down beside me. He has heard AH Frank's rant and his first words are, "Screw those lifers," and I laugh.

He is an interesting guy from southern California, maybe Riverside. He joined the Army for three years, just ahead of his draft induction date. This "forced' enlistment was the kind of stuff the Army and the Pentagon loved; they could pretend that the Army was getting substantial numbers of volunteers and not just forced conscripts. Who are they kidding? After some time, he took leave, but didn't return as scheduled and was AWOL. They caught up with him; he may have done some time in the stockade for punishment, but now he is with us at Uplift finishing up his enlistment. He has a great sense of humor and can tell joke after joke. We badly needed a guy like this. He had to extend his time here for several months to complete his enlistment. Any days AWOL don't count, and one must extend past the end of one's enlistment or induction to make up for them. As you might expect, he doesn't like the Army. Besides the usual "FTA," he also says "FTI." When asked what that meant he replies, "Fuck the Infantry," as he was in the infantry when he went AWOL.

So, with a devilish look in his eye, he says, "Why don't you go light those water heaters right now? By tonight the water will be scalding hot. You can set the lifers' fat asses on fire." I have an enormous smile now, nodding my head. "Yeah, why don't I?"

I leave the mess hall and head straight for the Officer/NCO showers. I bring a can of gasoline up the ladder with me and fill the gas tank to the brim. The water tank is only one third full, but I start the heater burning anyway, and I crank it up as much as I dare. I'll start the enlisted men's water tank later at noon.

I know the water tanker driver; he's a good, decent kid. I look for him in the motor pool and find him there as he fills the tanker's fuel tank with diesel. I tell him how AH Frank is all over me because he didn't think the shower water was hot enough last night. So, I ask as a favor, could he fill the shower water tanks right away. He tells me it's a little early for that, as he makes a few other deliveries first and asks if it can wait till noon, the usual time that he fills them. I offer, "Well, okay, but I really want to make sure Frank gets a good hot one." He pauses, and then smiles. "Okay, I'll be over there in a few minutes." He shortly tops off both water tanks.

Just after lunch, I start the burner for the enlisted men's showers and then check on the water tank for the Officers and NCO's; the water is already very warm. As it turns out, I have guard duty that night and will miss the outcome, but maybe it's just as well that I'm in a bunker on the line tonight. Right before 6:00 PM I check the water tank; it is hot to the touch. I lift off the cap of the filler pipe and I see steam coming out! I climb down and report for guard duty. We listen to the usual crap from some lifer about how we are using more ammo than an infantry company and to quit wasting it. We all stare at the ground for a bit and then begin loading the truck up with box after box of ammo, grenades, flares and machine guns as the lifer drones on. Of course, we will bring significantly less back with us in the morning, but who's counting? Not us.

He finally gives up and walks away; we jump into the back of the truck and the Sergeant of the Guard drops us off at our respective bunkers for a night on the perimeter. FTA and the Artillery. The night on the line is uneventful; a couple of flares are popped now and then along the wire. The grenade launcher comes out for just a round or two fired deep into the brush, having taken aim at the ghosts that haunt the place. The ghosts keep their distance.

But it is a near full moon this night and as I look to the western sky I see a fleet of B-52's high in the sky. They appear as dozen or two of tiny dark shapes that silently and evenly fly from north to south and they are many, many miles way. I see their long contrails stretching far behind them. Probably 15 or 20 minutes later, I feel through the earth to the top of our sandbag bunker the minute shockwaves as hundreds of bombs explode on contact with the earth. There is no sound of jets flying, they are too high and too far away and there is no sound of the explosions; you just feel hundreds of shock waves less than a second apart and this goes on for a few minutes. It's called "carpet bombing". The pattern and timing of the aerial bombardment is such that each bomb's explosions is so close to the next it is as if a carpet of explosions were laid down upon the ground. This is not the first or the last night I feel this. But I wonder what can be left after this. At 4 AM, I hand my shift off to the next guy and then sleep until the daylight awakens me.

The Sergeant of the guard comes out just after 6:30 AM in the morning to gather us and the ammo up, and we come back inside Uplift. We back the truck up to the ammo bunker and unload the machine guns, grenade launchers, claymore mines and assorted ammo of each, and hence ends our night on the wire. I head over to the mess hall, as I am already up, to grab some breakfast. It is still early, and there are only a handful of us in there. I go to the chow line and my cook friend serves me steak and eggs! I am dumbfounded, but he explains with a grin, "We only got a few steaks in last night. Not nearly enough for everyone, so it's first come, first served for breakfast until they're gone. Otherwise, the Officers would get them all." I tell him "FTA baby, FTA."

I take a seat at one of the picnic tables inside our crudely built mess hall, and it is the best breakfast I've ever had in the Army. Some minutes go by and the cook comes by my table, "Oh by the way, last night around nine o'clock, there was a big ruckus down by the Officers' shower." I respond, "Really, what happened?" He tells me, "They came running out of there squealing like scalded pigs in July. FTA baby, FTA".

Life goes on. From time to time, I am assigned for the day to drive somebody somewhere. It's usually down to base camp at Phu Cat, occasionally farther down to Quy Nhon, and sometimes up north to LZ English. The driving beats the work details, although on more than a few occasions while we are driving north up Highway 1 toward English, there's a little pop of dust beside the jeep and another just in front of it. You realize, far too late, that Charlie has just taken a few shots at us moments ago, and he missed. Perhaps the Buddha still keeps watch over me.

The highlight of the day is the evening, as we usually, maybe 5 or 6 nights out of seven, have a movie. It's shown at its usual place, the outside wall of the mess hall upon which a white sheet is hung. The projector is placed on a crude table, set back some distance from the mess hall wall; it's pretty basic, but effective. But on a rainy night, it is not as much fun, and it's a little tough on the projector as well. Just wait for the beginning of the monsoon season; then it will really suck.

On a few occasions, I drive the new XO someplace and I get to know him a little. He is a much more decent guy once we drive out of the gate. We have some good conversations on some of our hour-long drives. Oh, he is a lifer for sure, but an educated man and does not seem to be the desperate suck-up type, I'm sure he will at least make light Colonel, maybe even full bird. He is head and shoulders beyond "Shaky."

There is a very slow progression that is both irregular and yet constant. As a few guys near the end of their tour and leave to go home, they are simply replaced by new guys coming in. It is an endless cycle; the cycle is constant, but often erratic. No one goes for the longest time, and then several guys go on the same day. One new guy arrives by himself, but on another week five or six show up. I have only just passed the halfway point of my tour here. It discourages me to think I still have so far to go. A few guys count down every single day that they are here, but I think they are mentally ill. But that would not surprise me; the Army would take anybody. Because I am on the LZ most days now, instead driving the Operations Officer all over kingdom come, I begin to meet some of the characters.

There is a guy from the Midwest someplace. I don't think he knows, understands, or even cares that the Army and this LZ suck, as he is truly a kind, gentle soul. He works in the radio-communication section but it is a very odd shift; perhaps that has something to do with his persona. He has been here a couple of months, and I see him from time to time, but he doesn't stand out for any reason at all. He is the kind of guy that you could go through four years of high school with and would never ever remember him. The guys in the radio-comm. section work a rotating shift of 6 hours on and 12 hours off; every four days they cycle through a 24-hour time period. That alone might make you nuts, just for starters.

One afternoon another guy that I know slightly starts telling me I need to see the jar of bugs that this guy keeps in his pocket. He insists that I do this; he needs me to see it, because no one believes the story of the bugs. So, we are introduced and after ten minutes of small talk, I am coaxed into asking about his bug collection. The guy seems just a bit shy about it, but I tell him I would really like to see it. He stammers a bit and then says, "Well, okay, here you go." He pulls a pint-sized glass jar from his pocket and shows me.

I fight hard against the gag reflex. The jar contains hundreds of bugs of all types, all in motion, either of their own accord or being dragged around against their will by another bug. There is a long awkward pause, and I sense that I must say something positive about this horrific display or his feelings will be greatly hurt. I offer a low key, "Great, that's just great." He holds the jar up to the sun and proudly smiles. I see the bugs walking in endless tiny circles. I wish to incinerate it. But I guess that is how he copes with this place.

Now that we are friends, he asks if I want to see a picture of his wife. It's a small wallet- sized photo; she looks fine, but not necessarily my style. I ask how they met. He says he became friends with some guy he went through basic training with. At some point at the end of basic training, he was introduced to his friend's sister. Fair enough, but she was already pregnant from a relationship with another guy that went sour. He agrees to marry her anyway. I am stunned by his story, but he seems very happy. What the hell, he's happy, I'm not, he is surely one big step ahead of me.

There is another guy who loves music, but in a disc jockey sort of way. He doesn't sing or play a musical instrument, but he keeps a running history with his own commentary about each song that is popular during each particular week. He is happy, too. He works in operations, which is where the Captain I drove around works also, so I see him at his desk on occasion. The guy keeps a transistor radio on his desk and plays it all day, listening to the Armed Forces Vietnam Network and keeping little notes of what is played and when. One of the senior NCO's that he works for likes him, so he has the NCO's permission to play his radio all day. The only thing he is unhappy about is taking a shower.

He has a rather good and kind friend who comes by our end of our hooch and coaxes, encourages, and cajoles him into taking a shower. He seems bright enough, but what terrible personal hygiene. He is another guy who just never goes outside the wire. He too is from the Midwest someplace, but will spend his entire year in Vietnam very safe, never venturing outside once. Instead, he just keeps a musical diary of what is played on the Armed Forces Radio Network. He will leave Vietnam clueless. However, his last couple of months are not so happy; the lifer that he has worked for finished his tour and has gone back to the states. The new NCO, on his very first day quickly tells him to put the radio away, and that is that. He whines and sulks, what a wuss, but he never once gets his hands dirty. His only reference to this place will be a year's worth of pop music.

It is really a roll of the dice as to where you get stationed and what you do, but what amazes me the most is that people spending a year on the same tiny base could have such vastly different experiences. He is one of the guys who are exempt from guard duty; he has never spent a single night on the wire. It always comes down to that barbed wire on the perimeter; you're either safe inside it (usually) or…outside it.

The New Doc

Perhaps because the usual driver is away, AH Frank assigns me to drive our 1-ton truck down to Service Battery near the Phu Cat Air Base. The truck carries any outgoing mail and any personnel needing to get to Service Battery and it makes that round trip seven days a week. It's actually a good time as it gets me away from Uplift and away from AH Frank for the day. The trip down was uneventful as expected and I cannot remember what I did while waiting for the return trip in the afternoon. I probably bought "French fries" and perused the PX to pass the day. The return trip however was much different.

In the late afternoon, I begin to make the preparations for the trip back to Uplift. Check the gas, make sure we have the incoming mail put aboard the truck and grab any personnel that are going to Uplift. As three or four guys begin to climb unto the back of the truck, someone from Service Battery shouts "Hold Up" and escorts to us a last-minute straggler. He is a newbie for sure and has the look of a fawn in the headlights of a car at night. He starts to humbly walk to the back of the truck, but his escort quietly tells me that the newbie is our new battalion doctor. I decide he is too valuable a commodity to sit back there. I need to keep an eye on him; I will surely be blamed if he even gets a scratch on him. I walk to the back of the truck and tell him in a kindly manner he must sit upfront with me. Though he was instantly commissioned a Captain upon his induction into the Army, he is clueless. He responds to me "Yes sir, sorry sir" and climbs out of truck. I want to laugh, but just smile and tell him it's a much better view up front. He climbs in and I head for the gate. The Air Force MP's wave us through and I drive out to Highway 1 and then turn right to make the twenty-mile trip to LZ Uplift.

The guy has had little military training and was probably rushed to us as his predecessor had left Vietnam weeks ago. The whole thing must seem a confusing blur to him and I attempt to put him at ease with some conversation. But that doesn't work out. We have traveled no more than three miles up Highway 1 when we come upon a fierce firefight just off the highway to our right. There are not any front or rear lines in Vietnam, every place has the potential for combat, the whole country is a war zone. But I am a little surprised by the ferocity and the viciousness of this firefight so close to Phu Cat. Somebody is really going after somebody. There is a mix of tiny Vietnamesse buses and motor bikes in front of me, on both sides of the road, some of which come to a stop, and some keep going to escape. But I cannot stop, we are sitting ducks and so I weave my way around the stopped vehicles. The intensity of the firefight is stunning as hundreds of small arms rounds are exchanged just off the highway. There is no way I would stop for this, let alone stopping with our only battalion doctor. I cannot allow him to be hurt; certainly not on his first day in country.

I play it cool and just keep driving north. But I am sure the new Doc probably thinks I am oblivious to this close-by battle when he quietly asks, almost in a whisper "Do you hear the gunshots." I almost laugh at the absurdity of his question; yes, I can and it is dangerously close. But I just nod toward him and tell him "I do hear the weapons, but that it's just a bunch guys having target practice, nothing to be worried about." But he turns pale; I just keep driving north in and out of the stopped vehicles and the sounds of the firefight slowly diminish. Though he must be several years older than I, he seems such a young kid that is in way over his head at the deep end of the pool. I need to get him through his first day unscathed.

I make small talk with him for the rest of trip and he seems to relax just a bit until we near Uplift. But at this point in our trip, nearing the 5:00 PM hour, we are now the sole vehicle on the highway. Just a mile or two south of Uplift there is a culvert that allows a small stream to pass under Highway 1. Charlie routinely blows the culvert; it gets repaired and Charlie blows it again and again and again. It's a pain in the neck because you have to slow down as you drive through it. And you don't dare drive around it on either side of the highway as there is where Charlie will plant a land mine. I don't want the new Doc to be caught off guard, so as we near the culvert, I tell him "I have to slow down at that culvert up ahead, it pretty deep." He leans forward in his seat as he stares bug eyed out the glass of the front windshield. He quickly looks to me as if wanting further instructions on what to do next. I calmly tell him, in as a matter-of-fact manner that I can, "We are almost to

Uplift, but this is the most dangerous part of our trip." He grimly nods so I know he is listening. I then gently pat my M-16 which lies on the seat close to me "Do you know how to use one these?" I hear a slight gasp; he turns pale again and shakes his head no. I nod yes back to him "That's okay, I got us covered."

I down shift the truck and slow down a bit as we approach the deep culvert. And now driving with my left hand as I grab my M-16 with my right and point it out my window. I drive through the blown culvert as fast as I dare and hear the curses from the guys in the back of the truck as we bounce very hard. A few minutes later we safely enter Uplift. I escort the new Doc over to the medical section and wish him well.

The next morning Capt. T sends for me and I meet him in operations. He tells me "I met the new Doc last night and the guy can't stop praising you. He says you showed grace under fire." I just shrug "He's a newbie, I had to get him through his first day. That's all." From time to time, I would see the new Doc around Uplift, he would always smile and give me a big wave. He was a good guy; I hope he made it.

The Dice Roll My Way

The time moves slowly, the days drag, and my days and nights are just an unchanging series of shit work details and guard duty. There are the occasional day trips of driving somebody someplace, that being my only reprieve. But it is on one of those little day trips down to Service Battery near Phu Cat that, by the oddest of circumstances, went south, very literally south. Captain T, whom I once worked for on a regular basis in operations, grabs me in the late morning to drive him down to Service Battery. It is sunny and warm, as it usually is, the drive down is unremarkable, and whatever business that is attended to goes well enough. In the late afternoon, as we are about to leave Service Battery for the drive north up to Uplift, we are held up, as Capt. T is called into a last-second meeting.

He emerges in ten minutes and tells me that I have been temporally assigned to Service Battery to drive my jeep as an escort vehicle for a convoy of Service Battery trucks. The trucks will be towing six brand new 105 howitzers to Nha Trang, where our Alpha Battery is located; they will be leaving early tomorrow morning. I ask him, "Why are we doing this?" He replies with a smile, "It's not we, just you." I beg him to get me off this trip, but it is to no avail. "You have to go. They have already cleared with Uplift; there's nothing I can do."

It seems that "Alpha" Battery is in immediate need of new howitzers. If howitzers are fired enough times, they eventually wear out, and apparently that's what has happened. New howitzers have been ordered, and they have arrived in the port of Quy Nhon. Service Battery has already driven the 20 miles or so south to Quy Nhon and brought them back to Phu Cat. The Air Force was supposed to fly them down to Nha Trang about 150 miles south of Phu Cat, but at the last moment they do not have the planes available to do this. Now Service Battery must tow the six 105 howitzers to Nha Trang themselves. The Captain wishes me well. He'll go down to the Officers' Club back at the airbase for the evening; he's happy. I will spend the night in the crappy transit barracks and then start driving in the morning. I am furious about my situation. Just another shit detail, again.

Service Battery is in a mad dash to get ready. They are already stretched thin, as there are a fair number of their personnel stationed at Uplift to haul artillery rounds to the other batteries in our battalion up north. That "A" Battery is so oddly positioned, 150 miles to the south, makes a rapid response to them difficult. The sudden change of plans brought about by the Air Force's lack of planes has forced a last minute get-ready-go departure. I just gas up the jeep and check the machine gun and the radio, which is all the preparation I can perform. I cannot pack a few clothes or even a toothbrush, as I cannot go "home" to get them at Uplift. FTA.

A hundred fifty miles by road is a very long way to go in Vietnam. It will take two days for us to drive to Nha Trang. Highway 1 is not an interstate; it is in most places a two-lane blacktop, and a narrow one at that. When convoys pass by each other they slow to a crawl, if not a stop. The speed limit is 25 mph and is strictly enforced by the MP's. There have been thousands of casualties, both civilian and military, due to roadside traffic accidents. The highest-ranking man, not the driver, is the one who gets the ticket. No Officer would dare risk the ticket, as this speed limit has been set by the Commanding General himself. One of our Staff Sergeants faced court-martial and had lost a stripe due to an accident.

We will not be traveling fast. Besides, in many places the road is in poor shape, and driving at even ten mph is rough as hell. In other places, we will have to crawl up mountains at just five mph. And finally, we are not allowed to travel at night; in fact, we must be off the road before 5:00 PM. Army regulations, aside, it's dangerous as hell. Charlie works the night shift, and Highway 1 is exclusively his for the evening.

The Journey

I awaken shortly after sunrise as I begin to hear a diesel in a truck thunder to life and then stall. I know it's time to go. I dress quickly and then head to the service battery mess hall to grab a quick breakfast. As I enter, I am greeted by the Service Battery commanding officer. I have seen the man on several occasions when I have driven Capt. T to Service Battery, but we have never met. He speaks pleasantly to me, as he knows I have been conscripted into his service just hours before. "Are you all set to go?" I reply, "Yes sir, the jeep is all gassed up, the ammo boxes are full, and the radio is good. I'll be right out, just wanted to get some toast." He replies, "Good, good. All right, I'll see you outside in a few minutes. We'll do a radio check before we go." He will be in the lead jeep; I will be driving the rear jeep. I finish a small breakfast of toast, grape jelly, and coffee, and then join the others who stand near the lead jeep.

Captain Illinois, as I refer to him, was in the Illinois National Guard and I think has been called up for active duty. I come to like and respect the guy; he is a leader who cares about his men. He is always fair, but a no bullshit kind of guy. He calls us together and lays out our itinerary. The plan is to drive to Tuy Hoa by the end of the first day, as it is about the halfway point to Nha Trang. On our way to Tuy Hoa, as we pass south of Quy Nhon, we will have a MP escort as we travel through a valley infamous for its many ambushes. After that we will be on our own. He cautions us that on the rougher sections of road, if we encounter the "right" series of bumps, it's surprisingly easy to flip the single-axle howitzer on its side. He now tells us to mount up and that we will do a final radio check of each vehicle.

I walk to the back of our convoy: a lead jeep with the Captain, six deuce-and-a-half trucks with each towing a 105 howitzer, and lastly me. I am joined by two lifer Staff Sergeants who will join me in eating dust for the next one hundred and fifty miles. The radio checks start, and my radio sends and receives perfectly, but the radio in the truck just in front of us is not working. The Captain walks back to my jeep and blasts the two NCO's for not having prepared better. Their protest is weak and lame; I easily see through their bullshit, and so does the Captain. He warns them if they screw up one more time, they'll face a court martial.

Captain Illinois returns to the front jeep, and we start driving out of Service battery toward the main gate of the Phu Cat air base more than two miles away. The whole time, the two Staff Sergeants squeal and complain about their verbal beat-down by the Captain. "Well, fuck that mother fucker; I'll take the mother fucking court martial, and we'll see who the fuck wins." And the other: "Yeah, fuck that mother fucker, fucking National Guard, fuck him." They finally quit as we exit the Main Gate. They didn't do their job and they got caught; end of story. Jesus, I hate being in the Army.

We drive out the three-quarter-mile or so access road from the main gate to its intersection with Highway 1, turn left, and head south for Tuy Hoa. We make only slow progress as we near Quy Nhon; the traffic is stop and go in a few places. It is always so much easier traveling as a single jeep, as I could maneuver in and out and around the various obstacles in and along the roadway. But we must travel as a group, a convoy of six deuce-and-a-halves, each towing 105 howitzers, and it is painfully slow.

Just south of Quy Nhon, we rendezvous with our MP escort. They are in a couple of jeeps, but they have brought their big gun along. It's another deuce and a half truck, but centered on its back bed is a quad fifty, i.e., four fifty-caliber machine guns. This thing could level trees. But we travel through the valley of death without any incident, and after only 30 minutes our MP escort departs, and we continue on our own.

We are making progress, but our pace is slow, as we almost never reach the maximum allowable speed of twenty-five mph. The driver of the truck in front of us lags behind the other trucks, and now, as we round a curve, I can see that a large gap has opened up between the first five trucks and his. One of the Sergeants riding with me radios ahead to report this; the convoy slows down, and we now catch up. But after a short time, the convoy begins to pick up speed, and we slowly drop behind again as the truck driver in front of us fails to keep pace. We again radio ahead to report this, the convoy slows down, and we catch up once more. But as soon as we do, Capt. Illinois pulls the convoy over, and we take a brief lunch of C-rations. Capt. Illinois checks on every vehicle and spends a few minutes talking to the driver in front of us. The driver explains that he is fearful of flipping the towed howitzer on its side, but the Captain urges him to keep up.

We start again, and it goes well for a while. But as we near our max speed of 25 mph, the driver of the truck just in front of us continues his cautious ways, and the main body of the convoy begins to pull away from us once more. We radio ahead, and the convoy slows and pulls over to stop. Capt. Illinois is visibly upset; he hates the delays, and I suspect he is more than a little anxious about having to stop on the roadside, as we are such sitting ducks. He maintains his composure though, as he knows the driver is not purposely dragging us down. Nevertheless, he wants to changes drivers. But a little surprisingly, in a slap in the face to the two lifer Sergeants, Capt. Illinois calls me from my seat to discuss this with me and not them. My cursed leadership abilities still plague me.

We stand next to the deuce and a half, and he explains to all, but more for the driver and his two pals who ride shot-gun, that we must make it to Tuy Hoa before 5:00 PM. We cannot spend the night on the road. He cannot put everyone else at risk if they fail to keep up. He pauses as that sets in and then turns to me and asks if I would drive the truck. I immediately look at the deuce-and-half crew, especially the driver; they are mortified with embarrassment. The driver, a blond young kid from Kentucky, meets my eye and silently pleads for another chance. I look back to the Captain and tell him, "They understand a lot better now Captain," and then looking back at the truck crew, "They'll keep up now." The Captain looks me squarely in the eye, and nodding says, "Okay then, let's roll." I take a couple of steps with him and quietly promise, "If they can't keep up, I'll drive." He nods yes and says, "I know." I return to my jeep and climb into the driver's seat. My lifer companions bristle but say nothing.

We start again and Kentucky, knowing that this is his last chance, drives remarkably well and sticks with the truck in front as if towed. The rest of the day is uneventful, if slow. We pass by square miles of rice paddies on either side, a few tiny villages, or a few bigger towns where we slow to a crawl or even stop momentarily. We pass by other convoys where we flash each other the peace sign. Their destination is unknown to us; perhaps to Quy Nhon? It is often dusty at the back of the convoy, but I smile to myself knowing that my two Staff Sergeant companions are eating the same dust I am.

We finally near Tuy Hoa in the late afternoon. The military base we will spend the night at borders Highway 1, and directly across the road is a broad, magnificent oceanfront beach. It stretches for miles and the pale blue beasts, though smaller than the ones at the Perfect South Pacific Paradise Beach, crash against its shoreline as well.

We enter the base at 4:40 PM. It has taken the entire day to travel less than eighty miles. We are directed to some abandoned hooches at the far end of the base. This is our reward? The sandbag-covered hooches are reminiscent of the ones at Uplift, but these are in deplorable condition. Most of the sandbags have rotted away, and one of the hooches has partially collapsed. The place looks as if the French abandoned it back in the fifties, but the frayed plastic sand bags give it a much newer "carbon date." It was probably abandoned six months earlier by an Army artillery unit, given that a few of the hooches have the typical wooden bunks made from used crates that once held artillery shells. So, it's sleep on the wood or sleep on the sand? I take the wood.

There is no power and it will soon become dark, so we dine on canned rations, which might more aptly be named "crappy" rations, in the gathering dusk. The sunset, however, is stunning; oh, but for a bottle of wine. Though we are within a guarded base, we nevertheless post guards all night, and thankfully I am not one of them. It may seem amazing, but I sleep like a baby on the bare wooden bunk.

We are up at dawn and are offered purple or orange colored "juice." There is no correlation between color and taste, and in fact if blind taste-tested, one could not tell the difference. I pass and grab a couple of small cans of fruit cocktail; they are actually quite good. We leave quickly enough. We have only about seventy miles to go, but given yesterday's pace, we might not make that. We exit the base at Tuy Hoa and turn right onto Highway 1 and now drive south toward Nha Trang. We drive along the roadway, and to our left in the very early morning light, we again see the broad white beaches of Tuy Hoa; they stretch forever. But they seem to pass out of sight quickly as we cut inland a bit to climb over a mountain.

The geography of Southeast Asia seems surreal, at least in South Vietnam. In places the mountains simply smack up against the Pacific. There is nothing subtle where land mass meets ocean, no gradual incline, no neutral zone in between, just sheer cliffs against the blue infinity.

Soon we are miles back from the mountain's ocean edge, slowly creeping, straining to climb their steep grade at about four or five mph. Kentucky has no problem keeping up with this. We climb into clouds now, and it shortly begins to rain. I hear the lifers next to me groan, "Oh shit, here it comes," and now it pours down upon us, and we are immediately soaked. It's almost a little chilly. We continue on, and I wonder whether Charlie is asleep somewhere. This convoy of six deuce-and-a-halves towing howitzers, twisting, turning, struggling up a mountain road at five mph would be such an easy prize to take. What would we do; back down the hillside? But it only pours.

We finally crest the top of the mountain, and now with just a bit more speed our convoy descends the far side. But I stress that our descent is most modest and gentle, as the grade down is as steep as the grade up was. Partway down the mountainside, the rain stops and the skies slowly brighten. The grade lessens; we begin to level off and now safely pick up a bit more speed. We travel a few more miles on a slight downhill pitch, as unknown to us, the highway carries us back to the coastline. Now the highway flattens, and as we round a long curve, we see the blue Pacific close to our left as we ride along a cliff's edge. The sun breaks through the clouds. The scenery is so striking it seems almost dreamlike, as if we are in a movie, but we are not. The highway drops lower as does the cliff's edge, and we drive along just a few feet above sea level. We pass by coconut groves on either side of us and then very quickly we come upon a fishing village which straddles the highway.

It is still early morning as we drive through the village, the Captain slowing our pace to make our passage as soft and light as possible. The highway follows along the sweeping curving arc that forms the beach; what a picture postcard this would make. The view to our left, the ocean side, is now one of thatch and grass hooches, perhaps three or four deep, at the top of the beach. A single dog has heard our approach and stands at the back corner of a hooch; he sniffs the air and then barks two or three times to warn the village of our entry. But the alarm is not needed as we glide by at 15 mph. I look between the hooches and see, just beyond them, the modestly pitched yellow/white beach where the fishing village sits. I see a lone fisherman standing on the beach looking seaward. Not far out into the water, as if almost painted upon the sea, floats the village's fishing fleet. There are perhaps forty or fifty tiny craft; most certainly, every one of them is handmade. The gentlest of surf rolls in from the vast endless Pacific, but the boats barely rise as it passes under them. The surf finally reaches the shoreline, but it can be no more than a few inches high. The surf seems supple and soothing, as if it wishes to caress and sweetly kiss the land. There is no epic battle here, land and sea having made their peace eons ago.

There is of course no power here, or phones, or TV. This fishing village seems unchanged by this war; it has probably remained unchanged for the last thousand years. What could have possibly changed here? You build a small wooden boat, and you go fish every day. You come home to your family in your small grass and thatch hooch, and the next day you get up and go fishing again. Life is good.

I wish I had brought my camera along to capture this scene; but of course, it sits back at Uplift in a footlocker. I carried it with me in the jeep whenever I drove Capt. T around, but that was when it was my job to drive him around every day. I had no idea I would be making this trip, and I could not make any preparations. South Vietnam could be so strikingly beautiful and so horrifically ugly all in the same day.

I recall months back when AH Frank has just arrived. I have to drive him down to Quy Nhon and back for something; talk about a long day. Just south of Phu Cat we come upon a small bridge that crosses a stream. It is guarded at each end with a small tower manned by ARVN's. During the night Charlie has attempted to blow the bridge, but the ARVN's have fought them off. Now, in the middle of the road, lie the bodies of three dead Charlies, all dressed in black pajamas. It is a somewhat gruesome sight. I never get used to looking at the dead, though I see them often.

As we approach, one of the Charlies lies on his side facing us. But there is something very odd about him; he looks as if he is wearing a mask. As we get closer, we realize that he has no head, but only a face, and as we slowly go by him, it is confirmed. His head has been blown away; all we see as we pass by is the inside of his face. AH Frank tries to impress me that he is a tough guy by saying, "Get your camera out, you ought to get a few pictures of this." I briefly look at him and nod, and then continue driving. He is such a FAH. I think, "Yeah Frank, these are the kinds of pictures I want to take home to share with friends and family."

We pass through the fishing village. Captain Illinois picks up the pace slightly, and we travel at just over 20 mph. We are starting to make good time. Our convoy passes by other oncoming convoys. Everyone waves and flashes the peace sign back and forth, the universal hello of this war zone. Kentucky is doing quite fine, much more confident about towing a howitzer behind his truck. The sun is fully out now and becoming, as is the norm, rather warm. Our clothes dry quickly in the sunshine and the fluttering breeze of the jeep. There are a few hills to climb, on which we slow down, and there are a few places where we barely crawl along due to the small villages we pass through. On a couple of occasions, we very slowly maneuver around water buffalo as they plod along the roadway.

The closer we get to Nha Trang, the heavier the traffic becomes; it's a mix of tiny Vietnamese buses, motor bikes, and of course military vehicles. Our progress is now very slow. But suddenly the roadway goes from a narrow two-lane blacktop to four wide lanes, each lane marked by white paint. Clearly the Corp of Engineers has built this. Now many civilian vehicles pass us as we maintain our steady 24 mph. We must be getting close. Shortly we enter the city of Nha Trang. It is the first city I have been in since arriving in South Vietnam. This ain't no stinking hamlet! There is some stop and go traffic, but we enter the large military base at Nha Trang at just after 12:00 noon. By comparison with yesterday, it feels like we made record time.

We drive to Alpha Battery's location and drop off their brand-new howitzers. The trucks are now parked, and we have a late lunch in their mess hall. Their base within the bigger base is actually quite decent. In fact, it is much nicer than crappy Uplift. I have been to Charley Battery just north of Uplift, which I consider almost primitive. With that experience, I consider this to be almost a resort, though I am sure it was not quite that.

We are to be housed just outside their section in transient barracks of the Nha Trang Army base. The barracks are not too bad, steel bunk beds, but with real mattresses. Our housing now arranged; we are given the rest of the day off. There is plenty to do on the base: an NCO club, slot machines, a restaurant even, but what most of us want to do is to go into downtown Nha Trang itself. And this is granted, as the city is considered secure; however, we must return to our base by 9:00 PM, as that is when the evening curfew goes into effect. Most guys head for the main gate, walking briskly, but I hold back and grab Kentucky and his two traveling companions. They are the only people that I remotely know in Service Battery. I invite them to come with me, but I tell them to forget about walking, we'll take the jeep. They happily accept.

What Happens In Nha Trang, Stays In Nha Trang

I am not about to ask for permission to take the jeep into the city, as "they" will most likely say no. Besides it is my jeep, kinda, sorta…

At just past 2 in the afternoon, the four of us head out the main gate of the base. I drive; we have no particular destination in mind other than "downtown," wherever that is. I figure we'll find it sooner or later.

Nha Trang is an old French resort city set right against the Pacific. It sits on a stunningly beautiful bay, with superb world-class beaches. It was once an escape from the summer heat and congestion of Saigon, but by this time Nha Trang is more than a little down on its luck. It still possesses a little of the old-world European charm that the French brought with them, but barely so. The streets are laid out in an organized fashion, and there are a few broad avenues lined with tall palm trees providing a glimpse of the faded elegance of the French colonial period. But many of the trees are dead or even broken, with just a tall stump remaining. The war has taken its toll. There is of course the steady influx of GI's who come into the city, feeding the honky-tonks that have sprung up from nowhere. There seems to be no shortage of bars and massage parlors, some of which front Houses of Ill Repute. The French would barely recognize the place now. But the city is still alive, especially in the late afternoons and early evenings.

I drive slowly; we are in no rush. We simply explore the place. We do see some ancient towers, landmarks that are centuries old, and we catch a glimpse of a couple of the statelier old hotels which overlooked the bay. The city must have been spectacular at one time, but now looks run down and worn out. We pull in front of a nicer looking restaurant and park on the street. The headwaiter approaches and greets us in a most friendly manner, but he warns us that the jeep will soon be stripped by the street urchins if we leave it unattended on the street. He suggests that we leave and come back in a cab that will drop us off, and the taxi will happily take us back to our base later. He tells us that the taxis are plentiful, and I see that they are.

We promise that is what we will do, and we get back into the jeep, and I drive us away. But we are not hungry at all; we had planned only on buying a beer or two. We continue to tour the city. At one point one of the guys in the back of the jeep spots a steam bath /massage parlor to his liking, and I pull over to let him off. We promise to pick him up in an hour. We continue to drive slowly up one long block and then back down the next; we cruise most leisurely. It's actually a little fun; it almost feels-- but even saying "almost" is a stretch—as if we are cruising a beach town someplace back home on a Saturday night. But of course, we are not. We shortly turn a corner, and we come upon three young women who smile, wave, and say hello to us.

Perhaps it is only by chance, or perhaps by something far more profound, but my life is about to change; despite my best effort to refuse to go along with it. Fate, for lack of a better word, is about to intervene. My destiny is to be altered, as if divine intervention will now present an opportunity for healing and soothing at least some of the wounds, pain, bitterness and anger that have come upon me for the last year and a half. And yet I fight against it. Later, I will wonder whether the Buddha shook his head at my initial blind rejection and refusal of "enlightenment." He must see more in me that I see in myself, and he surely must wonder, what a damaged, battered child I may be that I cannot see more clearly. But maybe he knows I'm an idiot, and that life is a difficult learning curve for me, and therefore must provide me with second and third chances. Decades later when I look back upon this, I wonder whether Buddha may have called out to Jesus asking, "He's in my back yard and I'm doing all I can for him, but Jesus, he is one of yours, so how about a little help?"

My two comrades in arms smile broadly with anticipation at meeting these girls and tell me, "Pull over, pull over," but I keep driving slowly by them. They immediately demand of me "Hey! Why didn't you stop?" Their tone is less than friendly. I respond "Oh come on, they're whores, it's going to cost you money, it's just a business deal. It's not like we're cruising by the A+W back in Minnesota." Now my two compadres go ballistic on me. They shout, "How do you know; how do you know that? Quit being a downer, we just want to have some fun." I respond, "Okay, okay, I'll go back, but you'll see."

I drive around the block and come back by the three young women. They wave, smile and shout, "Hey GI." I pull the jeep over to the curb and stop right next to them, and I think only to myself, "Right, this is going nowhere."

My compadres and the ladies immediately begin to converse in a combination of equal parts of fractured English and Vietnamese, but I say nothing. My two companions grin and almost blush as they talk to the girls; I assume it's going well for them. I check the three girls out; I rate one as average, one as good and the third as …Oh My God…drop-dead gorgeous! I have to look twice, as this cannot be, but oh, it be… And as I look her over, she catches my gaze and flashes the most beguiling of smiles. It is a smile of a sensuous, beautiful young woman who undoubtedly knows and is most confident about her good looks, yet it is not a hardened or practiced smile. There is something that is still innocent about it, in a *Suzie Wong* kind of way.

But I look away from them and now just stare over the steering wheel of the jeep; I have yet to speak a single word. I am just not into paying a woman for sex. It's not any moral scruple; Sweet Jesus no, I don't have any. It's just that it would seem so cold, so impersonal, and just so lonely, just too…empty? I cannot bear to do that to myself.

So, I sit half turned in my seat, and with my left leg touching the ground, I look down the broad avenue watching a flurry of tiny three-wheeled Vietnamese cabs pass us by. A few minutes pass; the sun sinks a little lower, and by nuance, announces that late afternoon is ever so slowly giving way to early evening. A warm, moist, sultry kind of evening in the old French resort town of Nha Trang, which in better times might well have been a Vietnamese Riviera.

I drift back to the present and now hear parts of the conversation next to me, and then finally something like, "Okay, we'll follow you back to your house." Kentucky now slaps my shoulder and speaks to me. "They're going to take a cab, and we're going to follow them back to their place." He looks as happy as a lark. I respond with a less than enthusiastic, "Yeah, sure." Kentucky instantly frowns at me, so I quickly add, "Okay, okay, we'll go." But Suzie Wong, as she hears my half-hearted response, is not convinced. She, this "take your breath away Oriental Lily," walks from the curb, around the front of the jeep, and then positions herself next to me on the street side. She stands like a white orchid. She wears the Vietnamese "long dress" the "Ao Dai." It is white, silky and fits her as a glove; it covers her completely, but hides nothing. She holds a "Non La" in her left hand against her side. The "leaf hat," broad-brimmed and conical, is tan but has a long purple ribbon that can be tied under her chin. The tan Non-La and its purple ribbon is so flawless in its contrast with her white "Ao Dai" that if one separated the two, it would be a violation of art and life itself.

There is a light breeze blowing up the street from behind her, and an occasional puff is just strong enough to lift her very long jet-black hair around her shoulders, and I catch the faintest whiff of its perfume. She speaks warmly to me and asks in accented but good English "You are going to come back with us?" Her eyes smile at me. They are brown, bright and clear and though almond shaped, seem slightly rounded. Her nose is small, but not flat ... "Well?" she asks with a slight laugh. I answer quietly, evenly, "Yes, yes, of course," knowing my comrades will surely pummel me if I say no.

She is still not certain of my response, so she asks, "Promise?" I reply, sighing, "I promise." And now nodding her head and smiling that beguiling smile once more she says, "Then let's shake on it," and she offers me her right hand. It seems like such a silly thing to do, but I go along with it. I kindly grasp her hand... and the current begins to flow. And as we shake hands, and known only to me, Suzie Wong most discreetly takes her middle finger and gently massages my palm... and the current surges. Yes Suzie Wong, Miss Vietnam, Miss Saigon, Miss Nha Trang, I shall follow you home. Oh Grandma, you were right to warn me.

Suzie Wong looks to her girlfriends and speaks in Vietnamese. They most cheerfully say to my comrades, "Okay GI, you follow." They now step to the street as Suzie Wong, with a slight smile and even slighter gesture causes a cab to lock his brakes and to immediately stop. They pile into the back of the three-wheel taxi, and we begin to follow them. Kentucky, who is sitting in the front passenger seat, slaps me on the shoulder again, and as happy as that aforementioned lark, sings out "See, see, what did I tell you?" I reply "Yeah, yeah, you were right," and I smile as well. We go about two blocks when Kentucky stands up in the jeep and gestures to the girls in the cab to hold up for a minute. He shouts to me, "Turn here; we have to go back to the massage parlor." I have completely forgotten about Mr. Massage. I race down the street; it's only a block and a half, and we find him standing in front of "Nha Trang Special #1 Massage and Steam Bath." He looks clean and refreshed as he jumps in the back of the jeep. The jeep, with its short wheel base, allows an effortless U-turn in the street, and I drive back to the intersection where the tiny cab waits. The cab starts up again and I follow closely as Mr. Massage is brought up to date about this evening's plans. He seems quite disappointed to be the odd man out.

We follow along behind the tiny cab, our "dates" occasionally waving to us, Kentucky and his pals' waving back. We probably travel no more than ten minutes and pull in front of a small house in a rundown residential neighborhood. It's not the best part of town, but it is a quiet street and seems safe enough. We climb out of the jeep and follow Suzie and her two girlfriends into the house, which we quickly come to realize is the home of Suzie Wong. I have promised to come along, but I am not at all sure of what is coming next. I take a seat in a chair or maybe on a small couch, and decide to let things play out. I am a guest, and good manners dictate that I should not assume anything. But my three comrades linger just outside the doorway. They seem to be in quiet but intense negotiations with each other along with Miss Average and Miss Good.

Initially Kentucky has ended up with Miss Average and number 2 is to be with Miss Good, but as soon as the subject of money is brought up, number 2 drops out because he has none. Kentucky then decides to step up one notch to Miss Good, and Mr. Massage, who initially was to be left out in the cold, now happily is to have a "date" with Miss Average. Number 2 will drive the jeep back to the base, which is probably a very good thing. He will come back in the morning to pick us up. I take no part whatsoever in any of the negotiations or the final decisions. The whole time I wonder whether Suzie Wong will interrupt them to say, "Don't take the jeep back yet. No one is staying the night, and you will need it later." But in fact, she says very little at all, and money is never brought up or even alluded to in any manner. Number 2 walks to the jeep, and Suzie closes the door as Miss Good and Miss Average take their "dates" to a house across the street. Suzie Wong returns to the couch. She sits close and faces me, warmly smiling her beguiling smile. She speaks happily, almost singing, as she tells me her name. (I have withheld her name to protect her identity)

Out Of Body

We begin to talk of small things, where I am from, what did I do before coming to Vietnam. I ask where is she from, what of her family? It's the small talk, the bits and pieces that slowly emerge that begin to fill in the mosaic that makes us who we are. But we haven't gone too far down that path when she tells me with a slight laugh, almost teasingly, "You know, you need take a shower."

Now I am a little surprised by this and a bit annoyed. I want to say "Hey, I'm an American; we're always clean." But of course, I don't say that. I think I have gotten used to how I smell over the past several days. I allow that she may be right, as driving an open jeep in the rain does not constitute a bath. I don't want to screw this up, so I respond with, "Yeah, okay, I guess I do." She giggles as she rises from the couch telling me, "Come this way" as she leads me towards the bath. It's not an especially nice house, so I am apprehensive about what I will find there. It would be silly to be expecting much. Like the house, it's not an especially nice bathroom either, but it's okay. It's very basic, a concrete and tile floor that's missing some of its tile.

Suzie Wong

I wonder whether I will have to use broken, dirty bars of soap, but she hands me a brand-new bar of Zest still its box and wrapper. And then a moment later hands me a brand-new large bath towel. I feel much relieved and think, how kind of her.

She leaves, telling me over her shoulder, "See you soon." I remove my clothes and step under the shower head. It seems an antique; it's large and strongly resembles the spout of a watering can that would be used in a large garden. There is no water heater; the water comes directly from the shallow water main in the street. But it absorbs the ambient heat of the street itself; it is lukewarm and the pressure is modest, but it feels good. I soap twice, even using the Zest as shampoo. I step out and dry off with the towel and then start to put my shirt on, but it smells. She was right, of course. So, I wrap the towel around my waist and walk back to her tiny living room. She smiles, and I smile back, as I feel clean and handsome, but before I can sit down, she asks teasingly, "Did you brush your teeth?" Now I am getting annoyed with all these questions of personal hygiene. Besides I'm an American, we always have clean teeth. But I only shrug "No." She gets up, saying again, "Come this way," and leads me back to the bathroom. I fear she is going give me some old toothbrush used by who knows how many, but she hands me a brand spanking new Colgate toothbrush, still in its plastic case, with a matching unopened tube of toothpaste as well. Okay I'm an Idiot with a capital I, and she's got class!!! Strangely, I begin to feel honored. And I brush those pearly whites.

I return to her tiny living room still clad only in the towel, but she has moved to her bedroom; it's just an alcove off the main room. There is no door, but rather some gauzy drapes that she holds apart with her left arm as she stands just inside them. There is a light on behind her, and its light bathes her perfectly. She has changed into baby doll pajamas; they are silky, a soft white color, and most unquestionably not opaque. Her long hair drops like black silk down well past her shoulders to partially hide her breasts, but only partially. I cannot help pausing to take her in. Several seconds go by as my very young blue eyes feed a starving libido. She looks back inquisitively, as if wondering what my delay is. But then our eyes meet, she smiles her beautiful smile and turns her head just slightly to her right shoulder to reaffirm her invitation, and now beaming with happiness I walk to her.

She moves to the bed as I enter and then pats the far side of the bed, directing me to that side which is against the back wall. I lie down on the bed; its width is fine, but it is barely long enough for me. She moves next to me, and each of us places an elbow and then a hand to support our heads as we face each other. We begin to talk.

She seems quite bright, and I ask about her education. She is a graduate of a prestigious high school, and that alone puts her in the ninetieth percentile of Vietnam. She then went on to a two-year nursing program. Upon her graduation, she worked for a year at a government hospital. I ask how old she is. We are nearly the same age. I ask what she does now; but the question is not as awkward as it would seem if taken out of context. She answers me most pleasantly and tells me she sells "Saigon Tea" in a fancy bar, "It's much more money than a nurse." When a GI goes into a bar, the "bar girls" work them to buy them tea. If the "Tea" costs $2, the bar gets one dollar and the girl gets the other dollar. She tells me, "I only work at very best bar." I study her face and wonder if she is partly Eurasian. I am curious about her background, so I ask where her parents were from. She tells me her mother is Vietnamese, but that her father was half Vietnamese and half Filipino. I nod, and smile approvingly at the results of perhaps a distant Spanish donation to her gene pool. I think she must do extremely well, "only work at very best bar."

We talk a bit more. I don't want her to think that I want only sex, as desperate and as needy as I am. I am nervous about this and afraid of making the wrong move. But clearly, she senses this, and as I try to say something, she puts her finger gently to my lips. She kisses me sweetly and says, "Let's make love." The words are spoken in Vietnamese-accented English in that Suzie Wong kind of a way. I feel I am somehow in a movie.

She sits up as I lift the top of her baby dolls over her head; her long jet-black hair now descends past her breasts. I push this black silk aside to see her body better; she is so perfectly proportioned. I hold her breasts, she is most ample. As I then kiss and suck them, she murmurs deeply. She lies back, and I pull her bottom pajamas off. Her stomach is flat and firm; I am a little surprised that she is hairless. I pull my towel away, and now she takes hold of me and as she does, I hear that deep murmur. Though she is small, she is not tiny; still, I worry that I may be too large for her. She lies back to take me, but she does not display the least hesitation. I lie upon her as she guides me in; she is most wet and opens for me. I move slowly and at the halfway point, she stops me and wiggles underneath me as to open wider. She looks at me and now gently coaxes me in deeper. I go almost all the way but then stop. I back up a bit and then go in slightly deeper and back up and stroke again. She smiles and says, "Yes" and then places her arms around my back and pulls me toward her. I propel myself forward at the same moment, and this time I go fully and completely to the hilt. She arches her back to me and shudders as she takes it all. And now we fuck hard. We fuck softly. We fuck madly; we fuck with abandonment. We fuck as lovers might; we fuck as only youth can fuck. The techniques that come with experience are not there, but youth is. We fuck with lust, but we fuck caringly and sweetly.

I don't want to come too soon, so I hold a long time. But I want to be sure she is enjoying herself as well. So, I ask, "Are you getting near?" She replies, "Yes." But I cannot hold back anymore, and I tell her "I'm coming." Her response is immediate. "I'm coming too, I'm coming too." We climax together; she arches her back toward me as I pump my fluid deeply inside her. It feels like a quart. We cuddle together for a while, warm and sweaty. And shortly she rolls onto her stomach and falls asleep.

But I cannot sleep. I am tired, but my brain races to process the events of this evening. I wonder whether I am dreaming all of this. How could I be as lucky as this? It is not possible. I close my eyes in an attempt to drift off to sleep, but I only drift. I am at the edge of sleep, but I drift back and forth from barely conscious to barely asleep. I now float above, looking down upon myself and Suzie Wong. I see my deeply tanned back and pale white bottom and I see the oriental gem lying next to me. I see a side profile of her stunning face, the long black silk flowing from head down her back ending just above a perfectly proportioned round bottom. It feels out of body, how can I possibly float above and look down upon myself? At 21 I have had the best and greatest, the most sensual, exotic lovemaking of my life. I fall asleep but wake once more; I sit up slightly. Suzie Wong sleeps deeply next to me. I go back to sleep; it's not a dream.

Sometimes A Man Needs A Woman, Sometimes...

It is morning, we awaken together, more proof that none of this has been a dream. I pull her on top of me and Suzie smiles and giggles. We make love again. It is not with the same urgency or near-desperation as last night; this is just for fun. The sweet, wonderful, playing-with-my-best-friend kind of fun. We finish and rest for a few minutes and then slowly arise together. We head to the bathroom, both naked, holding hands. I turn the watering can shower head on and step under it. Suzie smiles as I do, but I grab her arm and pull her under the shower as she squeals with delight. Now we take that bar of Zest and soap each other up, and I take much pleasure in washing every inch of her. Her wet hair, now heavy with water, reaches to her sweet bottom, such a sight, so provocative, so Asian, so Oriental, so Suzie Wong. We dry off, and I dress, putting on my faded, fragrant uniform.

Suzie has opened the front door, and in the daylight of mid-morning I see a kind of covered lanai and then a street that must not have seen much maintenance in a decade. I see my jeep parked in front; Mr. Massage has found his way back to us. He talks with Kentucky and number 2, and I hear them laugh on occasion. Everyone is in a good mood.

I return to the tiny living room where she sits. She wears her baby dolls. We exchange smiles; how can I not smile? I take a seat and I tell her my ride has come and I must leave shortly. She nods; she knows this.

I want to acknowledge how wonderful this has been for me. But I stammer around a bit. I finally say, "You know, you have never asked me for any money." She gazes into my eyes for a seemingly long moment and then steps close to me. She speaks lightly in her Suzie Wong accented English. "Sometimes a man needs a woman; sometimes a woman needs a man." She nods her head ever so slightly and adds, "You understand?" I pause to take this in… I nod slightly and quietly say, "Yes." I think, what a moment.

I stand and we hold hands as we slowly walk to the door. I stop there and am about to say… but she places a small folded white piece of paper into my hand. I open it; she has written her name and address on it. It is written in Vietnamese; her handwriting is exquisite and delicate. Suzie Wong's accented final words to me are, "When you come back to Nha Trang, don't go to whore house, you come here." I silently nod yes. I place the folded paper into my shirt pocket and button it. And then walk to the jeep. I wonder how can I ever get back here.

The Rockets' Red Glare, The Bombs Bursting…

The jeep fires on the first crank, and I drive away. I look back at my comrades, they all smile and beam at me, and everybody is good. I tell them we'll take one last drive through downtown Nha Trang before we return to the base. I am not looking for another woman; I wish only to savor this moment before we go back. We drive around for about forty-five minutes sightseeing and then enter the base at the noon hour. We park the jeep inside Alpha battery and then head to the mess hall. We get lunch and see most of the other members of the convoy. They look as if they have been drinking most of the night. There is a brief meeting immediately after lunch. We are informed that we will be leaving early in the morning, so we are advised to get our vehicles and ourselves ready to depart on time; and further, we are restricted to the base. I'm slightly disappointed by this news, and especially the restriction, but it is very much what we all expected. Besides, maybe it is better this way. How can I ever top the night before?

I top off the gas tank in the jeep and check the oil. I travel the lightest of any man here, as I have nothing to pack. Everything I own I am wearing (again). That done, I waste away the afternoon. I do take a nap in the transit barracks as I am, proudly I might add, a little tired from the night before. I awaken just before suppertime and shortly head to the mess hall for the evening meal. I eat lightly and talk a bit with a few of my comrades. Later that evening, we head over to the NCO club. I have only three dollars, but at ten cents a beer, I do quite well on a half dollar. By 10:00 PM, most us head back to the transit barracks and fall asleep.

At around 6:30 AM, I am awakened by a powerful explosion. It is close by, and I jump from the bottom bunk and run toward the door to seek the shelter of a bunker. I am only a few steps from the door when I hear another rocket slam into the earth. I lie on the floor and then crawl to the door, but another rocket slams into the base, and I stop at the doorway. In the background between blasts, I hear the sirens wailing away. I feel I am in a newsreel of the London Blitz. Another rocket hits very close by. I hear shrapnel fragmentation hit the plywood and then see a few new openings. The transit barracks has only a tin roof and plywood sides, feeble protection for sure, but I don't dare leave it, as I do not want to be caught out in the open as I search for a sandbag bunker. Instead, I crawl to a nearby bunk and pull its mattress down over me, hoping that it might provide some protection from the shrapnel. Eight more rockets hit the base and then a brief pause. Now more explosions, but it is Alpha battery sending an artillery barrage back out to some target. Then quiet.

We gather ourselves up. We have suffered no casualties. But our departure from Nha Trang is delayed for at least twenty-four hours, and the city itself is under a curfew; we are not allowed into it. My convoy mates and I just hang around all day. Most of us have little money left at this point and are becoming a little bored. The day drags by slowly. We have lunch and play cards at the NCO club. In the late afternoon, we are gathered together and told that we will be leaving the following morning at 8:00 AM sharp, but we are to squeeze into the Alpha Battery hooches, as they are covered in sandbags. They are not rocket proof, but they offer much better protection from shrapnel then the tin roofs of the transit barracks. We have supper and then play more cards at the NCO club, but of course I would much rather be downtown. I am assigned to sleep in one of the cannoneer hooches of Alpha battery, as there is a spare bunk. It's a rather comfortable bunk, and I sleep well; this place is way better than Uplift.

At 6:30 AM I am abruptly awakened by the explosions of rockets raining in yet again. Another dozen or so rockets slam into the base. Maybe it's not so great here. Most everyone in the hooch immediately runs for their assigned howitzer and begins firing an artillery barrage at some target, but I stay inside. Fortunately, we suffer no casualties. As soon as it's over, I go back to sleep for another half-hour, as I know we are not traveling today. I get a little breakfast and kill the morning. At the noon hour we are called to another meeting. We are informed that several key bridges have been blown up during this morning's attack. The repairs will take many days, and therefore our convoy will be unable to drive out of Nha Trang. The vehicles are to be left behind at Alpha battery, and everyone is to be flown out of Nha Trang and back to Phu Cat on an Air force freighter-- everyone that is, but the drivers. I cannot believe my great luck. Everyone else is moaning and complaining, especially the drivers, but I smile. The rest of us, i.e., the drivers and a couple of lifer sergeants, are to remain behind until the bridges are repaired or some other alternatives are found. That could take days or a week, who knows, but now I'm as happy as that lark.

Almost immediately, those who are flying back to Phu Cat head over to the very nearby airfield. The rest of us, just ten of us now, have the rest of the day off. The city is still off limits, so I must bide my time, but hopefully Charlie is out of rockets, and tomorrow I will go find Suzie Wong.

I hang out with a few of my comrades passing the rest of the day and evening away at the NCO club. But they are just about broke and rather bored; they just want to get back to Service Battery at Phu Cat and be in their own beds, see their pals. They almost seem homesick. I don't care if I never get back to crappy Uplift and AH Frank. But of course, here, I have much more to look forward to. We leave the NCO club and walk back to our bunks in Alpha Battery. I fall asleep with anticipation of tomorrow.

I awaken the next morning, and all is quiet, no rockets. I get a little breakfast and then hang out for a bit. I check with one of the lifer Sergeants, asking if there is a plan yet. He tells me to take the day off, as there is no news to report. I tell him, "Okay, I'll check with you later." It is now late morning as I walk to the main gate. I ask the MP's whether Nha Trang is open. They respond, "Yeah, the curfew was lifted at 8:00 AM. Go ahead," and they wave me through. What a difference; at Uplift you wouldn't dare walk out the gate alone on fear for your life, and at Phu Cat, the MPs would arrest you if tried to walk in or walk out of the gate. Here, other than the 9:00 PM to 8:00 AM curfew, it's a good place to be stationed.

Suzie Wong

I stroll through the gate, and within a dozen or so steps several Papa sans in their tiny three-wheel taxis ask, "Hey GI, you need ride?" But I wave them off. There is a large bar across the street from the main gate, and I head there if for no other reason than to satisfy my curiosity. I enter the bar; it is a fair-sized building and can easily handle a hundred or more GI's. The bar's decorations are cheap and gaudy, the usual predictable strings of beads hanging from walls or the ceiling that pretend to designate areas of the larger room. There is a large and long rectangular bar against the back wall, behind which stands a lone bartender. He is Vietnamese, and he is stacking glasses on a back shelf; he barely looks at me. Otherwise, the barroom is completely empty but for one other customer. He stands leaning against the bar rail, and within just a few seconds of my entry he speaks to me. He has a short military-style haircut, but is dressed in civilian clothes and speaks with a neutral American accent that I cannot place. He tells me he's a Sergeant in the US Air Force stationed in Nha Trang, and then without pausing, asks, "What kind of drugs are you looking for?"

I have never really liked the air force personnel, especially the lower-level lifers. Oh, they are much better educated than the Army lifers generally speaking, but they are often a lot sleazier. The Air Force typically sets up large bases wherever they go; it's the nature of that branch of the military. To build and operate an airbase requires a huge commitment of resources, including a lot of personnel. There is no need to locate an airbase in the middle of nowhere, as the jets can quickly fly to anyplace within Vietnam; hence, the bases are often placed next to large cities. Given the huge investment of building an airbase, they become a semi-permanent fixture of the city, which means for their personnel an almost Stateside tour of duty, an almost nine to five job. They generally have it easy, and obviously some have too much time on their hands.

The first word out of my mouth to the Air Force Sergeant is, "Huh?" He responds, "I can get you heroin or opium," and then goes on to list a half dozen more drugs. I'm stunned and tell him, "No thanks, I'm just checking the bar out." His response is, "Okay, you must be looking for some bar girls. I can get you as many as you want; they're all clean too." I tell him no thanks and walk out of the bar. What an asshole; he needs to spend a little time in the boonies. He will be another one who will later brag about having served in Vietnam. He hasn't a clue.

I walk just a few steps to a group of waiting taxis and gesture to the nearest one. He smiles slightly and quietly says something in Vietnamese. I presume he is asking, "Where do you want to go?" I hand him the small piece of paper with Suzie's address, but he doesn't seem to know the location. He has his son with him, a boy of perhaps 10 or 11. He shows him the address, and the boy speaks happily, clearly, he knows, and points with his hand as if to make a left and then a right. The father nods yes and then gestures for me to sit in the back of his tiny three-wheel cab. We journey through the city and I am soon lost, but I am relaxed and confident about my driver and his young son.

It is sunny and hot, but the tiny cab has a roof which shades me, and its open sides allow for the air to move around me; it's kind of fun. Taxis honk at each other, and as we slowly go around one busy corner, I hear a chorus of voices singing, "Hey, GI." About twelve minutes later, we turn down a familiar battered street and now stop in front of Suzie's house. I pay the driver fifty cents in American military scrip and he smiles; I guess I paid him too much. I walk from the street through the lanai and then stand in front of the open door and simply say, "Hello." I hear some Vietnamese words spoken and then a young woman appears; she says something over her shoulder, and then I hear Suzie's voice responding inquisitively. I say "Hello" again, and now Suzie appears; she smiles her smile and says, "Oh, you come back!"

She brings me into her house, and I tell her of the rocket attacks at the base, of our repeatedly delayed departures, and now with the bridges blown, how everyone but the drivers have been flown back up to Phu Cat. She smiles and says, "Good, now you stay here." I nod and smile and think to myself, "Fine by me, Suzie Wong, that's just fine by me." I have little recollection of the rest of the afternoon, but around 3:00 PM Suzie and her house girl (the young woman who came to the door) go shopping. They return about an hour later and begin to make supper. I have no idea of what they will cook. Although I have seen Vietnamese food before, it never smelled or looked particularly appetizing. I am more than a little apprehensive.

We all move from the house out to the covered lanai, where they cook the food in a big wok over a tiny propane burner. At first glance I don't think I am going to like what they are cooking, but they shortly begin cooking a fresh chicken breast in the wok. Suzie tells me, "I don't think you like Vietnamese food, so I cook for you American food." I feel honored, but honestly very grateful; they have cooked some kind of nasty looking catfish for themselves that really smells. But my "American meal" is quite good. I have tomato and sliced cucumber, with a wok-cooked chicken breast, and this is washed down with a cold can of Coca-Cola. How kingly!

It's about 5:30 PM now, and Suzie tells me she must work tonight. She takes a shower, as does the house girl; I guess they are both working tonight. At around 6:30 or 7:00 PM they leave together. But before she goes, Suzie puts me into a chair, brings me a Budweiser, and turns the TV on. "You watch TV and drink beer. I only work at best bar. Not late; I come back." I reply, "Okay, have fun." To which she gives me a puzzled look. But I just smile back.

I open my Bud and turn up the volume on the tiny TV. It is small; probably not even 12 inches if I remember correctly, but it works fine, and I watch the Armed Forces Vietnam Network television station located on the Nha Trang Airbase. I can't remember what I watched, but it was the first television I had seen since leaving the US. I must have gotten into it, because I am somewhat surprised that nearly three hours had gone by when I hear Suzie's voice. And then I am really surprised. Suzie and her house girl have brought their "dates" back with them. Holy shit!

Standing behind Suzie and her house girl are two 2nd Lieutenants, the lowest rank of Officers. One is white, one is black, and their uniforms are very green, as if never washed. Obviously, they are very recent arrivals into Vietnam, perhaps only in their first week. They are more than a little staggered to find me here in this tiny house on some battered back street of Nha Trang. But they have no clue about my rank, as I sit in the chair wearing my Army issue, but rather faded, olive-green shorts and tee shirt holding a can of Budweiser. Clearly, I have been in country far longer than they have. I remain seated and calmly, coolly look them over. I doubt they are much older than I am, if it all, and I sense they think I may outrank them, as I could easily be a 1st Lt. or even a young Captain. I nod a hello to them, and they nervously murmur a hello back. But the great equalizer here is the fact that there is a 9:00 PM curfew for Nha Trang and all of us are equally in violation of it. They are not about to pull rank; they would end up in much deeper shit than I would.

Suzie comes to me and quietly asks that I come into another part of the house with her. I do and she says that each of their dates will pay one hundred dollars to spend the night. But I tell her not to worry, take the money. I will just sleep out in the front room. But she will have none of this. "I cannot let you sleep alone." I'm clueless as to what she is talking about, and I tell her, "I'm okay, I'll sleep out there." But she repeats, "No, no, I cannot let you sleep alone. It hurts my heart too much; you cannot sleep alone." I respond that it's not that big a deal, but she starts to put the rest of my clothes on me. "You get dressed; I have girl for you across street."

I yield to the moment at hand; she doesn't want me here, and I think it would be selfish of me to force a different outcome; a hundred dollars is a lot of money to her. So, I quickly dress, though I am uncertain what will come next. It seems very important to her that if I leave her house tonight, I must sleep with another woman? I couldn't make any of this up. Suzie now walks me across the street, where we are greeted midway by the woman I am to spend the night with. Clearly, Susie must have stopped there to make this arrangement before coming back to her own house with her date.

We are introduced, and I walk across the street with my new date on my right and Suzie on my left. I am glad I have had a few beers tonight. Suzie tells me I will be fine and that I must come back to her house in the morning. As she is telling me this, she very discreetly puts five dollars in my left hand as to "save face" for both of us. I barely have a dollar on me, and Suzie would then have to pay another woman to sleep with me. I smile a little bit to myself as she hands me the money, as it seems quite sweet of her to do this so discreetly. I suppose this is also flattering somehow, but I am not entirely comfortable with the situation, so I just go along. What else am I to do?

We reach the house; Suzie kisses me on the cheek and tells me, "You come back in morning." She turns and walks back to her house, and I go into the house of the girl next door. I hand her the money. She leads me to her bedroom, and I get into the bed and she shortly joins me, but I don't find her attractive. She is most willing to have sex with me, but her breath is not good; it smells like a dental odor, which is a turnoff. Besides, I feel I am going steady with Suzie now, and I should not touch this woman even if Suzie has given me the money to. I just go to sleep and I spoon her once or twice, but that's it.

I don't sleep well and I awaken early but wait until a respectable hour before I leave to walk back across the street to Suzie Wong's house. I don't want to walk into any unfinished business there. I think my "date" was slightly disappointed, but she tells me I can come back any time I want. Why wouldn't she invite me back? It was the easiest money she ever made.

I walk across the street and knock-on Suzie Wong's open door, and she immediately comes to the lanai and brings me inside. It feels good to be home, I think. I ask how her evening went, but she tells me she didn't like them because they were not nice and kicked them out in the middle of the night. I doubt they got refunds. Sweet Jesus, she is like a tigress! But she most graciously does not ask me how my evening went. There is little to report, and even if there were more, I am certain she would not want to hear any of the details. I sense she wants this to be lost and left behind us, and that is most perfectly fine with me.

I cannot remember the rest of the morning, but around 11:00 AM, I tell her I must go back to the base and check in. I will find out whether a plan has been made about when and how we might get back north to Phu Cat. I tell her we will not be traveling today, as we must have at least one day's notice to be able to bring back the rest of our comrades to ride shotgun with us. I tell her I will be back in a couple of hours. She understands but asks if I have enough money for the taxis. She knows I'm broke. I tell her I only have enough for a one-way trip. She now gives me money for the cab, carefully instructing me on how much to pay the driver for each leg of the trip. She sends the house girl to the corner to hail a taxi, and she very shortly returns with one. As I step from the lanai, Suzie tells me, "When you come back, we do something special." I nod and smile and then jump into the back of the tiny cab.

The taxi shortly drops me off at the main gate, and I pay the driver exactly as Suzie had instructed me. I approach the main gate, and the MP's wave me through. It is nearly noon, so I head for the mess hall to grab some lunch and check in. I spot a few of the drivers, and one of the lifer Sergeants. They ask jokingly, "Where have you been?" But I reply, smiling, "Oh, just hanging around." I ask if there is any news, but the Sergeant tells me, "Not a god damn thing." He clearly wishes to be out of here, as they all do. I reply, "Yeah, okay, I'll check with you tomorrow," as the Sergeant steps away from the table. I say this as flatly as possible as if I am disappointed, no sense rubbing it in, but I honestly don't care if I never get back to Uplift.

I chat a bit more with my comrades, but with the meal finished we go our separate ways. I don't know what they do with their time, be it day or night, but I tell no one of my newly acquired girlfriend-- no one except Big D. I leave the mess hall and head directly to the office at the transit barracks where I request writing material. The clerk wordlessly hands me pen and paper and a white envelope. I write to Big D; I have to tell somebody, and it may as well be my best friend.

Big D,

You're not going to believe where I am or what I'm doing. I got stuck driving my jeep as the escort for a Service Battery convoy to Nha Trang. I couldn't get out of it, what a long trip. But we can't get back because Charlie blew all the bridges leading out of Nha Trang. So, we're stuck here, but I don't mind because I'm living downtown with a beautiful girl. She's gorgeous! What an interlude. I'll tell you all about it when I get back to Uplift.

PS. Tell AH Frank "FTA"

I use the word "interlude" because that was the name of some sappy romance movie that we saw one night back at Uplift. At twenty-one, I think this to be quite a sophisticated and worldly use of the word to describe my situation. Captain T had watched the movie also and we discussed it the next day as I was driving him someplace. He didn't like the movie because he didn't think the woman was good-looking enough. He asked me rhetorically, "Why fool around if the girl is not that pretty?" I wanted to answer, "Because the guy was unhappy, and he wanted to change that." But I just said, "Yeah, right."

But none of that matters now; I'm not married and Suzie Wong is Jade East. I fold the letter into the envelope and then address it to Big D using our military address. I then write the word "Free" where the stamp would go. It is one of few good benefits of being in South Vietnam; our letters are delivered for free. I hand the letter to the clerk and ask, "When?" and his nonchalant reply is, "It will go tonight." I walk out of the transit barracks office and head for the main gate smiling to myself, thinking "wait till Big D reads this."

I reach the main gate, and the MP's wave me through; we're starting to know each other at this point. There are a dozen tiny taxis waiting. I grab the closest one and show the driver the address. He shakes his head yes and I jump into the back. Another cab ride into Nha Trang, oh what a lucky boy am I.

Afternoon Interlude II

It's becoming routine now, taking a taxi from the base and being dropped off in front of Suzie's house; I am starting to memorize the way there. I hop out of the back of the tiny taxi and pay the driver; he pulls away, and there sits Suzie and her house girl under the shade of the lanai. They are both dressed as if they are about to go out.

As I approach, she gives me the warmest of smiles, and I smile back. She tells me "Good, you are back now, but I have nice surprise. We must go right now." She speaks in Vietnamese to the house girl, who rapidly walks to the corner and almost immediately returns with a cab. When I look at Suzie for the explanation, she happily says, "I take you for good movie."

The three of us jump into the back of the cab; there is no front seat other than the tiny one the driver sits on. We go into a part of the city that I have not yet been to. The traffic is busy and the buildings are a little taller here, perhaps three or four stories. But we shortly pull up near a theater and step from the cab. Suzie pays the driver and then sends the house girl to purchase the theater tickets as Suzie and I wait on the sidewalk in a somewhat long line. It does feel like a real treat, and I feel I am being treated as royalty, despite the night before. I feel kingly, and standing right next to me is Queen Jade East. The house girl returns with the tickets, and now the line finally begins to move forward. I casually mention, "A lot of people here today," to which Suzie replies in her Vietnamese-accented English, "Oh, most popular movie in Nha Trang." She has trouble pronouncing "popular," but I only smile and say, "Good."

We enter the foyer and then through the left door into the theater itself. There are three sections, and we take seats about three quarters of the way down on the left side of the center section. Suzie sits to my right, the house girl to my left. But at 6-4, even seated, I tower over everyone. I feel bad for the people behind me, but I hear no complaints. The theater continues to fill, and it seems every seat is taken. I look around the theater. There is a balcony above, but the place looks as if it was built in the twenties and is more than a bit rundown. The crowd is noisy with anticipation, but then every so often I hear Vietnamese punctuated with the word "GI." I look around me slowly, and every few rows someone is pointing in my direction as they say "GI." I am feeling a bit uncomfortable hearing this. But after a while I realize they are simply curious about why a GI would go to a Vietnamese theater even if it were showing the most popular movie in Nha Trang. The movie starts, and everyone becomes still and focuses only on the screen now. As it turns out, it is not a particularly good movie, and yet I thoroughly enjoy myself.

It's a black and white and is a bit grainy, but it is a talkie; after all, this is 1969. It's a cops and robbers thing with a teenage girl heroine, who has a rather savvy German Shepherd who helps her solve crimes. It is the silliest, goofiest thing, as the cops and robbers are wearing uniforms from decades before. Judging from the way the actors are dressed, it appears that the production unit bought the entire wardrobe from a Charlie Chaplin silent movie; and I mean the grainy black and white doesn't help. But the crowd loves it. They ooh and aah, laugh out loud, and applaud wildly at every twist and turn of the action, be it the robbers robbing or the cops chasing them, which is played as if neither has an IQ in double digits. Of course, the biggest reaction is for the teenage heroine, who is wise beyond her years and her ever faithful, devoted and brave Rin-Tin-Tin.

At one point in the movie, though I cannot understand a word spoken, even I am laughing out loud. Suzie nudges me with her elbow, and as we look toward each other, she flashes her smile and gives me a wink. It is one of those brief moments you remember forever. She immediately goes back to the movie oohing and aahing with the rest of the crowd. But I drift; I think of Uplift, AH Frank, the Charlies in the school house, the horrific day as we left that beach, the coconut grove from Hell…I could walk away from all of that in a heartbeat. That war can go on without me…But Suzie nudges me now, I turn and smile, and she is laughing out loud at some scene on the screen. I cannot think of those other things now…and I go back to laughing as well. The movie closes to much applause, with both Suzie and her house girl enthusiastically clapping. In the end, this is the worst and the best movie I ever see.

Don't Cry For Me

We exit the theater, the house girl running ahead to fetch a taxi. We pile in and head home. Suzie pays the driver, and as we enter the house, Suzie asks if I'll have chicken again and sends the house girl out for some shopping. She returns soon enough, and the women begin to cook on the lanai. I just sit and take the whole scene in; it seems surreal, yet familiar; how odd.

Every one of us is in a good mood. As some of the Vietnamese dishes are being prepared, Suzie names them in an attempt to expand my limited Vietnamese vocabulary. I try to pronounce them correctly but it's not easy, and whatever I have said is so far off the mark that Suzie and her house girl roar in laughter. Susie, now speaking Vietnamese in a low voice, says something to her house girl that causes both of them to have deep belly laughs till they begin to hurt. I chuckle along with them though I don't understand the joke, only that I am the butt of it. Now I pretend that I am deeply hurt by their laughing at me and complain to her. Suzie stops dead in her tracks, as she thinks I am being serious and now floors me with her next words as she most somberly asks, "You want me cry for you?" I am stunned and now regret spoiling their fun. I reply softly to her, "No. Don't cry for me." They go back to their laughing; it's actually nice to hear.

We eat dinner; it is quite good, even better than yesterday's if it's possible. Around six the dusk slowly comes in and Suzie Wong prepares herself to go to work. She instructs me to watch TV and drink beer; she's a woman ahead of her time. "You stay with house girl. Not work late, it's only the very best bar." I smile and wave goodbye. I decide not to say, "Have fun."

Oh God…Not Again

I put the TV on. There is only one channel as far as I can tell, but I watch whatever the Armed Forces Vietnam Network is showing that evening and have a couple of beers. I see little of the house girl, though she is in the back ground somewhere. Time slips by; I can't remember what I was watching when Suzie Wong comes back from "working only the very best bar, not late." She has a GI with her; Oh god...not again.

He seems surprised to see me there, sitting very comfortably in a chair watching TV with a beer at my side. But he remains at the lanai entrance as Suzie directs him to stay there. She quietly asks me to come with her back into the inner room. She is most apologetic. She tells me the GI has missed his R+R flight; his story doesn't sound right to me, but in any case, he has paid her three hundred dollars for the night. I am stunned. Three hundred bucks is far more than a month's pay! I am about to say, "Okay, sure, take the money, but I'm not staying with that woman with the bad breath again." But she must know what I am thinking, as she says, "He paying for hotel, I only come tell you not worry." She grabs a tiny overnight bag, hugs me and then departs. She is gone before I can really react, but probably just as well. I'm not happy about this, but I know that three hundred bucks is a lot of money, especially to a young woman in South Vietnam. Who am I kidding? It's a huge amount! I think we only pay our workers at Uplift about a dollar a day; take the money, I think, you never know what's coming next.

I slump back into the chair and simply stare into the TV. I'm disappointed, for sure, but I think she did the right thing.

Comic Book Love

I look at the TV, hoping that something interesting will come on, but that's a fool's errand; why would anything interesting be broadcast on the Armed Forces Television Network? I finally give up and walk back to Suzie's bedroom. There is a light on and through the thin gauzy drapes I see the house girl in her baby dolls lying across the bed reading a magazine. Oh God...

As I enter, she begins to sit up as if to leave, but I tell her to stay, as I move to the back side of the bed. I lie on my side next to her, and, pointing to her magazine, I ask what is she reading. She speaks little English, so without answering me, she hands me the magazine. I take it from her and begin to thumb through it. But after flipping through just a few pages I realize it's actually a comic book, and I wonder, a comic book about love? I guess she is feeling a little lonely as well.

I look at the cartoons; they picture two attractive Vietnamese young women who seem to be talking to each other. One seems to be showing the other a photograph of her boyfriend and seems misty eyed as she speaks. I can't read any of the Vietnamese words in the captions, but I interpret the cartoon pictures as best I can, and I ask the house girl, "Is this about love?" She replies, nodding yes, "About love." She takes the comic book from me and then opens to a new page and points to a few more of the cartoons depicting the boyfriend returning to her and their happy reunion. And she simply says, "Love."

I ask her with some difficulty what is her age, we count our fingers, and she is nineteen. We move closer together, and I sense that it is okay to be in close physical contact. I pull the top of her baby dolls down; she offers no resistance and smiles. But I wrestle with myself and in the end decide to go no further. I am not sure if I should pay her, as money was never discussed and it seems so insulting to offer it. And even if she is giving herself freely, I feel as though I would be taking. Besides, I'm going steady with Suzie, sort of. I simply say, "must sleep," and then roll over. She puts the light off, and I doze for a while. Later in the night I awaken and find her with the light on reading her love comic book. She notices me and puts her love book away and shuts the light off. She is soon sound asleep, but I lie awake for the longest time.

The morning comes, but I find myself alone. I roll over and look out through the bedroom doorway, and I can hear Suzie talking quietly. I slowly get dressed, and as I am tying my boots Suzie enters the bedroom. She looks very tired, but she smiles very sweetly. She sits at the edge of the bed and speaks most pleasantly. "House girl say you sleep with her." I respond, "We sleep in same bed, but no boom-boom." She replies, "Yes, I know, but it's okay." I must look most puzzled, as I find her response so mystifying; does she mean I could have had "boom-boom," but no one is upset that I didn't? But she is already walking back toward the lanai talking about something else. Oh god…

I arise slowly and follow her out to the lanai; it's a little later than I thought. She greets me with a smile and tells me, "Not work tonight, plenty money. Tonight, I am with you." She looks deeply into my eyes; I know she means it. I smile back and laugh the tiniest laugh, then nod my head and simply say, "Good." She seems very relieved by my demeanor; there is no tension. She adds, "Tonight I take you special place."

She changes the subject now; she tells me she has received a letter from the U.S., and it has a check for two hundred dollars enclosed with it. She tells me it is from her old boyfriend, an Air Force Sergeant. She shows me his picture. He is dressed in civilian clothes, but there is nothing striking about the guy. He appears several years older than I, and is rather average looking, so unremarkable, and so mediocre. I don't see Suzie with him; ever! I ask if she loves him, but without any hesitation she tells me, "Not love him, he good to me, but never love him."

I reflect on at that for a moment. He is the third guy in just the last few days who has heaped money upon her. I, on the other hand have no money; she's given me taxi money, taken me to the movies, cooked great meals for me, and given me beer. But she made me brush my teeth and take a bath because I smelled so bad. I begin to smile and think; now that's love! She catches my smile and smiles back; she seems relieved, perhaps, I suspect because I am not jealous. But I am truly not, not in the least; I don't want to be as the others are, I am so much further ahead. Even if I don't fully understand why and how, I just know that I am.

Suzie asks if I can help her cash the check, she doesn't trust the Vietnamese banks and their fees are so high. I tell her, yes of course. She wants me to go to an American bank with a branch office in Nha Trang. I doubt that they will cash it, but I will try. After that, she will drop me off at the main gate of the base so I can check in to see whether there is any news about when and how we might get back to Phu Cat. The house girl is sent to the end of the street to hail a cab, and she returns shortly with a taxi, but only Suzie and I get in.

It is a beautiful day, very sunny, and it will turn rather warm I am sure, but at the moment it is quite bearable riding in a kind of motorized rickshaw. I have no clue where anything is, but if I am riding with Jade East, I don't care where we are going. The bank turns out to be located not far from the base; they must get plenty of American customers. I have Suzie endorse the check and then enter the bank. I walk to a Vietnamese receptionist and ask if I may speak with a manager. She is cheerful and walks me over to an assistant manager. He rises from his chair and greets me warmly. He is American, young, polite, and very considerate as I explain that I am trying to cash a check drawn upon a US bank. I add that the check is written to a Vietnamese national, who doesn't want to go through the Vietnamese banking system. He asks whether I have an account with his bank, and I tell him no. He tells me most sympathetically that the bank's policy is not to cash third party checks. The best thing that he can do is for me to open an account, deposit the check, and wait thirty days. Of course, there is no time for that, so I thank him for his efforts and walk back out to the tiny taxi. I tell Suzie what happened, but she seems fine; I think she knew this would be difficult.

But now she smiles her smile and tells me, "Before you go to base, I want to show you the night club I am taking you to tonight. It is best night club in Nha Trang." She gives the driver his instructions, and we now cruise along a wide divided boulevard that still has most of its tall palms planted alongside the roadway. At one time this must have been a spectacular city. The night club is slightly elevated from the street and just behind it is a view of the ocean. Suzie smiles her smile and holds my hand. She tells me "I wear my best dress for you." I smile as she has said this proudly in that Suzie Wong kind of way; but I also know it is a great compliment to me. This is going to be great. We ride along in the open-air cab with the wind whipping Suzie's long black hair; we are both beaming with smiles of anticipation.

We pull up just in front of the main gate to the base; it's about 11:45 AM. Our plan is that I will go check in and then come back out to the main gate and meet her at 1:00 PM. She will come back with the taxi to meet me then. I step from the taxi and wave saying "See you at 1."

I walk toward the gate. The MP's check out Suzie as she sits waving to me in the open-air taxi; they smile and wave me through. And I smile too. I am trying to imagine what she will look like when she wears her best dress for me. She will seem like such an exotically tropical, sultry package... I try to imagine walking into the best night club in Nha Trang with Jade East on my arm... Okay, okay, I know, I'll be wearing the same stinking, weather beaten, sun-faded uniform that I have been wearing for a week straight, but Suzie Wong knows this and she forgives me in advance. One must marvel at this vivid dissimilarity, how vibrant this juxtaposition, the contrast so brilliant. She is the lone orchid standing among the weeds. But despite the costume I wear, I know she sees more than just the cover of the book. This whole scene seems so movielike, but then so does every day here, and I star in my own personal movie called Vietnam.

Gone With The Wind

I walk; I jaunt, from the gate toward the Alpha Battery portion of the base, their base within the base. I wish I had told her to wait at the gate, as this isn't going take much time at all, perhaps ten or fifteen minutes, tops. Either they have a plan or they don't, but either way the earliest we can travel will be tomorrow morning. That is most unlikely, as they would have to fly a dozen or so guys back down from Phu Cat to ride back with us on the trucks as guards. We will be here for several more days at the very least. I am that happy lark. This war can go on without me. And unknown to me, it already has…

I walk into Alpha Battery, and I discover the trucks are gone, as is my jeep… I check the mess hall; none of my guys are there. I walk-- I run-- over to the transit barracks; they are gone. They are all gone, and they have left me behind… I am not panicking yet, but I sense I am in some very deep shit. I now walk as fast as I can, but I force myself not to run, back toward Alpha Battery; maybe someone there knows something. But by asking someone in Alpha Battery I will be admitting I am AWOL (Absent Without Official Leave). I know I am in serious trouble. My brain is racing trying to come up with some story to save me…and then I see a jeep coming towards me…it is my jeep.

One of the lifer Sergeants sits in the passenger seat and shouts, "Get in, get in," and I immediately jump into the back seat. He asks where I have been, but he doesn't wait for an answer, instead telling me that a Korean LST (a landing ship) will sail us up the coast from Nha Trang to Quy Nhon. "We got to go; they are loading the trucks now." The driver makes a U-turn, and we race to the main gate. We momentarily slow as the MP's wave us through, and I look about hoping to catch a glimpse of Suzie. But it is only 12:30 PM, far too early for her to be there. I never see her again. I feel rather sad about this, unable to say goodbye, unable to explain. I wonder how long she waited by the gate; maybe she assumed that I had to leave in a hurry. I hope she would know I would not leave without saying goodbye, if at all possible. But my thoughts are broken when the Sergeant tells me almost apologetically, "We had to tell them back at Head Quarters that you had gone missing. They've got you listed as AWOL. If I hadn't found you now, they would have listed you as a Deserter." I just nod; it wasn't his fault.

We drive through the city and head to the port area. There is a mass of ships there, but the one we are traveling on is easily spotted. Its large bow rests on the shoreline; its bow is open wide with a large long ramp extending from the ship to the shore like a tongue. We get in line behind our trucks, all of which are to be backed on to the ship. It goes fairly well, and we are soon boarded, but it is two more hours before we actually sail. The delay only saddens my mood, as I think there would have been time to say goodbye. But there is nothing I can do about this; reality has now, most unkindly, ripped me fully from my "Interlude."

The Koreans take us below and show us our sleeping quarters; they are just canvas bunks that fold down from the walls. Nothing plush about this, but everything is painted white and spotlessly clean. The air is very warm below deck, and there is a strong smell of cabbage and garlic; it is unbearable to me. I find a vent and ask a Korean sailor how to turn it on, but he speaks no English. I gesture at the vent, and he quickly understands. He locates a switch and the vent starts up; it is a bit noisy but tolerable if it will clear the air. But it only makes the situation worse, by pumping more of the cabbage and garlic odor around. I won't be sleeping here tonight.

I go up top and join some of my comrades; they are talking to three Korean sailors, who seem to speak perfect English. The two lifer Sergeants do most of the talking as they have both spent a tour or two in Seoul. One of the Korean sailors asks one of the Sergeants how long he had been in the Army, but before he can answer, the other Sergeant says, "Oh, he's been in for twenty years."

The Korean sailor is visibly shocked and says, "Twenty years and still only an E-6?" Everyone laughs. The Sergeant is both embarrassed and annoyed with the other Sergeant and says, "No, no only fourteen years." The Korean sailor is still not impressed and says "Fourteen years?" and he shakes his head disapprovingly. They continue with their banter, but I walk away and look around the harbor.

Finally, two hours after boarding, the LST closes its bow doors and eases off the beach. It is late afternoon now as we sail north to Quy Nhon. As we pull away, I stare back at Nha Trang. Oh Suzie Wong, I am indebted, you were kind, you nursed the bitterness from me, you made me laugh, and you made me feel alive. I thank you for showering me with your love, sharing your beauty with me; all of which you have done so freely in your own Suzie Wong kind of way. The other Suzies before you smile; I think all humanity smiles. I know I would have left Vietnam a very bitter man and you have saved me from that terrible fate.

I look back fifty years on this moment and I think I was far too young to truly appreciate and understand the impact of this episode on my life. But then after further reminiscing I realize I was precisely the right age; I was supposed to be here, this was meant to happen. **It's Cardinal Rule Number VI: Never Doubt When Thunderstruck, You Are Always The Right Age.** (Though circumstances may be heavily against you.) Not too long after I finally left Vietnam, there was a song written by Michael Nesmith simply called "Joanne". And among the lines he wrote and sung were these:

> And she touched me for a moment
> With a look that spoke to me of her sweet love
> Then the woman that she was
> Drove her on with desperation
> And I saw as she went
> A most hopeless situation

So gentle reader, give a listen to the song. And please tell me of more laconic, iconic and succinct words that could possibly better fit this moment of 21-year-old me. I have been asked what may have happened to her; I did try to contact her to no avail. And much like that tropical beach I was once upon, I know I could never go back, as it would never be the same. How could it? In a much larger view, the words also pretty much sum up the whole travesty called Vietnam.

Dusk slowly falls. I must have gotten something to eat, but I cannot remember. It was probably some c-rations, as I would not have eaten the Korean food served below deck in their galley. The night air is warm, and though never cool, it is most pleasant as we sail north up the coast of South Vietnam. There are some wooden benches on the upper deck. I put two of them together to form a bed of sorts and fall asleep. I awaken in the middle of the night; we are in the midst of a tropical shower. I move the benches under the shelter of a stairway in hopes of staying dry, but the shower ends shortly, and I fall back asleep.

I awaken in the morning to the sound of a grinder. I arise, no need to dress, the benefit of sleeping in your clothes. I walk toward the railing that looks down upon the front deck of the ship. There is a seaman with an electric grinder who goes from one spot to the next of the steel deck grinding off the rust. A second seaman paints the freshly ground places with a coat of reddish colored paint. I go below deck to use the head, as clean as it is, and I mean spotlessly clean, the smell of cabbage and garlic is punishing. I guess you have to be Korean. I return to the upper deck as quickly as I can. The ship doesn't seem to be making much speed, but then again, we didn't make much speed driving on land; I guess the biggest difference is the ship never stops. At late morning we finally pull into Quy Nhon harbor and gently land against the beach. Nha Trang is a much prettier city. The bow of the ship opens up, and the ramps are extended from the ship's bowels. All goes well, but it is nearly an hour before we finally drive off the LST. It will be about an hour's drive back up to Phu Cat. I was expecting there would be some Service Battery personnel to ride shotgun with us up to Phu Cat, but there are none. Poor planning and dangerous, I think.

I am last in line as the convoy drives out of the harbor, and I am alone. Who the hell wants to be last in line??? The traffic is stop and go in places, and in one area there is trouble. There is squatter housing on both sides of the highway, and as long as you are moving everything is fine. It is when you stop that the street urchins rush to the sides of the trucks to strip off anything they can. Usually there is nothing to strip, and there are almost always guards in the back of the trucks, but not today. But worse yet is my situation, I am last in line and alone; I am forced into breaking cardinal rule number one.

The street urchins rush to the back of the jeep and pull on the strap that holds a jerry-can full of gasoline. They make a couple of attempts to steal it, but I pull the jeep up a bit. But on the third try, they succeed, and I hear the heavy can hit the pavement. I grab my "Mattel Toy" as I jump from the stopped jeep. I may need that gasoline; if I run out, I don't want to stranded alone on the side of the road. I pull the bolt back and let it slam forward, putting a round into the chamber. Everyone sees this and hears the bolt pushing into the chamber, and the urchins run. I pick up the gas can and throw it into the back of the jeep.

I hate Vietnam again; it didn't take long. The convoy moves ahead a short distance, stops and then moves a little more. I hold my Mattel Toy in one hand keeping the urchins at bay. We finally get moving at a steady clip and leave wretched Quy Nhon behind us. The rest of the trip to Phu Cat Air Base is uneventful, and we finally pull into Service Battery in midafternoon. My comrades are now home, but I am not. I still must drive north another 20 miles to get to Uplift. I don't want to spend the night here if at all possible. I am in luck; the Headquarters' truck, which brings our mail to Uplift in the afternoon, is still there. I will convoy with them and will happily have a passenger riding shotgun.

We soon leave and the drive to Uplift is without incident. We pull into the main gate about quarter to five, and all is well. Once more, I am welcomed by my friends like a ghost coming back from the dead. Big D greets me warmly and asks where the hell have I been. I am astonished by his question and ask, "Didn't you get my letter?" He tells me no, so as we stand next to my jeep, I tell him briefly of my "Interlude," but he refuses to believe me. Oh, he believes the part about getting stuck going on the convoy, as he tells me once again, "If you are stupid enough to get into the Army, then you deserve everything that happens to you." He just won't believe that something good came from it.

We now walk towards the FDC hooch and as we do, the Major, the Executive Officer, the guy who metes out the punishment when called upon, calls me over. Big D smartly walks away from me. The Major smiles at me. I know he kind of liked me a little, as we became at least "road friends," when I had driven him on many a trip. In fact, just a few days after his arrival in Vietnam, I had to drive him down to Quy Nhon for some reason. As we were about to start the long return trip, he nearly fainted in the tropical heat and humidity, as he was badly dehydrated. I quickly bought him a cold soda. He had offered to pay me back, but I had jokingly told him that I would prefer that he remain indebted. "Besides, I want you awake if something happens on the return trip." He nodded his agreement then.

But now, though he speaks pleasantly to me, there is a tone in his voice as he says, "I hear you were missing." I respond "Oh no sir, never, not for a minute. That was just some miscommunication, sir." I make sure I put a couple of "sirs" in my response. He looks at me very carefully, and I smile back like the cat that eats the canary. He nods his head and, still smiling says, "Okay then, that's good;" he still has that tone in his voice. I reply, "Yes sir." And he starts to walk away. I am dying to tell him my story. I start to say, "Well sir," but as he turns around, I think the better of it, and I simply say, "Talk later sir." He nods and smiles; he's letting me off the hook, a very big hook; why push it? The cost of that cold orange soda is repaid with interest.

I get a hot shower and finally put on some clean clothes. I honestly don't know how my uniform has lasted a year. I have dinner with Big D and Bitter John, and then we all drink a couple of beers. All three of us brazenly fail to show up for AH Frank's motor pool maintenance show. We are lucky on that. Later we watch the nightly movie and then go to bed, and I sleep like a baby.

The More Things Change, The More...

I have made such a break with Uplift while I was away. Even last evening with my arrival back, I noticed that it was a little less light, the sun a little lower on the horizon. It surprises me that the sunsets are coming noticeably sooner now. But in the ways that it matters the most, it is the same old prison yard. I think at mid-morning AH Frank has me driving somebody someplace for a short trip. We return to Uplift by midafternoon, but as I have that funny feeling, I decide to check the guard roster. It is as I thought; AH Frank has me on for tonight; Sweet Jesus, I hate guard duty.

One good thing does happen a few days later. After supper one evening as Big D approaches me, he holds in his hand the letter I had written to him the week before from Nha Trang. It has gone all the way to the Army Post Office (APO) in San Francisco, where it was processed and then sent back to South Vietnam. He smiles, shakes his head with envy and says, "Son of a bitch!"

Time moves slowly but steadily. Days become weeks, and as we move into the Fall, it begins to rain. Not much at first, occasionally only light showers, but they come sometimes in the morning now, as we no longer get the late afternoon thunderstorms. Then it is clouds and drizzle for three days, then sunny for a few days. But then it's back to the three days of rain, not constant ever, but off and on. The monsoon is coming. Now the "guard duty plus the rats suck factor" goes off the top of the misery scale, as does the sand bag detail. But unless you are one of that sub-group that pulls guard duty and the other assorted "shit details," the weather is meaningless. Everyone else who has a job to report to on a regular basis, be it FDC or Radio Communications or Medical station, reports to a dry, sandbag-protected hooch. The rest of us are at the mercy of Mother Nature and AH Frank. And he's still quite the AH.

Late one afternoon, Captain Illinois shows up at Uplift. Obviously, he will be staying overnight, probably to meet with the Colonel about some military crap, as there are a few other Officers here that I rarely ever see at Uplift. But he spots me at about the same time I see him and now walks towards me with a big smile. We simultaneously extend our right hands and shake like old friends. I have not seen him since our journey down to Nha Trang, not even when I returned to Phu Cat, as there was barely enough time to drive back to Uplift that day. We ask each other how we are doing; he asks how I liked Nha Trang. Clearly, he has heard I was "missing" for a bit, and I reply, "Oh, I liked it a lot." He smiles back and then, nodding in the direction of the Operations hooch, says, "I've got to go to a meeting now." He gently pats my back and adds, "Thanks for helping out like you did," and walks away.

The whole time, I can see in the corner of my eye AH Frank watching us talk, and he now comes over in a rage. "Didn't you see he's an Officer? Why didn't you salute him?" I reply, "We served together before; he's an old friend. Besides, it's the Colonel's orders, we don't salute inside Uplift." AH Frank already knows this, but it is now that I realize how mentally ill he is; he is psychopathically jealous. Of course, it doesn't help matters that when Captain Illinois walked past AH Frank, the Captain ignored him. Captain Illinois had little tolerance of incompetence and lifers, and it showed. I walk away from AH Frank. He is seething, but there is nothing he can do. I ask myself rhetorically, "Why aren't there more Officers like Captain Illinois?"

But there are some changes in the works. One day, four or five new guys show up at LZ Uplift reporting in to HQ Battery. They are not greenies; they have been in country for many months. Their unit has just been pulled out and sent back to the US, yet most of its personnel remain in Vietnam. They are simply transferred into other units, including ours. The number of military personnel in South Vietnam peaked at slightly over 543,000 five months earlier, but now the US is slowly pulling out. The "Vietnamization" of the war, as the Pentagon called it, is just starting.

About a month later, most of HQ's Battery is moved back to Phu Cat. We are to move in next to Service Battery at the extreme north end of the Phu Cat Air Base. A Command Group has been sent back stateside; we will take their place. The actual reduction in numbers of personnel is negligible, but it starts the long decline. For us it is meaningless; in fact, things worsen and morale plummets further. We move into rectangular wooden barracks, but without sandbags on their roofs or sides, they provide no protection from rockets. We were far, far safer at Uplift. Worse yet, AH Frank now has barracks that he can inspect on a daily basis. Further, we now have morning and afternoon formations; AH Frank is overjoyed. His whole life's purpose is to be a bully, and now he blossoms.

One of the better things about living somewhat isolated back at Uplift was the almost nightly movie that was shown on the ragged sheet that hung on the back wall of the mess hall. The nightly movie was a sort of social hour that brought everybody together at least for a little while. Many of the junior officers and most of the enlisted attended; it created at least a modest sense of community. But that immediately disappears once we move to Phu Cat; we never see another movie for the rest of my tour.

Instead, we get 8:00 AM and 1:00 PM formations. AH Frank stands in front us twice a day now, complaining about one thing or another, assigning us to whatever shit detail that comes up. He is somewhat on the short side, red-faced as always from his bout with the bottle the night before and has a steadily growing paunch. The Brylcreem in his hair dates him to another time; he would be pitiable if he were not such a prick. He is universally despised; I wonder at every formation why someone hasn't killed him yet.

Big D and I now share the same area of the sleeping barracks. It is a large open room with partial partitions that pair off two bunks and a single tall metal cabinet in which we stow our clothes and other personal items. The barracks holds about forty guys, and AH Frank strolls through every day to nitpick about any perceived infraction of the rules. What else do desperate lifers do all day, anyway? But we are never there to see him do any of this, as he repeatedly assigns us to riding as guards in the back of a deuce and a half on day trips to nowhere and back.

The only advantage to moving down to Phu Cat is that we can use the Air Force facilities on the Phu Cat Air Base. I made an appointment to see an Air Force dentist at the air base. It took about a week to set up, but on the day of the appointment AH Frank again sends me off as a guard on a day trip convoy. I tell him about the appointment, but he won't let me go to it. He tells me to make another appointment. This of course, violates Army regulations. He's simply a prick. The next day I go to the Sergeant

Major of the Battalion to complain. He announced upon his arrival that he is "all for the men," but in the end he does nothing. He listens to my complaint and agrees that AH Frank should not have prevented me from seeking medical attention. But then tells me that it's AH Frank's first time as a 1St Sergeant and that he is new at this and still learning. The Sergeant Major is just another lifer bull-shitter protecting one of his own. Everything is a cover up; no one leads.

Phu Cat Air Base is a large base and its perimeter ran for ten miles. It is in the middle of nowhere. Phu Cat is just a small village less than a mile from the front gate; there is nothing there. Our corner of this dog patch gently slopes down to the perimeter and then looks out upon a vast marsh that is at least a mile deep. We still have guard duty at our end of the base but we have more guard bunkers to man now, and therefore the frequency of guard duty does not diminish. Even combining the personnel of Service Battery and one other HQ Battery next to us with ours, our numbers are only a quarter of the size of Uplift. The very ends of the runways are nearby, but the main portion of the base is miles away. In many ways we are more isolated than ever. So, despite our relocation from Uplift to Phu Cat, things only worsen. It is a new location but still just a prison yard, and the guards, the lifers, only torment us more.

There was no longer any nightly movie. It could easily be re-instituted, but neither AH Frank nor our Battery Commander can be bothered. Morale is not important to them. Our only possible outlet for any kind of relaxation is back at the EM and NCO clubs in the main portion of the Air Base. It is more than a two mile walk each way, as we are not allowed to drive vehicles there. Yet on many a night we walk there, often doing it in just 40 minutes. It is something to do; we get away from our prison yard and for a few hours we have just a little bit of freedom.

The Drugs Of The Monsoon

Unless we have guard duty, which is frequent, we walk into Phu Cat Air Base and spend the evening at the NCO club. It is twilight as we begin walking there and of course pitch black when we walk back to our battery. I suppose if nothing else, it keeps us pretty fit walking all those miles. Many of us are E-4's, which means enlisted grade 4. Technically we are considered NCO's (Non-Commissioned Officers) and therefore we are granted entry into the NCO club. It isn't that we are champing at the bit to drink with the lifers; it is that as E-4's we are barred from the EM (Enlisted Men) club, which is open to E-1's, 2's and 3's only.

The Air Force NCO club at Phu Cat is in a large non-descript rectangular building. There is a long bar against the longest wall and a bunch of tables and chairs spread throughout the rest of it. You can buy food there as well, but the item we buy the most of is French fries. It seems quite the luxury to us.

The Air Force generally welcomes Army guys like us there, though at times they seem just a little reluctant. I suppose you can't blame them for not being overjoyed when we walk in; we almost always look a little sweaty, grubby, and rough at the edges, and our uniforms are "well worn." The Air Force personnel always look clean and crisp. We, on the other hand, look more like a pack of tramps. Their base and its facilities feel somewhat "stateside," especially compared to the cave-like setting of Uplift, where everything is covered in sandbags. Even the food they serve in their mess hall is better than Army food, and we occasionally eat there. But that is the nature of each branch of the service, as each branch plays a different role. Of course, there is one other huge difference; the Army has hundreds of thousands of forced inductees, while the Air Force has not a single draftee. No wonder they consider us a little rough around the edges.

Occasionally, there is some live entertainment at the Phu Cat NCO club. The timing of this is a little sporadic, but then again there is a war going on. It is usually some unheard-of garage band from the States; they are never that good. We even see some Australian band; they are lousy, but at the same time we are happy to have the entertainment, and we applaud no matter how bad the performance.

One night, by sheer chance, we walk into the NCO club to find the Corn Fed Bare Blond Band performing. We stay for the entire evening hoping for her sweet and patriotic dedication to all the brave men in Vietnam. The band hasn't improved any since I saw them a few months back at Uplift on that scorching Sunday afternoon. But I'm really not listening to the music as much as I am watching her. In any case the Blonde keeps her top on. Maybe she learned her lesson from the last time she took it off. I would think she felt much safer performing inside the enforced decorum of an Air Force NCO club. But maybe she felt they were not as worthy as that collection of tramps on the barren hillside at Uplift. May God Bless Her, America and the Constitution of the United States.

As November comes upon us, the rains of the Monsoon become almost continuous; it often rains for ten days in a row. It is almost chilly in the evenings, which makes for good sleeping, but otherwise it is no fun. We never walk back to the NCO club any more. It's too long a walk in the rain just to get there. And then having to walk back again in the rain makes this nearly impossible. The nightly movie had stopped when we left Uplift and now, we have nothing to do in the evening, whether enlisted man, NCO, or Officer. The hard-core lifers do what they always do; they stay inside their hooches and crawl into their bottles. We see them in the morning, with blurry blood shot eyes, nursing their headaches and occasionally the "shakes."

Instead of alcohol, we turn to drugs. While drug use had been common at Uplift, it quickly becomes contagious here, and then epidemic. I don't think I know any enlisted man who is not smoking pot. It is readily available, easily obtained and very cheap. Besides, no one ever wakes up with blood shot eyes or a hangover. The only side effect is getting the munchies, and that is satisfied by opening one of the small cans of Elberta-Cling peaches that Big D has received from home. They are so delicious.

We don't smoke inside the hooches and rarely smoke during the day. It is almost always at night, and the most common place is down in the motor pool. The motor pool is somewhat away and downhill from the mess hall and the other hooches we sleep in. The lifers are not about to walk down there at night, especially in the rain, to see if they can catch us smoking. We select two or three, deuce-and-a-half trucks that are parked at the far end of the motor pool and climb into the back of them. They're covered by their brownish-olive green canvas tarps, which not only conceal us but also keep us dry during the unending monsoons. Two or three of us walk down and then we are shortly joined by two or three more guys. A few more wander in, but seeing that the truck is a little full, simply climb into the truck next to us.

There can easily be a dozen or two of us in the motor pool blowing weed. As much as anything else it is a social gathering. Somebody might have a joke, or a tale of some "lifer" encounter that took place earlier in the day. Sometimes we talk of what we might do when we get out or what we did before we were drafted. But there is never any trouble, only jokes, laughter, and a rather strong buzz. Most of us don't toke up during our nights on guard duty; we aren't suicidal. A night on the line is still a spooky experience, and most don't want to be impaired by anything. But other than that, almost every night we light up.

But for some of the lifer NCO's, it is a much different story. Some of them drink very hard, and fist-fights break out between them. On one occasion, I am working the night as "driver of the guards," which is slightly better than the guard duty in a bunker on the line.

I drive the Officer of the guard around from time to time during the night just to check on the bunkers. Sometimes I just do it alone if he doesn't want to come out in the rain. But on this particular night the Officer on duty comes running to me and tells me to grab my M-16, load it, and follow him. We rush to one of the NCO hooches where a fist-fight is going on. The duty Officer, a Captain, tells me as we are about to go through the door, to shoot if I need to. Oh god, just what I need!

The Captain enters first, with me one step behind him. He shoves the two main combatants apart, but there are already bruised and bloody faces on several of them. There are six or eight Sergeants, including a few senior NCOs, and they are all heavily intoxicated. There is an overturned table as well as chairs and several whisky bottles scattered about. The room reeks of stale booze and cigarettes. The Captain demands, "What's going on?" There are several versions of the main event shouted out, which of course completely contradict each other and none of which is delivered coherently. The best that can be determined is that they were all playing poker, when one of the senior Sergeants was caught, allegedly cheating. That's when the fight started.

The principal accuser is the one enlisted man in this group; and the Captain asks for his side of the story. He gives his version of the events, and it sounds believable, but it's difficult to know exactly where the truth lies. Though it appears he came out on top in the fight, he has lost his money. The Captain orders everyone to his bed, if not; he will get the Battalion Executive Officer out of bed. Everyone begrudgingly complies, and it's over, at least for this night. These guys ought to smoke pot; they would live longer.

I hear later that the NCOs were given reprimands, which means that nothing happened except that they have used up their one "get out of jail pass."

None of the senior NCOs, or especially the Officers, seems to want to address the rampant drug or alcohol use or any of its underlying causes. Looking hard at anything in Vietnam would require courage. So much so, that it seems the brass really doesn't give a shit about anything. Undoubtedly the war is already lost; the Pentagon has just started to pull troops out. Even if it is only a trickle now, which later becomes a torrent, the message is loud and clear. The officers' attitude seems to be just go along with the flow, don't make waves, make it seem as if all was well, so as to correctly position themselves for that next promotion. Just don't be the one that causes an embarrassing problem by pointing out an inconvenient truth.

Of Mice And Men

Life goes on, but it is a miserable life at times. Frank the AH seems to become meaner by the day, becoming almost cruel at times. He is greatly frustrated by what he perceives as his lack of complete control over us. He has become obsessed by a frantic need for power and respect, which always eludes him. The harder he tries to squeeze us in his hands, the more we resist. When we were back at Uplift, he was desperate to hold his morning and afternoon formations, but of course he was stopped by our former battery commander Capt. "Good." I'm sure AH Frank felt great frustration by this, but probably told himself it was the Army's fault, not his, that he was denied his entitled position of power with all its trappings of awe and respect.

But Frank was almost giddy with excitement when we first moved from Uplift to base camp at Phu Cat. I am sure he had great expectations of how things were going to be now. He would be able to hold us at his morning and afternoon formations, inspect barracks, rant, rave, and demean us as often as he could. One day I drive my jeep into the motor pool after returning from a day trip to somewhere. He is holding an enlisted man by the shirt with one hand and slapping him with the other. As I approach, Frank lets go of the guy, the motor pool clerk, and walks away. The clerk is just a young kid of perhaps twenty who, not so coincidentally, is much smaller than AH Frank. I tell the clerk to report this and that I will back him up, but he never does; he is probably too afraid. He knows the "Army" doesn't give a shit about him, that they will only protect one of their own. But sooner or later Frank will get his....

America should have cared more about its Army; maybe then the Army would have cared more about its soldiers. In early November a new guy arrives from Germany. He's a big strapping kid and has probably enlisted at age seventeen. After basic training and a mechanics school, he has been sent to Germany. But it only takes ten or fifteen minutes of conversation with this kid to conclude that he is more than clinically depressed; he is unstable and mentally ill.

While stationed in Germany, he had a traffic accident with an Army truck that totaled a civilian's car, a Mercedes no less. The Army requires him to pay them back for the cost of the damage. But as a private first class, he is paid below the poverty level and cannot possibly pay for the damages. The Army has a retention program through which it will pay up to a ten-thousand-dollar bonus if a soldier reenlists for six more years. I doubt the Army paid him that much, but nevertheless, he is forced to re-enlist for six more years and is sent to Vietnam. He arrives here at age eighteen, with at least six years, but perhaps eight years, to go on his enlistment. Hell, if it was me, I wouldn't be just depressed. I'd be suicidal.

We soon learn that we have to be careful when talking to this kid. He is so depressed and oversensitive, feeling that the entire world is against him, that if he says hello to you, you must immediately respond hello back. If you hesitate for a moment, he assumes you have snubbed him and goes off in a huff promising to get even. The real problem is that we all carry M-16's; we figure he might snap some night and use his.

But the poor guy has great difficulty at making any friends. Finally, one of the house boys who comes in during the day to clean our hooches gives him a brown puppy. He immediately names the puppy "Brownie." The poor kid is a little simple at times. All I can think of is a character in "Of Mice and Men" who loved puppies but pinched his puppy's head when it bit him, killing the dog. This guy never has done anything like that as he is a kind soul at heart; but after this, I refer to him as Lenny whenever I speak about him with Big D.

Lenny lives in our hooch and keeps his dog with him in his bed. But the dog wanders around the hooch at night and chews on people' socks or boots. There is often much screaming in the morning when one of us finds that Lenny's puppy has chewed on his socks during the night. They often threaten to shoot the dog. Lenny just can't stay out of trouble with anyone. He should keep the dog on a short leash, but he never does, and this causes daily problems.

Lenny takes his puppy to work in the motor pool, but he always let the pup run free, much to the distress of everyone there, as the dog is always walking in front of vehicles. One late morning, AH Frank has me get the jeep to drive somebody to Quy Nhon. As I pull out of the motor pool, I stop to let a couple of guys get in to give them a ride back up to the barracks area. But partway there, we come across Lenny's dog lying in the middle of the road. I toot the horn, but it doesn't move. So, I slow to less than 5 mph and I pass the dog on the left side of the road. But as I pass ever so slowly by the dog, it gets up and walks under the rear tires of the jeep. Oh god, we hear a yelp, and I stop. Lenny's dog is quite dead. The two guys with me tell me Lenny is going to kill me, but I tell them if they say one word, I'll tell Lenny that they killed his dog. They swear their silence and we drive away.

Later in the day after I return from Quy Nhon, the motor pool clerk asks if I have heard the news about Lenny. I play dumb. He tells me that at lunchtime, Lenny went looking for his dog, and finding the dog dead in the road, he went berserk with grief. After some time, he gathered himself together and buried his dog, but with full military honors, including a twenty-one-gun salute. When everyone heard Lenny firing his weapon, the alarm was sounded, and everyone went to battle stations. It was quickly called off when Lenny had emptied his clip at 18 rounds and walked back up to get more ammo to fire off three more. He got chewed out, but nothing more, given his mental state.

But only a week or two goes by and in early December, the house boy brings Lenny a black puppy. Lenny quickly names the dog "Blackie," keeping things simple. But Lenny now keeps a much closer watch on his new dog and takes him everywhere he goes by carrying him inside his shirt. This causes some problems in the mess hall, as the dog gets away from his shirt and walks on the dinner plates holding food. Lenny is chastised and then leaves the mess hall, taking a bowl of milk with him. He sets it on the ground in front of the door, and the puppy laps up about half of it. Lenny then lifts the bowl to his mouth and drinks down the rest of the milk. Watching this makes us want to retch, but it also demonstrates how severely ill Lenny is. I doubt he'll be able to complete his year tour.

Like A Ghost Returning

Less than a week later, on a late Sunday afternoon we are informed that we will have an opportunity to meet a Professional Football Player at suppertime. The NFL has put a program together in which the League wishes to demonstrate its appreciation and support of the troops. The League has sent players to Vietnam for a couple weeks to visit various units and boost our morale. We are unimpressed, and this goes over like a lead balloon. We would much rather have the Bare Blonde Band in the mess hall. We walk back to our hooches asking one another the rhetorical, "What the fuck? What do we care?"

At the dinner hour a few of us walk down to the mess hall for our evening meal. Sure enough, there's a very big guy dressed in civilian clothes sitting alone at a table. We get some food and eat our dinner quietly, talking among ourselves, just another forgettable meal on another forgettable day, the best part of which is that we don't have guard duty that night. As we walk toward the exit, the football player says hello to us. We stop a minute, so as not to be rude, and say hello back. There's an awkward silence. I suspect he is disappointed by our rather low-key reception and doesn't know what to do next.

I finally ask who he plays for, but I cannot remember his answer, as none of us cared. More silence, so I ask for how long, and he may have said three years. I would like to ask him why isn't he in the Army. I want to ask how much he makes each game, because I get about 8 dollars a day, but I don't ask. After more awkward silence, we finally ask in a friendly way if he wants to go smoke some pot with us. He responds kindly, saying, "No, no thanks." We nod okay and then walk away. As we exit the mess hall, we find Lenny behind its corner; he is just finishing off a bowl of milk with his puppy. I don't know who thinks this crap up. But I wish *they* wouldn't do this to us, none of us leaves with his morale boosted; hell, we feel worse now. Why don't *they* help Lenny instead? About an hour later, we see the football player getting a short demonstration ride in our small observation chopper; I guess our pilot is boosting his morale?

Another week passes; it is mid-December now and the rains are less frequent. We actually start to have a few sunny days now and then. We occasionally now walk the near five-mile round trip to the NCO club in the evening. Just the sunshine alone helps our moods. And now that we are able to walk to the NCO club in the evenings, without getting soaked, it allows us a slight respite from our drab, bitter, Army lives.

One afternoon I walk into one of the small barracks to see and listen to a stereo that one of our comrades has bought at the PX. It doesn't sound that great, as the speakers are covered with a clear plastic tarp in an attempt to keep the red dust of our camp off of them. They sound terribly muffled. It is at this moment that I see Grandpa. It takes a few moments for me to recognize him. He seems ghostlike. His head is shaved; he has lost weight and looks much older than when I last saw him so many months before. It is painfully obvious that his time at LBJ has taken its toll. I see him before he sees me, and I walk slowly to him and ask, "Grandpa? What are you doing here?"

It takes him a long moment, and then he smiles as he recognizes me. I ask when did he get in, and he tells me the day before. I tell him I thought I saw him yesterday but decided it could not be him. He tells me that he has finished his term of imprisonment at LBJ and the next step is to return to his old unit to continue the process of his discharge from the Army. It will of course be a dishonorable one. In the meantime, he just stays in the hooch, as he has no function to perform. I tell him I must go now, but that I will come by in the evening and we will talk more then.

Later that day I ran into Big D and a couple of others who were there back at Uplift when Grandpa was taken away. There are only a few of us still remaining here from that time, and I tell them Grandpa is back.

That evening I go to Grandpa's hooch and suggest that we walk to the airbase and go to the NCO club. I tell him to wear a jacket that will hide the sleeves of his uniform; this will conceal his absence of any rank, as he has been permanently demoted to private E-1. We begin our walk into the base, and slowly he tells me his story. After his conviction, he was stripped of his rank, with forfeiture of all pay and allowances. He was sentenced to six months hard labor at LBJ and is to be dishonorably discharged from the Army. He was immediately taken to the Army stockade at Long Bin. The conditions there were very crowded and very hostile, and he feared for his life. So, he took a top bunk that no one else wanted; the bunk lay under a bare light bulb, which hung from the ceiling. It is a scene out of "Cool Hand Luke." The bulb burned twenty-four hours a day and it kept him safe. He will be in Vietnam another two or three weeks while his paperwork is processed in personnel. He tells me that his parents are upset, as is his girlfriend back home, but that they have been supportive in their letters to him.

I ask what he now does all day and he tells me, "Nothing." He is, in effect, an official leper. He is not allowed to carry a weapon; therefore, he cannot leave the base or pull guard duty at night or do any other duty; even AH Frank leaves him alone. He simply bides his time until they put him on the plane to take him home. He will process out at Ft. Lewis, Washington, in a day and then be released from the Army completely. The worst part is behind him. We have a couple beers and talk of other things and then make the long walk back to our end of the base.

Have Yourself A Merry Little Christmas, Frank

Just a few days before Christmas, I receive a package from home that my mother has sent to me. It is just before supper that the mail comes, and I sit on my bunk across from Big D as I open it. It's a cardboard box wrapped in the usual Christmas wrapping, and it arrives in pretty good shape, considering the distance traveled. It has some home baked cookies and a few small gifts and trinkets. My youngest sister, as a joke to me because I am in the Army, has sent along a small sailor doll dressed in a navy-blue uniform. I show it to Big D, laughing out loud at this family joke, but as he sees it, he says "Hey, let me have that," and grabs it from my hand. He smiles a rather nasty smile and says, "Don't worry; I'll take care of this." I don't see the doll again for twenty-four hours, although later that night he does ask me for instructions on how to tie a hangman's noose. I reply, "I'm not sure, but I think that the rope should coil or loop thirteen times around the noose." He nods, "Yeah, yeah that's right."

The next evening, as I open the tall double doors of the metal locker that we share, the doll comes swinging out on a perfectly tied hangman's noose. The little sailor now has Sergeant stripes on both his arms, and across his chest is written the name "FRANK". I roar with laughter. I suppose some might call this a voodoo doll, but that's a good thing.

The next afternoon, which is Christmas Eve, we gather in a formation to greet the arrival of Santa Claus. Actually, our unit has received gifts from a very kind group of ladies from Illinois, I think. It is really a rather decent gesture and one I will always remember. The tiny gifts are passed out by Santa, who is the same Captain who broke up the fight among the lifers a month earlier. He is a short-timer, meaning that he only has a few weeks to go before he leaves Vietnam and the Army for good. He tells every one of us, as he hands us our gift, "Fuck you." I think he is trying to be funny, but I'm not certain of that. I get a small address book; Big D gets a small flashlight. They are all small gifts, but the kindness and decency of that unknown group of ladies back in the States is not lost upon us. Grandpa does not attend the festivities, but maybe just as well. I have guard duty that night, which seems especially odd to me for some reason, but it is a quiet peaceful night, fine by me.

I sleep in for a few of hours the next morning after coming off guard duty. I grab a little lunch with Grandpa at noon. Because it is Christmas Day, I suggest to him that we walk back into the Air Base and spend the rest of the afternoon at the bar in the NCO club. He thinks this a great idea, as he has absolutely nothing to do today or tomorrow or the day after. We slowly walk down there; what's the rush? Not a single truck passes us as we walk. The place is actually crowded, but we have no real problem getting in. The NCO at the door does look suspiciously at Grandpa, as he has no visible rank that would allow him to enter. But I tell the Air Force Sergeant, "He's with me. They lost all his laundry." He looks stunned by this news and says, "They did the same with my laundry; come in, come in." And we enter with smiles on our faces.

There are several Christmas Day Specials on drinks, and we take full advantage of that. We leave a few hours later, well lubricated, and begin our long walk back to our end of the base. We get partway back and pull out some reefer, some really potent joints that have been purchased in Phu Cat. Hey, you got to support your local grower.

About a mile and a half away, at the very same moment we light up, something else is about to light up this Christmas Day. AH Frank and his pal the Sergeant Major are walking across the compound of our tiny base. As they walk by a hooch, someone pulls the "pin" on a fragmentation grenade, and the grenade is thrown underhand toward AH Frank. The grenade handle, now free of its "pin," closes and ignites the fuse, which has a four-second delay. The grenade hits the ground, rolls a short distance, and then explodes.

We toke up, but finish smoking well before we enter our small isolated compound. We giggle and laugh loudly about some silly joke as we walk by a hooch in front of which stand several lifers. Each gives us the dirtiest of looks, but we ignore them completely, which seems to grate on them even more. I take a quick look back at them; a couple of them are shaking their heads most hatefully. We are clueless.

Grandpa and I walk into my hooch, which is abuzz with loud and raucous conversation. Everyone is ecstatic. We spot Big D, and he nods his head with an enormous smile as he tells us both, "Somebody just threw a hand grenade at AH Frank." We all shout

"Merry Christmas" to one another and laugh out loud. Everyone in the hooch is joyful, as if let free from a prison.

Only an hour later, we happily head down to the mess hall for our evening meal, but we hear some disappointing news. AH Frank was not hurt, though the Sergeant Major who was walking next to him caught a small piece of shrapnel in his hand. We have no sympathy for the Sergeant Major, as he has been unwilling to control AH Frank. The grenade rolled a bit too far past the nearby hooch, and most of the shrapnel went into the wooden sides, with no other injuries. We also hear the rumor that Grandpa and I are the prime suspects, because after all, Grandpa is a convicted killer. But neither of us is worried, as we have a solid alibi.

The next morning there is the usual formation. AH Frank does not come to it but remains hiding in his quarters. The morning passes, and we get lunch. At 1:00 PM there is the usual afternoon formation, and after we are assembled, AH Frank finally appears. He looks awful and is probably drunk. He stands before us and screams at the top of his lungs, "We've found the pin (to the grenade), we found the pin, and we've sent it to the FBI for the fingerprints."

There are probably forty or fifty of us standing there. The absurdity of his statement overwhelms us, and we instantly and simultaneously roar with sidesplitting laughter, including all of the other lifers standing in the formation with us. Frank goes beet red; I am not sure which stings him more, us laughing at him or his fellow lifers. He seems close to a stroke as he tries to speak, but then bellows at the other NCO's, "March, march, I want these men to march." We are called to attention, then right face, and then forward march. We march back and forth for about five minutes, most us fighting hard not to laugh. Some of the lifers realize the stupidity and futility of this and grin also. We are finally stopped and then dismissed. Our hatred of AH Frank is even more intense now. It was an opportunity for him to learn that something is very wrong, but he refuses to see his own cruelty, and instead he makes things even worse. We hope he dies soon.

The day after this I go to see the Battalion Executive Officer, the same Major who had let me off the hook after I was briefly reported as AWOL. His clerk gives me some crap about why I need to see the Major. The clerk is a prick; he seems to think he is quite the cat's meow working for the Major. He was drafted like most of us, but had already completed college. It was strongly rumored that his family had some political pull and that he had been sent to clerk school to be kept safe, what a wimp. As the Major's clerk, he is exempted from guard duty or any of the demeaning crappy grunt work details. But he is a bit too arrogant for most of us; he is just another snotty elitist shit who will leave here clueless about what it was like. He'll never spend a night in a bunker on the line or ever set a foot past it. Yet I am sure he will brag later about how he was a combat veteran of Vietnam.

The Major recognizes my voice and shouts from his office for me to come in. As I enter, he makes a face and waves his hand as if to dismiss his suck-up clerk. He then speaks in a loud voice to be sure that his clerk hears him in the outer room. "Sit down and tell me what I can do for you." I smile at his friendly welcome. I speak quietly and tell him that things are becoming unbearable here. He nods his head yes in agreement, though he doesn't say anything. I tell him that I would prefer a field assignment someplace else and ask if he can help. He pauses a moment and asks how much time I have left; I tell him just under two months.

He begins, "I could get you sent out on a long-range patrol. They usually last three or four weeks. They are always looking for a few guys to do this." I nod my head. He responds, "You think about it and let me know." I stand and thank him for his time. "I'll get back to you, sir." He nods his head and then, lowering his voice to almost a whisper, says, "Think about it very carefully." I silently nod my head and leave. I catch his meaning: "You're going home in seven weeks, don't do it in a body bag." I wrestle with this for a couple days and decide the Major is right.

New Year's comes and goes. It is half-heartily celebrated. I have guard duty that night, though a couple of pals walk down to the guard bunker I am in to say Happy New Year. But of course, nothing changes on the first day of the New Year; why should it? It is the same old Army.

AH Frank is trying a new tactic now. He tells us either individually or in small groups, "Do it for the BC." Be it guard duty, a guard of a day trip convoy, or any other shit detail, he says, "Do it for the BC." BC stands for Battery Commander, as if that is reason enough alone to cause us enthusiastically to go all out in whatever task we have been assigned. It is AH Frank's attempt to shift any responsibility for being a loathsome bully to the Battery Commander. He tells us, "I don't understand why you men don't want to move up in rank. It's more money every month." Or on other occasions, "Don't do this for me. Do it for the BC. Make him proud." Big D would rage when he heard this. He would say, in the evening, "Do it for the BC? What kind of a stupid fool is Frank anyway?"

Why should we do anything for anybody other than to stay out of the military stockade at LBJ? We are in somebody else's war that no one seems to know how we got involved in to begin with. We are led by a military command that has botched the war from the beginning, a war they have now decided they can't win and are slowly withdrawing from to have peace with honor. We get paid between six and eight dollars a day and are mistreated and bullied by cowards and ignoramuses. Yeah sure, we'll do it for the BC.

And as to our BC, our Battery Commander? Oh, he is a pleasant enough guy, but he never does anything to rein in AH Frank. He should, but he exercises no leadership. He just goes along, no point in making waves by pointing out the inconvenient truth; he's just another lifer. In the end, all we can say to each other is, though 99.99% of the time it was Big D saying it to me, "If you're stupid enough to get into the Army, then you deserve everything that happens to you." And then we laugh (usually).

I have yet to take my R+R. This official Rest and Recuperation is a week's paid vacation outside Vietnam. You are supposed to wait six months before you take it, so as to be on the downhill side of your tour when you return. You cannot go home to the mainland US, though; the Army figures that too many of us would not get back on the plane to return here, and I have to agree. You have your choice of about a dozen different places; most of the married guys go to Honolulu to meet their wives there. The rest of us went to Bangkok or Hong Kong or, in my case, Sydney, Australia.

I have timed my R+R so that when I return to Vietnam, I will have only 29 days left. And in the end, I am glad I have waited so long, as the re-entry back into Vietnam is tougher than I thought it would be. I put the paper work in with personnel and within only a couple of days my confirmation for my R+R to Sydney comes back. It's a short flight from Phu Cat to Cam Ranh Bay, which is the jumping off point from Vietnam to anywhere else in the world. I spend one night in Cam Ranh Bay before we depart the following evening for Sydney. Regulations require us to wear civilian clothes, and we are most happy to comply. There is a large PX at Cam Ranh Bay, and I buy some new clothes. We are further advised, several times, not to bring drugs with us to Australia, as we will be searched at the airport in Sydney and arrested on the spot if we do.

We board our plane in the late evening and fly nonstop all night. Our flight is uneventful, except for an invitation from the flight Captain to come up front and visit the flight deck. Everyone else is asleep at this point, so I alone visit the flight deck. The Captain is most welcoming and explains some the functions of the various dials that are displayed completely across the cockpit. It was a very kind and generous thing for him to do. I thank him for his courtesy and return to my seat. It takes a while, but I finally drift off to sleep.

We are awakened by the Captain's announcement that we will be landing shortly in Sydney; it is barely dawn. The airport does not open until 6:00 AM, and we circle once before the controllers bring us in. We are the very first plane to land this day. We taxi to the terminal, but before we are allowed to disembark the plane, an Australian Customs Inspector enters our plane. He is most welcoming and in a rather kindly manner explains that we are subject to a possible body search, and definitely a luggage search, for drugs. He urges us that if we are carrying drugs, to please place them in the large paper bag he holds in his hand. There will be no questions asked, but once we step off the plane, if we are found with drugs, we will be arrested on the spot. He hands the paper bag to someone in the first row and it slowly makes its way back down the plane. The bag reaches me and it is empty. As far as I know, nothing is placed into it. He retrieves the bag and folds its top and then very politely thanks us for our cooperation. We now slowly exit the plane.

Meet Joe Friday (With An Accent)

I have only minimal luggage, just a nearly empty duffel bag with a few clothes in it, a small plastic bag of personal hygiene stuff, and my camera. I clear customs very quickly, though the inspector does a methodical and meticulous search. However, he is most pleasant and wishes me a good time. Almost everyone else has several bags of luggage, and it takes them much longer. A few have packed so much that I wonder if they are planning on going over the hill (AWOL).

I stand nearly alone with my one piece of luggage as I wait for the rest of my comrades to clear customs. I smile in anticipation and think how glad I am to have packed so lightly. But that must have sounded alarms bells to someone, because almost immediately a guy resembling a Joe Friday / FBI agent is standing directly in front of me. At the same moment, I sense the presence of others around me. I look left and then right; there are two more clones standing on either side of me. All three are terrible dressers; they look as if they bought their cheap suits in the same place. "Joe Friday" asks me in an even voice, but with a very distinct Australian accent, "Would you mind following us? We have a few questions." I am certain that they think I carry drugs, but I fear nothing and respond, "Sure, but I'm not holding." He seems unimpressed, and I now follow him down a hallway. I carry my duffle bag, with my two escorts on either side only a half-step behind me.

We don't go too far before Joe Friday opens a solid wooden door and all four of us enter a fair-sized windowless room. I am a little surprised to see at least another dozen agents sitting around a very large oblong table. They're lousy dressers too; there must been a fire sale on cheap suits and narrow ties. I smile at everyone, as if this has got to be some kind of joke. But nobody smiles back.

The guy seated at the head of the table, who is apparently in charge, politely asks me over to him and requests that I put the duffle bag on the table. I think my only response is, "Sure." The bag is passed partway down the table, where two agents take everything out. They thoroughly go through every piece of clothing and my shaving kit, even releasing a little bit of shaving cream, as another turns the green canvas duffle bag inside out, convinced there are drugs inside it somewhere. I just shrug and shake my head no. The head agent now asks if I will put my hands on the table, as they will now frisk me. One of the agents aggressively gropes and feels every inch of me but of course finds nothing. I smile and shrug toward the head agent, as if to say, "See, I told you I have no drugs." They all look at each other, perhaps wondering whether they have made a mistake, when one says, "Shoes, check his shoes." I remove both shoes; they hold them, shake them, and squeeze the heels;

and nothing. I put my shoes back on, thinking we are done, and I still smile.

But we are not done. One of them says, "We need to look in your camera," to which I immediately respond, "But I have a new roll of film in it" Oh shit! They all murmur and smile and nod their heads, convinced now that they finally have me. One of them says "You're not supposed to have film in it." Which sounds stupid, but I say nothing. I re-wind the film and then pop open the camera and hand it to the head agent. He looks in it. There's nothing there. The room is now filled with a deafening silence of great disappointment. The head agent briefly holds the small spool of 35mm film, and then hands it to me. He tells me, but in a kind manner "Just go to any Camera Shop and they can fish the start of the film out and you'll be able to use it." I gather up my stuff and walk out the door, thinking, "Just another bunch of lifers."

Now unescorted, I head back to Customs. There are just a few guys left to be cleared. Soon we are gathered together and are led to the street exit. We are advised we can either take taxis or a group bus that's free that will eventfully take us to the hotel we have chosen from a list back in Cam Ranh Bay. Big D has already been here on R+R and suggested the Hotel Charles where he stayed. Last, we are reminded to not miss our flight back to Vietnam, which kind of puts a damper on things. I now wonder again whether a few my comrades, who have packed so much, are going over the hill.

I opt for the cab; they are plentiful, and I just want to get to the hotel. The cabby makes a couple of attempts to strike up a conversation, but his accent is so thick I can't understand a word he says. I keep asking him to repeat himself, which he does, but I still can't understand him. I try to guess what he's saying and respond with, "Oh yeah, sure," or "Gee, I don't know." He finally gives up; it isn't a long ride anyway. I check into the hotel and don't remember the rest of that day. In the evening I have a steak dinner in the hotel dining room; the steak is disappointing. I am seated next to a couple also having dinner. They both look as if they bought their clothes at the same department store as the drug agents. And their date isn't going well. They both smoke cigarettes, to look more sophisticated and cosmopolitan to each other. But there isn't a lot of conversation going on, and I wonder what the hell they see in each other. Maybe they are thinking the same thing.

I pay my bill and then head out for the evening. I stop at the front desk and ask the receptionists were might I go, and they offer the names of few places that are close by. I step out the front door into a splendid summer evening; it is warm but with less humidity than South Vietnam. And I easily walk just a couple of blocks to the first pub. I cannot recall its name, but somehow Buddha has once again guided me well. The pub is fairly busy, and the atmosphere seems friendly enough. I feel like having a beer, but I am uncertain which brand to order. Just in front of me at the bar, two local guys have ordered a "Middy," and the bar keeper pours a beer from the tap into a glass mug. I speak up now and tell the bartender that, "I'll have the same thing." The bartender asks me, "A Middy?" and I shake my head yes. He pours it quickly, hands it to me and I thank him and pay immediately.

Of course, everyone within earshot recognizes my American accent, and the two guys who have just ordered their "Middies" begin conversing with me. Smiling, and in a most friendly manner, they begin, "What have we here, sounds like you're a Yank." I smile and tell them, "Yes, of course," and we chat each other up. At some point, I mention that this "Middy beer" is pretty good, but they look to each other smiling and tell me, "It's not a brand, Mate; it's the size of the glass." I laugh with them and then tell the bartender, "Let's have three more Middies." I have another round with them. They have to get going but offer to show me around Sydney the next day. They ask the name of the hotel I'm staying at and promise to pick me up mid-morning.

I now start conversing with another local bloke, and he insists on taking me to another pub. We drive a short distance and enter a much bigger pub where he buys the next few rounds. The rest of the night is a blur, but I think we went to a couple of more places, before he dropped me off in front of the Hotel Charles in the middle of the night. I stagger in somehow and I sleep like a log.

I awake at mid-morning to the sound of bells, but I have not a clue what they are. The bells sound twice, then pause for a moment, then sound twice, then pause, and so on and so on. At some point I realize that this is the sound of the phone ringing. I reach for the phone and meekly say, "Hello." It is the front desk; the clerk tells me I have two visitors. I ask who they are, and the clerk tells me their names to which I respond, "Who?" There's a pause and the clerk slowly speaks, "They say they met you last night." It finally clicks. It's the Middy brothers, and I tell the desk clerk to "Send them right up."

The Middy brothers soon arrive, and we joke about my poor memory, but I blame the Australian beer. I grab a quick shower and dress quickly. The three of us head out to tour the town, and this becomes the best vacation ever. In fact, I never spend another night in the Hotel Charles. The Middy brothers are of course only beer brothers, but seem to be longtime good friends. They are about my age. One is an only child, but is not a spoiled brat by any means. He is not working at the moment and has grown a brown bushy beard. His best friend is blond and clean-shaven and has a couple of siblings. He is working somewhere but happens to be on vacation at the moment. When he returns to work, he will give a two-week notice. They plan on heading across Australia to Perth and working out there. How nice to be so carefree.

I can remember little of the day, but at some point in the evening, after picking up another one of their friends, we hit a few more pubs. Well past midnight, as we are leaving a pub, Bushy Beard spots an all-night pool hall and insists we play a few games. We all happily oblige him and enter the pool hall. Beard has some kind of pool game that the four of us play for a small wager. But only two or three shots are taken and the game is over; I have lost before I have even taken a shot. Blond, and especially Beard, are embarrassed, as it looks as if he has deliberately cheated me, though I know he has not. But I make the most of this moment, saying, "Oh sure, bring the Yank to play some pool and then take his money." Beard is mortified, but we all laugh and then immediately play another round of whatever pool game we are playing. We have a great time and now finally leave the pool hall and step out on to the street in bright sunlight; we have been up the entire night. We are a bit shocked by the sunlight, but quickly decide there is no point in going home at this point. We all agree to go to the beach.

As we drive through some suburb of Sydney, we spot a milkman making home deliveries. We are ravished with hunger and pull up behind the milk truck. All four of us jump from the car and unintentionally scare the daylights out of the milkman. I'm sure he thinks he's about to be robbed, but when we pull money out of our pockets, he quickly calms down. We buy several bottles of chocolate milk and then continue to the beach.

We pull into an empty parking lot; it is only a little after 7:00 AM. We walk to the beach, and because we are feeling tired from being out all night, we all lie down. I pull my shirt up over my face to block the sun and soon fall asleep. I awaken four hours later as I hear the buzz of numerous conversations around me. I pull my shirt back down as I sit up and now see that I am surrounded by thousands of people who have come onto the beach. I am more than a little stunned. I stand up and wonder how I will ever find my friends. I begin walking down the beach, but in only a few minutes, I hear my name shouted, and there they are. We spend the rest of the day there. In the late afternoon as we reach their car in the parking lot, we find that it has been broken into, and among other things my wallet and money have been stolen. My friends are most sympathetic, but it becomes a blessing in disguise. They simply bring me into their homes. We first go by the Hotel Charles, and I check out, getting a refund on the unused days. This gives me some cash for the rest of the week.

We must have gotten something to eat somewhere and then more pubbing. Very late that evening Blond brings me home to his house, we quietly enter and climb the stairs to a spare bedroom, and once more I sleep like a log. We awaken in the morning when I hear Blond's mother calling him to breakfast. I follow him downstairs and now meet his family; they seem a bit surprised to see me. I forget what his father did, but he sits at the table in jacket and tie as he reads the morning paper. I suspect he does fairly well, as it is a nice home in a nice neighborhood. Blond's mother very kindly offers me some breakfast, and I am introduced to Blond's brother. He's a few years younger. He's a bit shy but my quick read is that he's a nice kid. It almost seems to be the Australian version of "Leave it to Beaver."

We don't linger long; I sense his parents are not enthusiastic about the late hours their son seems to be keeping, even if he is on his vacation. I can't remember the rest of the day other than that it was a lot of fun. In the late afternoon, Beard brings me home to meet his mother and father. We immediately hit it off, and they open their home to me as if I were their long lost second son. Never in my life can I remember a family taking me in so warmly and enthusiastically. I am given the best room in the house, and I am treated like royalty. I spend the rest of my nights here and have truly a wonderful time. I sleep late, as does Beard, though it seems I am up well before him. His mother and father seem to adore me and cook a nice breakfast for me every morning. When I ask where Beard is, they tell me I better go wake him up and I do. He laughs when I wake him and tell him his parents sent me to get him up. What a loving home and family.

We have dinner here each evening with his family, and it is just after dinner that I meet the neighborhood dog. It is the biggest dog I have ever seen, and it wanders into their back yard. He is a mixed breed of sorts, but I am not sure which breeds. He is short-haired with big shoulders and a head the size of a small cow. He must weigh 160 pounds. But he is a happy guy and approaches most confidently. Beard and his father tell me the dog is making the rounds of the neighborhood and that he's especially fond of beef bones. Beard hands him a bone that his mother has taken from the refrigerator, the dog takes the bone in his mouth, and all we hear is crunching. The dog crunches and then swallows; just imagine your leg in those massive jaws. Beard laughs loudly, but the dog is most civil. He gives us a few wags of his tail and then walks toward another back yard, continuing his rounds; life is good here.

The next day Beard tells me his parents are especially mad for KFC, which has just arrived in Australia from the U.S. He thinks it a good way to reciprocate their kindness to me. It turns out to be a great idea. I get a bucket that afternoon, which we have for dinner. His parents love it and think I am quite grand, but I need to thank Beard for this; it was his idea.

And John Cameron Swayze Says

I am down to my last two days, and at some point that mid-afternoon Beard, Blond, and I end up at Bilgola Beach, just north of Sydney. It's an especially gorgeous midsummer day in January at a beautiful crescent-shaped beach that has rocks and cliffs at each end of its curve. The surf is fairly strong, but doesn't seem dangerous, as I can see other people swimming in it. Blond offers me one of his swimming fins, as he thinks the currents may be a bit strong. But with much bravado, I decline with all the cockiness of a young foolish American male. We enter the water, and it is absolutely perfect in temperature and clarity. I find swimming in it easy, especially going down the beach in a southerly direction. But as we turn around to go back up the beach, I soon tire, as I am swimming against the rip current.

I soon fall behind my friends, who use swimming fins on their feet. I know now that I should have counter intuitively swum further out from the shore to be out of the rip current. Free of the rip current, one can easily swim back up the beach and only then swim into the shore but of course I do not know that. Instead, I try to swim in toward the beach, and as I do so I am taken farther down the beach by the current. I am now in very big trouble, as I end up among huge rocks which the incoming surf now bashes me against. I climb up upon one of the rocks, but only thirty seconds later, another swell comes in and sweeps me off it. I see it coming and take a big gulp of air and hold my breath as it thrashes me about. I come to the surface and swim back to the rock and drag myself up upon it. I stand up to catch my breath, but only twenty or thirty seconds go by, and now another wave sweeps me off the rock. I take a gulp of air just before the wave hits me and I hold my breath until I come to the surface; it seems to be the longest time. There is a cliff behind me, but I know the surf will immediately crush me to death against it. I don't think I have the strength to swim back out into the surf, and so I swim back to that same rock.

I am near exhaustion, and I know I will die here. I know panic will not serve me and refuse to give in to it. I drag myself up on to the rock and shakily stand, but less than a half minute later, I am once again swept from the rock. I take a gulp of air as the wave hits me and takes me under water. I hit other rocks, as I had earlier, and I finally come to the surface. I have so little left. I get back onto the rock and get to my feet, which now hurt from this constant banging around against other rocks. I see the next wave coming towards me, and I know this will be the last one. But I do not scream or cry out, as it seems senseless to do so. As the wave hits me, I take my last and final gulp of air and I am now swept away. I go under the water and I am thrashed about but remember little of what came next.

I do vaguely recall Blond pulling my left arm and then later Beard grabbing my right hand. They shout words, but I cannot understand them. Together they swim up the beach against the current, dragging me between them; I may have tried to help, but I suspect I was limp with exhaustion. As we near the shore, they stand and half lift me, half drag me onto the sandy beach where they lay me face down. I cough and spit up water; I am barely conscious. They start to do chest compressions on my back, but I move my right hand, to say no. I slowly come around as I lie there. My first conscious memory is a ticking sound in my left ear. I lift my head slightly and see that Seiko self-winding watch on my left wrist. I do not recall the time at all, but I am so stunned to see the second hand sweeping with such keen and even precision across the dial face. I say in a weak voice, "It takes a licking and keeps on ticking." But I hear Beard say in his Australian accent, "Poor mate, must have hit his head."

I am pretty well scratched and banged up, but nothing that requires medical attention. We probably had a low-key evening and I am sure I must have slept like a rock that night. My last day was some sightseeing and a last supper with my friends. I spend the last night sleeping at Beard's house and in the morning say goodbye to his parents. Blond comes early with his car; he and Beard will take me to the airport. The three of us stand together for one last picture and they now depart. They drop me at the gate, and we say good bye; what great friends to have made. I wish I could have stayed; what adventures the three of us would have had. But I know I can't. I simply board the plane, and it is a long and depressing ride back to South Vietnam. About half way back, I notice that there are a few empty seats; maybe a few guys did go over the hill. Good for them.

We fly all day and arrive in Cam Ranh Bay in the late afternoon. We change back into our drab Army uniforms, part of the re-entry process. I stay overnight there and, in the morning, catch a very early morning flight up the coast to Phu Cat. I must have caught a ride to base camp, as I don't remember walking. I am feeling a bit let down. Why shouldn't I, coming from Sydney back into this? Our camp is rather quiet and I realize it is Sunday morning. I look for my pal Big D, as his bunk is empty, but someone in the hooch tells me he had guard duty last night. I head for the mess hall thinking he is probably getting some breakfast, but I doubt he will be any fun, as he is just coming off from another night on the line.

The Hitch-Hiker's Guide To South Vietnam

The mess hall is nearly empty, but Big D is there, sitting alone at a table. He looks up as I approach, and we are glad to see each other. He asks how my R+R went, and I tell him great. He asks if I stayed at the Hotel Charles, and I tell him just for one night as I made friends and they took me home to their families. He smiles and nodding his approval says, "How to go!"

I ask where Grandpa is, and Big D tells me the day after I left, he finally went home. We pause a bit. But now Big D changes the subject. He tells me, that a few days earlier, he had heard some great news; there is a Korean Whore House housed inside the Korean-run laundry. The Koreans have secured a big military contract to wash the Army uniforms we wear. It's near Quy Nhon, and he has exact directions to it. He asks, "You up for this?" I should have asked him who exactly has told him this, but I don't. No need to be a downer, I think, having learned that lesson in Nha Trang. I will not disappoint my friend, and I respond, "Yeah, of course. When do you want to go?" Big D lights up with a huge smile. "Right now".

We exit the mess hall and walk back up to our hooch to make preparations, which are pretty simple: grab your ammo bandolier and your Mattel Toy. We tell none of our hooch mates where we are going, as they would probably want to come along. That would make it more difficult to disappear discreetly for the day, and a large group makes for tough hitch-hiking. We definitely weren't going to tell any of the lifers either, they would only say no and give us some shit detail to do. We just quietly and most nonchalantly walk out of camp and head for the main gate of the airbase two plus miles away. We ended up walking the whole way to the main gate, since there's not any traffic on an early Sunday morning.

At the main gate the MPs are there as we expect. The first rule of hitch-hiking is that you must exit the base in a military vehicle. The MPs won't let you walk out the gate on foot, and if you push it, they will arrest you. So, we patiently stay back about fifty feet waiting for a passing jeep or truck. It takes twenty minutes, but finally a small Army truck stops, and we get in. They are headed north to Uplift, and we are headed south so they can take us only the three quarters of a mile to the intersection with Highway 1, but at least we get out the gate legally. You're not supposed to hitch-hike on any of the roads. Besides the Army's prohibition, it is a good way to get killed, as any Charlie would love to pick off a single guy. We don't dare take that chance going north toward Uplift, but going south to Quy Nhon is much safer; Phu Cat is the dividing line.

We get let off at the end of the access road, where it intersects with Highway 1, and we walk a short distance to be just south of the intersection. There are whore houses in tiny Phu Cat town, but they are so low class; Big D wants only top shelf. We wait for our next ride, but it doesn't take long, and another small Army truck stops and we jump in the back. They are only going a few miles, but at least it's in the right direction. They stop where they are turning off, and we wait once again on the side of Highway 1 for our next ride. It arrives soon, and we climb up into the cab of a tractor pulling a tanker-trailer. The tanker-trailer is escorted, but its driver motions us to get in the cab with him. He's a good guy and is pleased to have a little company for his trip back to Quy Nhon. He tells us he hauls jet fuel from Quy Nhon to Phu Cat and back almost every day. He asks where we're going, and Big D tells him to the Korean laundry, but no more. The Army trucker smiles and nods his head knowingly.

We ride along at about 20 mph staying under the strictly enforced 25 mph speed limit. You never get anywhere fast on the ground in Vietnam. Despite our gentle speed, it is a bouncy ride. The driver tells us the truck rides better when it's full of fuel, but I respond saying, "But probably less dangerous now that it's empty." The driver shakes his head no; "It's the fumes that explode, not the fuel." Maybe his job is not so great.

We ride with the trucker for close to an hour, and well within Quy Nhon he pulls over near a main intersection. He points to the right and tells us, "It's just down there, maybe a quarter mile, it's that gray building." We jump down from the cab and thank him for the ride. The tractor-trailer noisily pulls away, followed by the jeep escort, and we quickly get off the highway and head down the side road before any MP's spot us.

We are soon there, but it is a bitter disappointment. The building is quite large and two stories tall; its wooden siding is painted a dull blue-gray. Oh, it's a Korean-run laundry, and it does house a Korean-run brothel, but we are greeted as we approach by Vietnamese ladies at the second-floor open windows saying, "Hey GI, we make love. Number 1 good time."

Big D curses under his breath, "Oh shit." We stand around for a minute or two, but I finally say to Big D, "Let's get out of here; there's nothing new here." And then, using the Vietnamese fractured English slang for "just like this," I tell him "It's *same-same* Phu Cat." Big D responds unhappily, "Yeah, yeah, let's go." We head back towards Highway 1. We walk rather slowly, as that "bubble of anticipation" has burst. We walk to the edge of the roadway; there is no traffic of any kind, and we cross to the far side to hitch our way back north up to Phu Cat. About five minutes go by, and the very first Army vehicle to stop is an olive drab colored jeep. It has two large letters painted white on its hood that read **MP**. As the jeep rolls to a stop, both of us whisper in perfect unison a somewhat desperate and dispirited prayer, "Oh fuck...no"

But the MPs are merciful. "You guys know you're not supposed to be hitch-hiking here. Where are you going?" We respond, "Phu Cat," and the passenger-side MP says, "Okay, jump in the back, we're going right by there." Most thankfully, they do not inquire what we were doing on the side of the road.

We cruise along Highway 1 with the MPs up front and Big D and me sitting in the back seat. It's not a bad way to go riding with the MPs; at least no one is going to stop us. We travel for about 25 minutes but then come upon a small accident on the opposite side of the road. The MPs pull over to the right, stop, get out, and walk across the highway without saying a single word to us. It's as if they have forgotten we are with them. We sit for about five minutes as they do their thing, but it appears they will be there a while. It's getting hot sitting in the sun, so we get out of the jeep and begin walking up Highway 1. We get about a half-mile, and the MPs pull up next to us and say, "Hey buddy, you know you're not supposed to be hitch-hiking". But I respond, "We were riding with you until you stopped back there." The MP responds with a laugh, "Oh yeah, I forgot, jump in the back." We ride another ten or fifteen minutes to Phu Cat, and at the intersection with the access road to the air base, they pull over and let us out. We shout thanks as they drive off, and one of them waves. But as soon as the MPs are out of sight, Big D pulls my arm, "Come on, we got to at least buy some pot," and we enter the first whore house on the corner.

The building is non-descript; it looks like any other on this corner of Highway 1 and the Air Force base access road. The buildings, and by calling them that, gives them more credit than they deserve, are usually only one story tall, jammed together, and built of poor-quality concrete. They are all painted a grayish white, which makes them appear dirty; maybe they are. There are few windows in them, as windows are too expensive to buy. Therefore, the buildings are most uninviting. the thatch-roofed hooches by the coconut grove were so much warmer and inviting. Though Highway 1 is paved with high-quality asphalt put down by the Army Corp of Engineers, there are no sidewalks between the edge of the asphalt and the buildings. There is only a patch of dirt, which is often muddy and almost always thickly littered with assorted trash: tin cans, pieces of plastic, and cardboard. Talk about zero curb appeal.

I quickly realize that buying some pot was Big D's pretext to get us into the whorehouse. As soon as we enter the whorehouse, we are both quickly surrounded by the Madame K ladies offering their services. We do buy some pot, which later turns out to be very good stuff. However, as soon as the pot transaction is completed, Big D is led, grinning, down a dimly lit hallway accompanied by at least three chatty girls. I shout after him, but he only waves me off. I take a seat on a beaten wooden bench; it's not even painted. The Madame K ladies stand in front of me and urge me to pick one of them, but I politely refuse. I will not pay for this. I cannot, as I would find it so crushingly depressing.

The interior of the building is most austere, just masonry walls and floors that are painted a weak pale green that seems lifeless. There is little furniture, a single small table, a couple of wooden chairs, and a few wooden benches. The air seems stale and smells partly of tobacco smoke but more heavily with the odor of the cheap perfume of smoldering wicks.

After a few minutes all the girls give up and leave me alone, except for one. Seeing that the others have given up, she must assume I will now choose her: "Oh GI, me number one girl." But I shake my head no and tell her, "I'm waiting for my friend."

She will not give up and continues her attempt to coax me along. I politely tell her no; it's not her fault. After all, I am the one sitting in a whorehouse in Phu Cat town; she's done nothing wrong. But she is persistent.

I finally say to her, as much as a stalling tactic as anything else, "Okay, show me your stuff." She pulls her shirt up to reveal her breasts. I am not impressed, but I was not expecting to be. I frown slightly and shake my head no. I hope this discourages her and that she will walk away, but she defends herself saying, "No sweat GI, I have beaucoup baby-sans, that why. Now we make love!" I shake my head no as I say the words, "No can-do Mamma-san, no can-do". But she continues anyway, telling me of her expertise, hopeful that I will eventually change my mind. I now ask her to show me her lower gear; I am sure that will anger her; she will say no and walk away. But instead, she pulls her black pajama pants down. I wish I had not asked her to do this, for it debases her and it debases me. But at the moment I asked, I of course did not foresee this outcome. On the inside of her right thigh, just beneath her crotch, is a large blistering scab. It is awful-looking, and it is the size of my hand.

I hold back the gag reflex and will not allow myself to shout, "Oh shit!" I don't think it's her fault; she's just trying to stay alive. All I see is another casualty of this war. But I emphatically shake my head no, and I tell her in an even voice that we cannot do boom-boom, because she is "beaucoup dow" (very sick), and I point at her thigh. Undeterred, she responds cheerfully in Vietnamese-accented English, attempting to reassure me, "No sweat GI. We make love, you catch number ten, you go come back, I give you money back." Despite her promise of a money-back guarantee, I again politely decline. But I want to leave this place now. I stand up from the bench and begin walking down the hallway that Big D has disappeared into so that I might find him and take him with me.

The Madame K, with the open sore on her thigh, walks next to me. She grabs one of my arms, attempting to pull me into one of the many small rooms on either side of this hallway. It seems mazelike. I call Big D's name, but I get no response. I look into each very small room; there are no doors but only strings of blue beads hanging from overhead at each entrance. They do not allow much privacy. There is no furniture in any of the rooms; only the thinnest mattress lies on the bare masonry floor. It is not at all appealing.

I round a corner. The building is larger than I thought, but there are only two more rooms, and in the last one I find my friend. He is just finishing and calls me a son of a bitch for the interruption. But I simply say, "Let's get out of here." I walk back to the front room of the whorehouse, and only a minute later Big D appears. He's still a little pissed at me, but I say "I'll tell you about it later." I never actually do. I decide I don't want him worrying about something already done that may not have any consequences anyway. Why ruin his good time?

We walk out of the front of the whorehouse and step toward the street, but though it is only a few feet away we never reach it. An Army jeep immediately pulls up in front of us, and a 1st Lieutenant steps out from the front seat. Oh shit...we are hitch-hiking, coming from a whore house, and now carrying pot. Big D and I look at each other and then back at the Lieutenant. He looks back at both of us and says, "Well?" I quickly look at Big D and then in unison we look back and shrug our shoulders as to wordlessly ask, "Well what?"

The Lieutenant now asks in an exasperated voice, "Well, do you want a ride or not? You know the MPs will arrest you at the gate if you try to walk back in on foot." Big D responds, "Oh right, right, thanks a lot," and we climb into the back of his jeep. A few minutes later we enter Phu Cat air base. Our ride pulls into the PX, and we jump out saying thanks once again. We walk over to the NCO club and get a beer. Later that afternoon we walk back to our tiny, isolated compound at the far end of the base. In the end, just another *dead heat on a merry-go-round.*

The Final Month

One thing that shocks me was how quickly I adjusted to the "good life" while on R+R in Sydney. The day after my return, I am assigned to drive Captain T perhaps down to Quy Nhon. We exit the Air Force base and are driving out along the access road toward Highway 1. As we draw near the intersection, there is a large but eerily silent crowd on the right side of the road. I slow to less than five mph, and for some reason, perhaps because I am driving so slowly, I seem to see for the first time how much trash and garbage line the sides of the road. It is a warm and humid late morning, and the stuff is almost nauseating as it is so offensively ripe.

As we pass, we now see a woman on her knees next to a dead body. She wails in terrible grief for her son or husband? He is dressed in black pajamas. He was VC, no doubt, and probably has been shot trying to get through the wire surrounding the Air Force base. Almost all eyes in the crowd turn and focus on us as we pass by. We immediately feel uneasy, and I speed up just a bit to get away from this scene. The Captain says something like, "Life is cheap for these people." I say nothing, but he is very wrong. There have been many lives lost here on either side, but they all have been lost at very high cost. We ride in silence for the longest time. Sweet Jesus, I hate this place. I can't wait to leave it.

With just under a month to go, you might think that the time would pass more quickly, but of course it does not. It's just more of the same crappy "make work" work details, riding shotgun as guards on one-day convoys to nowhere and back, and of course the never-ending guard duty. Frank the AH seems depressed, not that he ever lets up being who he is. But my sense of it, despite his best efforts to bully us into getting us to kowtow to him, is that he is slowly seeing that it has not worked. He will never be that esteemed, loved, and worshipped great leader of men, or whatever delusional dream he has of himself. He still goes off on his rants and then swings wildly back pretending to be a nice guy.

We still have the little sailor doll with Sergeant stripes on his arms and FRANK written across his chest, and it still swings on a hangman's noose from our metal locker. Frank punishes Big D over something trivial and puts me on KP for a day during the Vietnamese Tet holidays, when our local ladies who work in the kitchen take a few days off. He had no cause to do this, as I am one of the most senior guys at this time, having been in country among the longest. It is just a deliberate way to screw me in his spiteful hateful way. Despite having been "fragged" on Christmas day and having been perhaps the luckiest man alive to have survived it without injury, Frank the AH has learned nothing. I am certain he will never make his year. Someone will get him; I only wonder, who?

The only highlight is a letter from Grandpa. He finally left Vietnam and after just one day at Ft. Lewis, Washington, he was discharged from the Army. He was now back home in Kansas or Missouri. He was starting his life anew, and he sounded good. It was kind of him to remember us. He tells us that upon leaving Vietnam, that on the very moment when everyone on board the chartered jet felt the wheels leave the runway of Cam Ranh Bay, there was a spontaneous cheer.

The days slowly count down. I am down to my last two weeks, but in early February, the Phu Cat Airbase is hit that night with two separate rocket attacks. We hear the strong blasts and run into some nearby tiny bunkers, as our sleeping barracks are made only of pine boards with tin metal roofs. There are a dozen plus casualties, including one dead serviceman at the Airbase. We were lucky, as just one rocket coming through our tin roof would have caused many deaths. We were so much safer at Uplift.

I do not obsess about death being so random or so close by, but think I would surely be pissed off to have "bought the farm" having come so close to the end of the tour. As I get to my final week, someone in personnel at Service Battery sends word for me to report there to begin the processing-out paper work. They are right next door to us, and after the morning formation, I walk over. It is not a difficult procedure, just updating information, signing a few forms, and then carrying a few forms around for other signatures.

One of the signatures I must get is that of the re-enlistment NCO. It's here that the Army gets one last shot at getting you to re-enlist and sign up for a few more years. But as I enter the tiny Re-Enlistment Office, the NCO lifer immediately sizes me up and knows I'm a lost cause; he's smart enough to know he shouldn't waste his breath. But he speaks in an even tone and offers me a chair and then asks for the paperwork. He flips through it and quickly finds the pages he needs. He wordlessly signs off and passes everything back to me. I am a little disappointed, as I had hoped to hear his pitch and then say NO! But I move on.

I return to personnel a couple of hours later and hand all the paper work back to the clerk. He looks it over and tells me, "Everything is good." But then tells me something surprising. "You were put in for an Army Commendation Medal, but you are not going to get it. When AH Frank heard about it, he went crazy. He's out to get you." He never did tell me who had put me in for the commendation, but I think it might have been somebody in Operations for the time I was in the bush. The clerk continues. "I checked, and you've got a spotlessly perfect record, why does he hate you so much?" I respond, "Because he wants me to kiss his ass and I won't do it." The clerk responds, "I'm glad I'm personnel, I never have to deal with him. But you're right about sucking up. I've got three weeks left, and they offered me a bump to E-5 for the little bit of time I have left, but I turned it down. What's the point of that? They could have promoted me six months ago."

It was an old Army trick. Each unit is allotted so many E-5's; but they hand the rank out just as somebody is leaving. Once they go, their allotment comes back and they hand the E-5 to the next suck-up. They all take it for the last two weeks they are in the Army, like it means something. But this kid has guts and class; he tells them, very politely of course, to shove it. Why would anybody, other than an ignoramus, want to stay in the Army? Your entire future career is subject to the whims of someone like Frank the AH.

The clerk finishes everything up and tells me I will leave Vietnam from Cam Ranh Bay, but that I cannot report there any sooner than 36 hours and no later than 12 hours before my departure day. Therefore, he tells me, "You can leave Phu Cat between Monday afternoon and Tuesday afternoon." I tell him I'll probably go on Tuesday morning, but he responds, "Either way is fine. Everything is ready; just walk over here on the day you want to go, and we'll give you your personnel file. And you are good to go."

I don't remember much of my last weekend there. I think I had guard duty on Saturday night, but I cared little, as I knew it would be the last time that I'd be spending a night in a bunker on the wire. It was a quiet and uneventful night anyway.

The Last Detail

Monday morning rolls around. I arise and get dressed and then stand as I look around the hooch. For the most part, all I see is a bunch of kids. They are half awake as they dress. I see Lenny sitting on his bunk. He speaks lovingly to his small black puppy as he holds the pup in his lap. The pup gnaws on one of Lenny's fingers, but he must have bitten down too hard, as Lenny now shouts, "Hey Blackie, no, no, don't do that." I only hope he doesn't pinch the dog's head. That poor bastard Lenny, he is nineteen years old now, only a private first class, and faces at least six more years in the Army.

I cannot see how he will ever make it. Sometimes I think he won't make it to next week.

Tomorrow, I will say good bye to Big D; he has been a good friend, and we have had some adventures together. He will stay about a month and a half longer than I will. He has voluntarily extended his time in Vietnam by about two months in order to reach the magic number of 19 months total time in the Army. When he returns stateside, he will have only five months left on his 24-month conscription, and the Army will discharge him on the day he returns to the States. I will have spent 22 months in the Army, three months longer than he. I will be sorry to leave him behind here, but he will spend three months less in the Army than I have; he's the lucky one.

Big D and I head down to the mess hall. I just get toast and some coffee, as does Big D; everything else sucks. When we leave the mess hall, we spot Lenny and "Blackie" drinking a bowl of milk together. Oh god… We walk back to our hooch and straighten up our area to make it semi-presentable to AH Frank. At eight o'clock we walk outside and get into the morning formation. Apparently, my section has a new lifer Sergeant in charge; he must have shown up over the weekend. Old Sergeant Patterson had left a few months ago; this is his replacement; more Army dead wood. I walk to the end of my section and fall in line.

AH Frank makes a couple of announcements that no one cares crap about, but he does like to hear himself talk. Next, he shouts out the names of a few people who will be convoy guards, and Big D is one of them. He'll spend the day riding in the back of a truck as a guard. He hates these trips, but he'll be away from AH Frank for the day, so it's actually a gain. Finally, AH Frank asks four different section chiefs to select one man each for the garbage detail. The four men chosen will now take a deuce and a half truck and pick up the garbage around the camp and haul it off to wherever it goes. My new lifer section chief picks me, my last and final shit work detail.

AH Frank starts to say something to my new lifer Sergeant about its being my last day, but I just shrug at AH Frank that it's okay. The morning formation ends a moment later. Big D tells me for the 656th time, "If you're stupid enough to get yourself into the Army, then you deserve everything that happens to you." We laugh, and he heads off to the hooch to get his Mattel toy and ammo, and I start to walk towards the motor pool to hook up with the garbage detail.

But I only get half way, for as I walk there, I decide I have had enough. There will be no "last detail." I will not work another GD shit detail. I walk back to my hooch, but Big D has already left, and I cannot say goodbye. I have pretty much packed everything I am taking over the weekend. All that's left to do is to pack up my toiletries and take my poncho liner off of my bunk and place them in my duffle bag. I put my constant companion, my M-16, aka the Mattel Toy, Widow Maker, and Little Black Death, under Big D's mattress for safekeeping. Oddly, I feel somewhat sentimental leaving my assault rifle behind. It sounds laughable now, but back then I truly felt I was leaving "my constant companion" behind, as if it were a betrayal of trust. It was kind of a friend that had come with me everywhere and had gone through everything I had. But I have almost never picked up another weapon since that day...I guess the thrill was gone.

I write Big D a short letter goodbye.

Big D,

Sorry I didn't say goodbye. I thought I would be here until tomorrow, but I decided I couldn't do one more of AH Frank's shit details picking up the garbage. So, I'm leaving now. Hey, FTA. Please turn my M-16 in to the armorer, it's under your bed, I don't want to be seen walking with it over there. I'm sneaking over to Service Battery now to get my paperwork from personnel and then heading straight to the air base to wait for my flight to Cam Ranh Bay. I'm sure there's a flight this afternoon. I'm leaving the little sailor with you, so take care of him. Please tell Frank to go fuck himself. I'll write when I get home. Take care and Adios MF.

Tokyo Bound, You Always Go Home Alone

I take a look out the back door of our hooch. The coast is clear, and I walk over to Personnel and pick up my personnel file and then begin walking toward the air base terminal. I am soon picked up by one of our guys in a truck who drives me all the way there. I check in, confirm my flight and time, and then walk over to the NCO club to await my flight. I order French fries; what else is there?

I catch my flight to Cam Ranh Bay and spend two nights there. I fly out at mid-morning on Wednesday, Tokyo bound; it's the first leg of the long trip home. It is another Flying Tigers charter, but fortunately was not especially crowded this time. And just as Grandpa wrote, when we feel the wheels lift off the runway of Cam Ranh Bay, every one of us cheers.

We fly for about four hours to Tokyo, where we re-fuel for the long non-stop flight to Seattle. We deplane for the refueling of the plane; that process probably takes an hour and a half. We are allowed to do a little duty-free shopping in the airport, which helps to kill our time there. The Japanese salesmen's English fluency is astonishing. I buy a small bottle of Joy; hell, I have to. Besides, the price is great.

But at some point, we simply sit around the airport gate area passing the time. I stare out huge plate glass windows. Below me, I watch the ground crew standing next to the wings of our plane as the fuel is pumped aboard. It's a gray and wet afternoon. A steady drizzle falls, and it must be chilly, as I see the breath of the ground crew as they speak to one another. They all wear yellow rain coats that fall well past their waists. They seem just as short as the Vietnamese, but much stockier. The scene does not depress me in the least; hell, I'm on my way home. But across from us sit a couple or three hundred guys who wait for their plane to be refueled as well. They look very quiet and somber. The weather outside cannot be helping their mood, as their plane will shortly take off to complete their journey to Cam Ranh Bay, Vietnam.

They are our replacements. This scene is the mirror reflection of where I sat exactly one year ago. They look very young to me. They are "greenies;" their uniforms are brand new, as yet unwashed, and still deeply green. They stare wide-eyed at us. The year before, when we left for Vietnam, we were given four shirts and four pairs of pants. But we and our uniforms are so much older now. We wore them every day for a year, never mind the many, many nights we slept in them. I look back at this and wonder how the fabric of the material stayed together as long as it did. To say that our uniforms are well worn and faded is not some ill-conceived understatement. In fact, most look see-through, threadbare, weather-beaten, and tattered. My own is among the worst, as my shirt has a tear in its upper left sleeve and several small holes chest high across the front. But far worse, to their eyes, is the number of us on crutches, with arms in slings, or with casts around legs, and there are a couple of guys with head bandages.

When you return from Vietnam it is never as a unit; it's just a bunch of guys who happened to finish their tour on the same day. When your time is done, you just go, even if there's a raging battle going on. And you always go home alone. Not a single one of us knows any other. We are a large group of misfits, and I know we look like a bunch of banged-up Army tramps. We must appear very hardened to them, and we must give the impression of a pretty much undisciplined lot as well; and hell yes, we are all of that. We carry chips on our shoulders the size of bricks, daring anyone to knock them off. We have been sucked in, chewed up, and-- having survived-- are now about to be spit out. We are only a day and a half from freedom; don't get in our way.

But I grow restless as we wait for our plane to re-fuel. So, I stand and walk in long slow circles, watching through floor-to-ceiling plate glass windows as the ground crew continues their preparations. After some time, I become aware of the many eyes following me as I limp around; my left knee is killing me. I am one of the walking wounded, and I realize I am scaring them.

But there's no point in scaring them; they haven't done anything to us. Hell, they are in the same stinking boat we were in a year ago. I take a seat again, and now I smile benignly at them. About ten minutes passes, and a young Black kid walks directly toward me. He smiles, and I return it. He looks about nineteen. He asks how I am doing, and with that we begin our conversation. We make small talk for a bit, where are we from, that sort of thing. He tells me he's from Detroit; I don't think there can be anyone left there.

He then asks a serious question, but his voice is hopeful and optimistic. "I hear everyone gets along" (meaning black and white). I assure him that we did. And I emphasize that I had many brothers as friends. But I smile as I tell him, "We all hate the lifers," and he smiles as well. I tell him he'll be okay, that there are always a few who are never going to change, but not to worry about that. I urge him just to be himself; he will make many friends. I tell him there will be extra money in his pay every month, as everybody gets combat pay no matter where they are stationed in Vietnam. (He is a private first class; he makes about four dollars a day and will get another two dollars a day for combat. Try to imagine how poorly we were paid.) I tell him to save his money and send it home, so that when he gets back, he will have something. And smiling once more, I tell him the old Army maxim "Never Volunteer." But I do not dare to tell him the Cardinal Rules.

My plane is now called for boarding and I wish him well. I hope he made it. Despite the Administration's and the Pentagon's earlier decision slowly to withdraw from South Vietnam, troops are still being sent there to replace those who rotate out as their time there ends. The American involvement in the war will go on for three more years; Saigon will fall two years after that; tell me it's not a crying shame.

I and my comrades in arms board our plane; but there are plenty of empty seats. The year before, my plane going to Vietnam was jam-packed, without a single empty seat. But in this past year, there are 12,000 of us who have been killed and tens of thousands more who have been wounded and hospitalized; none of them will be returning with us. Our plane is only half full. But now there is a certain sadness that seems to overcome all of us. I think it is the realization that we are not just leaving Vietnam, we are also leaving our friends behind us.

We pull away from the gate and taxi to the very end of the runway. We begin to roll, slowly accelerating for nearly a mile and a half, and finally, without any sense of urgency or hurry, we gently lift off from the Tokyo airport. We cheer once more, but with much less enthusiasm. We fly across the North Pacific into the coming darkness of night and twelve hours later land near Seattle. I doubt any of us gets much sleep. It is barely dawn as we land; but at this point we are too exhausted to cheer; the whole thing is so anti-climactic.

The Last Day In The Army

We land at McCord Air Force base and as we exit the plane, we grab what little luggage we have, usually just our drab green duffle bags. Somebody from the Army greets and directs us to buses that take us for a very short ride next door to Ft. Lewis. It's a little chilly, and suddenly it hits us that it is February.

We enter a reception area and are divided into two groups. The smaller group by far is for the few guys who still have some time left on their enlistments and who will not be processing out of the Army.

No point in holding them up, as they will no doubt go home for some well-deserved leave before reporting to their next base.

But the rest of us will begin a multi-step, day-long marathon of physicals and mountains of paper work. Our guide through this process is a young but educated and bright Sergeant. Surely, he will not be staying in? He tells us we must do each step of this process as a group. He knows this may seem frustrating, as some may complete each step faster than others, but this way no one is left behind. And he promises, "I'll have you all discharged by the end of the day." To that we all cheer.

The first step in this process, he tells us, is to discard all of our old uniforms and combat boots from our luggage; it has something to do with the Dept. of Agriculture. They do not wish for us to unintentionally bring any nasty insects into the country. I am happy to comply, as we all are, to get rid of this stuff. The young and bright Sergeant has an assistant. He is also a Sergeant, but he's an old lifer. God, he looks elderly. He says something nasty like, "And I'm the one who's going to do the inspection." Until that moment we are a hundred and twenty-five individuals who happened to arrive here on the same plane. Now we are instantly united. He has given shit to the wrong group, and we turn on him like a pack of lions about to take down a stray wildebeest and that would show not the slightest mercy. Every one of us looks loathingly at him, and there is a loud chorus, shouted as hatefully as possible, "Fuck you, lifer." He shuts up instantly. It's a good thing we left our M-16's in Vietnam; we can barely keep our rage in check. The young Sergeant tells him he will take it from here and tells him to go take a coffee break. We never see that lifer again.

Before we begin the next step, our young Sergeant guide asks all of us one seemingly innocent and routine question. One question that in reality is a cruel hoax about to be played upon us, and which in later years our answer is very detrimental to us. Our young Sergeant asks, "Do any of you have a physical ailment or injury you wish to make known now?" Probably half of us or more, myself included, raise our hands, as my knees are achy as hell. But our Sergeant now quickly adds the caveat, "Understand that the Army will hold up your discharge for sixty days while your injury is investigated." And to a man, every single one of us lowers his arm. How awful of them to play this dirty trick on us. We have left Vietnam behind us (or so we think) barely 18 hours ago. We are all very young, and our freedom, promised to us once more, is just eight hours away. I am 21 years old. The last 22 months, some of which were hellish, have felt like a prison sentence. I, like everyone else in that group fresh off the plane from Vietnam, just want to be out of the Army. But there is no one there to speak on our behalf, no one there to explain that now is the time that you must record your aches, pains and injuries. If not, they will close the books, and good luck later on if you want to file a claim for disability. I lower my arm. What a misfortune. How shameful that the Army does this to its soldiers.

So, we begin. As a group we are pinched, probed, and poked. We see dentists, nurses, and doctors. We are given more shots, and we sign our names to more forms than I think could exist. At some point, measurements are taken for new uniforms. We must have been fed lunch, but I don't recall. The day drags on, and it begins to get dark, but our ordeal goes on. Very late in the evening we are given dinner. It is 11:00 PM, and we actually eat a fabulous steak, in fact, the Army cook comes to us individually to ask how we would like them cooked. After dinner we get our new uniforms and now change into them. We of course turn in our old uniforms, and it honestly felt a little sad when I turned in mine. The uniforms will be incinerated; the USDA aside, maybe it is just as well. They are not much more than rags at this point anyway, and to keep them would keep alive some things that maybe should lie at rest.

The very last thing that the Army does is to pay us. We are paid travel money back to our place of induction, wherever that may be, as well as for any unused leave time we have accrued. And then we are paid for the first twelve days of February. At this point it is now 2:00 AM Friday the 13th and we are entitled to one more day's pay. This is not lost on any of us. Our guide, the young Sergeant, who has stuck with us all day and has done a great job, apologizes to us. We are correct, he tells us. Our pay and benefits were calculated up to the twelfth, but having gone past that date, we are indeed due one more day's pay. But he tells us we must wait until 9:00 AM when the finance center reopens in the morning. A few guys say they will stick around till then, but I am too exhausted to do that. Most of us murmur, "well FTA," and bitterly walk out the door. I soon have a killer headache. We board a jammed bus that will take us to the Seattle-Tacoma airport. It cost eight bucks, which is more than a day's pay for me; no more free rides. Imagine, an entire day's pay spent on a bus ride to the airport.

The Home Coming

I finally catch a cross-country red-eye to New York. I wanted to wear civilian clothes on the flight, but I am flying Military Stand-By one last time, as it is cheap, and one is required to wear their uniform. I board my flight and take a window seat mid-way back. A few minutes later, my would-be seatmate arrives; he is perhaps a half dozen years older. He sees my uniform, shakes his head, gives me a look of disgust, and immediately takes another seat. No words are exchanged, but his revulsion and hostility are abundantly clear. Welcome home, soldier. I feel insulted, so fuck him, he can go to the next war, I never will. But I soon have a pounding headache. I am glad it's a night flight, but I get no sleep. I change planes in New York and arrive home in mid-morning. It is sunny and bright, but I shudder with the cold temperatures of mid-February.

My family comes the airport to pick me up. We return home and have a somewhat formal dinner which some of my extended family attends. But more than anything I just want to be left alone; there is much to process. I have been sucked in, chewed up, and now thrown back out on the street. I'm twenty-one years old, but a part of me feels a hundred and ten. And while I have been away, life has gone on without me, and nobody gives a shit.

Meet A Civil Servant Lifer MF

I want to take some time off and apply for unemployment benefits. It doesn't go well. That mid-morning, I have taken myself to the unemployment office and brought along my discharge papers. I approach the main counter to explain my purpose there to a semi-well-dressed woman in her late thirties. But her clothing dates her; she's not quite the Queen of the Office she thinks she is. I am still 21 years old, so the age difference is just enough to be generational. Her peers seem elderly by comparison.

She hands me a two-page form to fill out and directs me to a nearby table. I give my full name, address, DOB, the name of my last employer (US Army) and, under the reason for my unemployment, I write the word "discharged." I return the form to her, but she almost immediately reprimands me for not completely filling the form out. She hands the form back to me, telling me to put the address where I was stationed and what I did there (a terrible question to be asking any veteran returning from Vietnam). I return to the table to add more information. Under address I write the words, "Binh Dinh Province, South Vietnam," and then under dates of employment, I write the day I got there and the day I left.

I return the form to her once again. She glances through it but demands more information. She raises her voice, almost shouting,

"What was your job? What was your job? You must have done something! What exactly did you do?" Her tone is belligerent and accusatory. She rides a high horse and insists on picking this wound. I return to the table and, under the heading of job title, I considered the words "fucking grunt" but leave it empty. Under the heading of "duties and responsibilities, please provide details," I get pissed. I write the words "participated in the burning of villages and their destruction including its men, women, and children."

I know as I wrote this that it is over the top, but all I want is to be left alone, as I have only been back five days from Vietnam. I return to the counter and hand the form to the woman. She reads it and screams, "This is sick. This is sick. You're sick." (What a prick, I think. She'd be perfect for Capt. Fruit.) But I say nothing and simply stare back at her. Her boss runs over and takes the form from her and tells her he will handle this now. He seems about 30. He is much more professional and is much more sympathetic.

He takes me to the Veterans Placement Counselor and hands him the form. The counselor reads it as I take a seat. And then he begins; he points a finger at me and says, "You guys, you guys, you're all the same, every one of you guys is so pissed off, but I don't know why. Hey, I know what it was like; I'm a WW II veteran myself. It was tough, but we won it." I think, what a fool, he has no idea what it's like to return to a country that disrespects us for having gone to Vietnam. He was honored when he returned; we get to listen to everybody's shit when we return.

He's another member of the "greatest generation" who is convinced of their collective wisdom but cannot see the forest for the trees. I suppress the violence I wish upon him and the woman in the outer office. He rambles on, checks his files, and then tells me he has no job(s) for me. He hands me back my discharge forms and tells me, "The Army paid you for 17 days of unused leave time, as far as we're concerned, that's like being employed for the next three and a half weeks. You're not eligible for unemployment." I reply I was only paid six bucks a day. He tells me it doesn't matter, but he is sending me to another office. "They might have something for you." And then adds, "The sooner you are working the sooner things will be better."

On that subject he is right. I do go to that other office, and they do have a solid lead on a job. I am working within a week. It is the best thing for me. I get going again and slowly get on with my life. It is a long period of adjustment, but I needed to start that journey.

Letters From Vietnam

I write to Big D about two weeks after I got back. I think I tell him it is cold and snowy; but I don't write much about myself. I am not having that much fun and am having some difficulty adjusting, and I don't want to convey any of that to him. Mostly, what I write is asking him how he is doing, what has been happening there and to say hello to a few of the other guys. About two weeks or three weeks pass and then I get a letter from Vietnam.

It feels strange to be on the other side of this now. I was somewhat guilt-ridden when I wrote to Big D a few weeks earlier. I was out of there, no more lifer tormenters, at least no Army lifers. I was home safe; he was not. I wish we could have left on the same day, but then I would probably be worried about someone else we had left behind there.

And now to receive a letter from Vietnam, a place and yearlong surreal event that shapes me in ways I have yet to realize, let alone understand. The presence of the letter stuns me; just touching the envelope feels current-like. The whole envelope is water-stained and smudgy; the return address is no longer legible. But in the upper right-hand corner of the envelope where the stamp should be is the barely legible word "FREE." Now there is no doubt where it came from. It has the look and feel of a letter written from a South Pacific war zone; but then, why shouldn't it?

I go to my room to be alone and open the letter. I am immediately drawn back into Vietnam as if I had never left. It is from Big D, and he is well; he has only a couple of weeks left. But he has a mixed assortment of stunning news. Lenny, that poor bastard with the puppy, has had a complete breakdown. It seems that late one evening, poor Lenny discovers that his wallet is missing. He tears through his belongings but cannot find it. He is convinced that someone has stolen it and tears through everyone else's things looking for it and making a shambles of the hooch. Unable to find the wallet, he runs towards Headquarters and jumps the Officer on duty. Lenny, who is a big strapping kid, pins the Lieutenant to the ground with his knees. He puts both hands around the guy's throat and begins to strangle him. He cries hysterically as he shouts, "They took my money. You have to help me. You have to help me". Just as the guy is about to pass out, Lenny is pulled off him. The Lieutenant lives, and Lenny has been sent to a hospital. The word is that the Army will send him home; Lenny will be given a medical discharge.

But now there is even more stunning news. There has been a mutiny at Headquarters Battery. I knew this would happen sooner or later; there is only so much abuse we can take. AH Frank had started a new procedure at the start of guard duty. He had started making the guards do a flag ceremony just before they were dropped off at our bunkers on the perimeter. It was just one more piece of bullshit that AH Frank used to harass people. But on this particular early evening, he pushed the wrong guys. AH Frank dressed them down over some supposed infraction, but none of them was aware of what the supposed infraction was. This caused AH Frank to get even crazier, and he was now screaming at the top of his lungs. One of the guards threw his M-16 at AH Frank's feet and told him he could pull guard duty. Before he finished speaking, all twelve of the guards threw their rifles to the ground as well, and they all walked back to their hooches. Frank started to chase after them, but then got on his knees and begged them to come back. He finally threw himself on the ground, crying, "The men hate me; the men hate me, why do the men hate me so much?" AH Frank was relieved of his duties and hospitalized as well. None of the guards were punished; it seems AH Frank may have been drunk.

I write back to Big D telling him how happy I am to hear that AH Frank was finally done in, and that it was by his own hand is an extra bonus. I get one last letter from Big D; he is down to his last five days, and he will be out of the Army forever in less than a week.

We stayed in touch for a little while off and on, but we lived a thousand miles apart. Life, as they say, goes on.

Still Bitter After All These Years

I work at my job for the next six months and then return to school. It is a long tough haul, I assure you, and I am not the brightest bulb. But four and a half years later I earn a BS Degree. The GI bill has helped, but not that much; it is only a $175 a month for each month I am in school. That is supposed to cover tuition, books, and room and board; it never comes close. I take out student loans and accrue debt that takes ten years to pay off. It is not our father's GI Bill of WWII; Congress is stingy.

But an especially painful moment comes about four months after I return from Vietnam. I happen to run into the father of one of my boyhood friends. He is a veteran of WWII. He asks me about my experience in Vietnam and what do I think about the slow but steady withdrawal of the US Military from there. I attempt to tell him that the South Vietnamese government was generally viewed as corrupt as hell and that there was little support for it in the countryside. We are only propping them up; they will soon fall after we left. I tell him that if we are going to go to war, then we should go to win it. If not, then get out, and the sooner the better; the longer we stay, the more blood lost and to what end?

While one would think that we are all entitled to our views, he is completely disgusted with me. He most scornfully and loathingly tells me that this is all part of the extreme leftist propaganda. He shakes his head at me, telling me I have fallen for all the lies, that I had been duped by the **world-wide communist plot** just like all the other young people, and what a disappointment I am to him. I just walk away; so much for the welcome home and expression of gratitude from a fellow veteran. I see the guy from time to time over the next several decades; I am civil, but I never forgive him.

The worst thing is how extraordinarily hypocritical he is. He has two kids, one my age, one a year or two older. Neither of them has gone. He has made sure to keep them out of the military. He is all for the war, but let someone else's kids fight it. Of the seven or eight kids I grew up with in my neighborhood, I am the only who got sucked up by the draft, the only one who got the complete tour. Their parents were all the same, they supported the war, but kept their kids out of it.

One good friend had grades in high school that were not good enough to get him into college. To keep him out of the draft, his father sent him to a prep school for a year in order to keep his student deferment. After the year in prep school, he was able to get into a college and of course his father is most pleased that he keeps the student deferment. He dropped out of college once the draft ended, but I was never angry with my boyhood friend. In fact, I was never angry with any of them for not having gone through what I had. What if they had been hurt or killed? I would find no joy in that. I came back in one piece, though not quite the same as I went in, and certainly with some hard mileage on the odometer. But some others never came back. A couple of years later, as the 1972 Presidential election approached, all of the parents in my neighborhood thought Nixon was a saint and that no-good George McGovern was going to end the Vietnam war. I wish I had asked if they thought Vietnam was such a good idea, why they didn't send their own children. Of course, by March of 1973, there were no combat troops left in Vietnam anyway. By August 1974, Nixon had resigned, and 58,000 American deaths later, Saigon fell in April 1975. What do they think of their hero now?

In the end, I consider my time in the Army as somewhere in the middle of the scale. I have a good friend whose entire time in Vietnam was spent on the large safe base at Nha Trang as a personnel clerk. He was able to take six R+R's. Whenever someone failed to show up to take theirs, he would take the unfilled slot; no need to have an empty seat on those R+R flights. He was smart and lucky, and I am happy for him. But I knew another who spent his entire year on an isolated fire base, humping ammo into a 105 howitzer; his hearing loss is profound. And I have another good friend who spent his year slogging through the Mekong Delta region, and it was hellish for him.

For decades, I didn't like talking about Vietnam. Unless you were there, no one knows what you're talking about anyway, and fewer even care. It has taken most of four decades until I could more easily speak of my time there. Most emphatically, I do not see myself as any kind of hero. The names of those heroes are listed on a long black granite wall in the District of Columbia or on the rolls of the VA hospitals. I was just a young punk of twenty who manned up when I had to and survived my time without committing any personal atrocities. I was hardly innocent, and I admit to being part of the bigger atrocity called Vietnam. And I am still a little bitter.

Dealing With The Veterans Administration

I have no clue about the workings of the United States Veterans Administration, and my very first experience does not go well.

My first summer out of the Army, I attempt to make use of my VA benefits, in particular my health care benefit at the VA Medical Center. One morning, as I go to take a glass from a shelf in my mother's kitchen, I step on a braided rug. Most unfortunately, the rug holds a pin (sewing) in a vertical position, and as I unknowingly step onto the rug, the pin goes fully into the bottom my right heel. I am of course in terrible pain but cannot see what had caused the pain, as the head of the pin is now beneath my skin.

After two days of intense pain, I take myself to the VA Medical Center. It goes badly. The doctor who examines me can't see anything obvious and so does not even bother to order a simple x-ray. They dismiss me. After two more weeks of continuing intense pain, I go to a non-VA physician who tells me I have a wart and, after numbing my foot, burns the supposed wart off. The numbing gives temporary relief but the next day the pain is back. After six more weeks of slowly diminishing pain, my sock catches something as I take it off one late afternoon. In the sunlight I see something reflecting the light; it is the top of the pin just protruding from the skin below my ankle. I return to the physician, and he sends me to a hospital for x-rays which reveal a sewing pin in my heel. The pin is removed, but I feel the VA Medical Center failed me terribly and do not return to the VA for any help for the next 25 years.

When I finally go back to the VA system, the system has improved some, but still some things are a battle. I complain about my hearing loss, but I am told I need to show the results of a hearing exam taken on the day I got out of the Army. This is so it can be compared with a hearing test on the day I went in. I was never given a hearing exam on that last day in the Army; a comparison is impossible.

Forty years after my discharge, at the strong urging and browbeating of a fellow Vietnam Veteran, I join the Veterans of Foreign Wars organization and begin the process of filing disability claims for injuries suffered so long ago. The VA has changed for the better. As an example, the VA now accepts that if you served in Vietnam, you were exposed to Agent Orange. Before, you had to provide the serial numbers of the aircraft that sprayed it on you. My hearing loss disability is granted almost immediately, because I served in combat and my hearing loss is severe. But the knee injury is denied. There is no record of it in my medical file, because I was "on loan" to another unit when I was injured.

Thus, begins a near eight-year battle of claims and denials, appeals and denials, and more appeals and denials. At some point, as my claim moves up the chain, it comes before the Board of Veterans Appeals in Washington, DC. This sounds like progress, but in fact, there are 114,000 claims ahead of me, and I am quite discouraged. Years go by, and finally the Board of Appeals directs the local VA Medical Center to perform a complete examination of my knees. It takes six months before an exam is given. Nine months after that exam, and 7 years and 11 months after the time I filed the claim, the VA reverses its decision. They find it more likely than not that my injuries were caused by that jump/fall from that Chinook in August of 1969. I receive the official notification almost exactly to the day 50 years later in August 2019.

In the interim, the VA Health Care systems improves greatly from where it was years ago. It has, to the astonishment of many (including me), become the model of what a health care system should be. I state without reservation that I am now well cared for by the VA Health Care system. It has taken nearly a lifetime, but I (we) finally get some recognition and respect, appreciation and some understanding for fighting a war already lost. We were so unintelligibly, unintelligently and incompetently led by the generation ahead of us that could not see the reality of what we faced. So much for the "greatest generation's" self-congratulations; they did a terrible disservice to the country by taking the country to war in Vietnam-- the same country that required just 2% or 3% of its population to do its dirty work for them. And as to their treatment of Vietnam Veterans: how shameful and deplorable......I guess I'm still a little bitter after all these years.

The Impact On My Life

It is not just the bitter taste of two years lost fighting an unwinnable war. We were betrayed and stabbed in the back by our supposed fellow countrymen. We were most unfairly judged and looked down upon for not winning it, and then further judged and had been collectively found guilty in the public's eye for being killers that committed atrocities. (yes, some committed unforgivable atrocities, I know because I was there, but most of us did not.) As painful as that betrayal is, it is as much, if not more, the aftermath of a lifetime trying to catch up to where you might have been if not drafted. I was determined to go back to school and earn a degree, but as I attend my classes I find I am years older than all of my classmates. I am out of sync with life. I am of course emancipated and therefore without the financial support that a typical college student gets, so it is a financial struggle. The GI Bill helps, but barely, as Congress was stingy. And even after the completion of my BS degree, my employers are taken aback, that at age 27, I have only just now graduated from college. They had assumed and expected I had several years of professional work experience by that age. One never quite catches up to where they might or should have been, so there are years lost with little or no income. My working career is marked by a life time of limping, a loss of 50% of my hearing, tinnitus, and eventfully a titanium knee replacement. For all of that

I was paid two dollars a day for combat. Did Vietnam affect me? It has never stopped affecting me.

I try to hold a philosophical view of the nearly two years of lost youth, misery, plus the mistreatment and injuries: Because I went to Vietnam, it meant someone else didn't have to go. But that is a difficult position to hold, as I think most that escaped the draft by one means or another are convinced that they were entitled not to have served. Those of us that were drafted or enlisted were somehow considered of less value: so, they have little or no appreciation at all of those that did serve. They caught a free ride on the backs of those that did, but still look down on us. Maybe Big D was right all this time.

And One Last Thing

As I end my story, I share but one last thing: Despite some of the gut wrenching events I saw and was part of, there were also some positive ones. And of all the positive ones, there was none bigger than the gift of love from Suzie Wong. So, from time to time, as I walk down the aisles of a supermarket, I will pause at the bar soap section. I'll pick up a bar of Zest, hold it to my nose and take in a small whiff. The magic is still there. But to this day I could not ever buy it. To do so would be a violation. I always gently and with reverence place that bar of Zest back on its shelf and I walk away…and the Buddha smiles upon me…

Acknowledgement

I wish to thank the following for their help, love, encouragement, decency, and kindness at various times and places in my life's arc. The names are listed in no particular order, but they all gave far more than they took. This book would not be possible without them. They all helped me heal.

Tore W.
Lisa B.
Helen P.
Nancy M.
J. J. B.
Janis L.
Nila T.
Jules M.
Tracie S.
B.J. Hunnicutt
Raymond D.
Frank L.
and Suzie Wong

Made in the USA
Monee, IL
17 May 2022